Investing in ETFs

Second Edition

by Russell Wild

Investing in ETFs For Dummies®, Second Edition

Published by: **John Wiley & Sons, Inc.**, 111 River Street, Hoboken, NJ 07030-5774, www.wiley.com

Copyright © 2023 by John Wiley & Sons, Inc., Hoboken, New Jersey

Published simultaneously in Canada

No part of this publication may be reproduced, stored in a retrieval system or transmitted in any form or by any means, electronic, mechanical, photocopying, recording, scanning or otherwise, except as permitted under Sections 107 or 108 of the 1976 United States Copyright Act, without the prior written permission of the Publisher. Requests to the Publisher for permission should be addressed to the Permissions Department, John Wiley & Sons, Inc., 111 River Street, Hoboken, NJ 07030, (201) 748-6011, fax (201) 748-6008, or online at http://www.wiley.com/go/permissions.

Trademarks: Wiley, For Dummies, the Dummies Man logo, Dummies.com, Making Everything Easier, and related trade dress are trademarks or registered trademarks of John Wiley & Sons, Inc. and may not be used without written permission. All other trademarks are the property of their respective owners. John Wiley & Sons, Inc. is not associated with any product or vendor mentioned in this book.

For general information on our other products and services, please contact our Customer Care Department within the U.S. at 877-762-2974, outside the U.S. at 317-572-3993, or fax 317-572-4002. For technical support, please visit https://hub.wiley.com/community/support/dummies.

Wiley publishes in a variety of print and electronic formats and by print-on-demand. Some material included with standard print versions of this book may not be included in e-books or in print-on-demand. If this book refers to media such as a CD or DVD that is not included in the version you purchased, you may download this material at http://booksupport.wiley.com. For more information about Wiley products, visit www.wiley.com.

Library of Congress Control Number: 2023941071

ISBN 978-1-394-20107-5 (pbk); ISBN 978-1-394-20108-2 (ebk); ISBN 978-1-394-20109-9 (ebk)

SKY10051370_071823

Contents at a Glance

Table of Contents

Introduction

Every month, it seems, Wall Street comes up with some new-fangled investment idea. The array of financial products (replete with 164-page prospectuses) is now so dizzying that the old, lumpy mattress is starting to look like a more comfortable place to stash the cash. But there is one product that is definitely worth looking at, even though it's been around not even 30 years. It's something of a cross between an index mutual fund and a stock, and it's called an *exchange-traded fund* (ETF).

Just as computers and fax machines were used by big institutions before they caught on with individual consumers, so it was with ETFs. They were first embraced by institutional traders — investment banks, hedge funds, and insurance firms — because, among other things, they allow for the quick juggling of massive holdings. Big traders like that sort of thing. Personally, playing hot potato with my money is not my idea of fun. But all the same, over the past not even 20 years, I've invested most of my own savings in ETFs, and I've suggested to many of my clients that they do the same.

I'm not alone in my appreciation for ETFs. They've grown exponentially in the past few years, and they'll surely continue to grow and gain influence. I can't claim that my purchases and my recommendations of ETFs account for much of the growing but global $9 trillion-plus ETF market, but I'm happy to be a (very) small part of it. After you've read this book, you may decide to become part of it as well, if you haven't already.

About This Book

As with any other investment, you're looking for a certain payoff in reading this book. In an abstract sense, the payoff will come in your achieving a thorough understanding and appreciation for a powerful financial tool called an ETF. The more concrete payoff will come when you apply this understanding to improve your investment results.

What makes me think ETFs can help you make money?

>> **ETFs are intelligent.** Most financial experts agree that playing with individual stocks can be hazardous to one's wealth. Anything from an accounting scandal to the CEO's sudden angina attack can send a single stock spiraling downward. That's why it makes sense for the average investor to own lots of stocks — or bonds — through ETFs or mutual funds.

>> **ETFs are cheap.** At least 250 ETFs charge annual management expenses of 0.1 percent or lower, and a few charge as little as 0 percent a year! In contrast, the average actively managed mutual fund charges 0.63 percent a year. Index mutual funds generally cost a tad more than their ETF cousins. Such cost differences, while appearing small on paper, can make a huge impact on your returns over time. (I crunch some numbers in Chapter 1.)

>> **ETFs are tax-smart.** Because of the very clever way ETFs are structured, the taxes you pay on any growth are minimal. (I crunch some of those numbers as well in Chapter 1.)

>> **ETFs are open books.** Quite unlike mutual funds, an ETF's holdings are, by and large, readily visible. If this afternoon, for example, I were to buy 100 shares of the ETF called the SPDR (pronounced "spider") S&P 500 ETF Trust, I would know that exactly 6.37 percent of my money was invested in Apple and 5.92 percent was invested in Microsoft. You don't get that kind of detail when you buy most mutual funds. Mutual-fund managers, like stage magicians, are often reluctant to reveal their secrets. In the investment game, the more you know, the lower the odds that you'll get sawed in half.

News flash: Regulators are still debating just how open the portfolios of the newer actively managed ETFs will have to be. For the time being, however, most ETFs track indexes, and the components of any index are readily visible.

If you've ever read a *For Dummies* book before, you have an idea of what you're about to embark on. This is not a book you need to read from front to back. Feel free to jump about and glean whatever information you think will be of most use. There is no quiz at the end. You don't have to commit it all to memory.

Most of the heavy technical matter is tucked neatly into the shaded sidebars. But if any technicalities make it into the main text, I give you a heads-up with a Technical Stuff icon. That's where you can skip over or speed-read — or choose to get dizzy. Your call!

Keep in mind that when this book was printed, some web addresses may have needed to break across two lines of text. Wherever that's the case, rest assured that this book uses no extra characters (hyphens or other doohickeys) to indicate the break. So, when going to one of these web addresses, just type in exactly what you see in this book. Pretend that the line break doesn't exist.

Foolish Assumptions

I assume that most of the people reading this book know a fair amount about the financial world. I think that's a fairly safe assumption. Why else would you have bought an entire book about ETFs?

If you think that convertible bonds are bonds with removable tops and that the futures market is a place where fortune tellers purchase crystal balls, I help you along the best I can by letting you know how to find out more about certain topics. However, you may be better off picking up and reading a copy of the basic, nuts-and-bolts *Investing For Dummies* by Eric Tyson (Wiley). After you spend some time with that title, c'mon back to this book — you'll be more than welcome!

Icons Used in This Book

Throughout the book, you find little globular pieces of art in the margins called *icons*. These cutesy but handy tools give you a heads-up that certain types of information are in the neighborhood.

TIP

Although this is a how-to book, you also find plenty of whys and wherefores. Any paragraph accompanied by this icon, however, is guaranteed pure, 100 percent, unadulterated how-to.

WARNING

The world of investments offers pitfalls galore. Wherever you see the bomb icon, know that there is a risk of your losing money — maybe even Big Money — if you skip the passage.

REMEMBER

Read twice! This icon indicates that something important is being said and is really worth committing to memory.

TECHNICAL STUFF

If you don't really care about the difference between standard deviation and beta, or the historical correlation between U.S. value stocks and real estate investment trusts (REITs), feel free to skip or skim the paragraphs marked with this icon.

Where to Go from Here

Where would you *like* to go from here? If you want, start at the beginning. If you're interested only in stock ETFs, hey, no one says that you can't jump right to Chapters 3–6. Bond ETFs? Go ahead and jump to Chapter 7. Sample ETF portfolios? Head to Chapter 9. It's entirely your call.

1
Getting Started with ETFs

Find out how exchange-traded funds (ETFs) work and how they're different from other investment options.

Look into the pluses and minuses of ETFs to determine whether they're a good fit for you.

Get the pieces into position for ETF investing, from starting an account to finding a brokerage house.

Understand the indexers and exchanges in the ETF world.

Chapter **1**

ETFs: No Longer the New Kid on the Block

anking your retirement on stocks is risky enough; banking your retirement on any individual stock, or even a handful of stocks, is about as risky as wrestling crocodiles. Banking on individual bonds is less risky (maybe wrestling an adolescent crocodile), but the same general principle holds. There is safety in numbers. That's why teenage boys and girls huddle together in corners at school dances. That's why gnus graze in groups. That's why smart stock and bond investors grab onto exchange-traded funds (ETFs).

In this chapter, I explain not only the safety features of ETFs but also the ways in which they differ from their cousins, mutual funds. By the time you're done with this chapter, you should have a pretty good idea of what ETFs can do for your portfolio.

What the Heck Is an ETF?

REMEMBER

Just as a deed shows that you have ownership of a house, and a share of common stock certifies ownership in a company, a share of an ETF represents ownership (most typically) in a basket of company stocks. To buy or sell an ETF, you place an order with a broker, generally (and preferably, for cost reasons) online, although you can also place an order by phone. The price of an ETF changes throughout the trading day (which is to say from 9:30 a.m. to 4 p.m. Eastern time), going up or down with the market value of the securities it holds. Sometimes there can be a little sway — times when the price of an ETF doesn't exactly track the value of the securities it holds — but that situation is rarely serious, at least not with ETFs from the better purveyors.

Originally, ETFs were developed to mirror various indexes:

>> The SPDR S&P 500 (ticker symbol: SPY) represents stocks from the Standard & Poor's (S&P) 500, an index of the 500 largest companies in the United States.

>> The DIAMONDS Trust Series 1 (ticker symbol: DIA) represents the 30 or so underlying stocks of the Dow Jones Industrial Average (DJIA) index.

>> The Invesco QQQ Trust Series 1 (ticker symbol: QQQ; formerly known as the Nasdaq-100 Trust Series 1) represents the 100 stocks of the Nasdaq-100 Index.

Since ETFs were first introduced, many others, tracking all kinds of things, including some rather strange things that I dare not even call investments, have emerged.

The component companies in an ETF's portfolio usually represent a certain index or segment of the market, such as large U.S. value stocks, small-growth stocks, or micro-cap stocks. (If you're not 100 percent clear on the difference between *value* and *growth*, or what a micro cap is, rest assured that I define these and other key terms in Part 2.)

Sometimes, the stock market is broken up into industry sectors, such as technology, industrials, and consumer discretionary. ETFs exist that mirror each sector.

REMEMBER

Regardless of what securities an ETF represents, and regardless of what index those securities are a part of, your fortunes as an ETF holder are tied, either directly or in some leveraged fashion, to the value of the underlying securities. If the price of Microsoft stock, U.S. Treasury bonds, gold bullion, or British pound futures goes up, so does the value of your ETF. If the price of gold tumbles, your portfolio (if you hold a gold ETF) may lose some glitter. If Microsoft stock pays a dividend, you're due a certain amount of that dividend — *unless* you happen to have bought into a leveraged or inverse ETF.

WARNING

Some ETFs allow for leveraging, so that if the underlying security rises in value, your ETF shares rise doubly or triply. If the security falls in value, well, you lose according to the same multiple. Other ETFs allow you not only to leverage but also to *reverse* leverage, so you stand to make money if the underlying security falls in value (and, of course, lose if the underlying security increases in value). I'm not a big fan of leveraged and inverse ETFs.

Choosing between the classic and the new indexes

Some of the ETF providers (Vanguard, iShares, Charles Schwab) tend to use traditional indexes, such as those I mention in the previous section. Others (Dimensional, WisdomTree) tend to develop their own indexes.

For example, if you were to buy 100 shares of an ETF called the iShares S&P 500 Growth Index Fund (ticker symbol: IVW), you'd be buying into a traditional index (large U.S. growth companies). At about $70 a share (at the time of this writing), you'd plunk down $7,000 for a portfolio of stocks that would include shares of Apple, Microsoft, Amazon, Facebook, Alphabet (Google), and Tesla. If you wanted to know the exact breakdown, the iShares prospectus found on the iShares website (or any number of financial websites, such as https://finance.yahoo.com) would tell you specific percentages: Apple, 11.3 percent; Microsoft, 10.3 percent; Amazon, 7.8 percent; and so on.

Many ETFs represent shares in companies that form foreign indexes. If, for example, you were to own 100 shares of the iShares MSCI Japan Index Fund (ticker symbol: EWJ), with a market value of about $69 per share as of this writing, your $6,900 would buy you a stake in large Japanese companies such as Toyota Motor, SoftBank Group, Sony Group, Keyence, and Mitsubishi UFJ Financial Group. (Chapter 5 is devoted entirely to international ETFs.)

Both IVW and EWJ mirror standard indexes: IVW mirrors the S&P 500 Growth Index, and EWJ mirrors the MSCI Japan Index. If, however, you purchase 100 shares of the Invesco Dynamic Large Cap Growth ETF (ticker symbol: PWB), you'll buy roughly $7,100 worth of a portfolio of stocks that mirror a very unconventional index — one created by the Invesco family of ETFs. The large U.S. growth companies in the PowerShares index that have the heaviest weightings include Facebook and Alphabet, but also NVIDIA and Texas Instruments. Invesco PowerShares refers to its custom indexes as *Intellidex* indexes.

A big controversy in the world of ETFs is whether the newfangled, customized indexes offered by companies like Invesco make any sense. Most financial professionals are skeptical of anything that's new. We're a conservative lot. Those of us who have been around for a while have seen too many "exciting" new investment ideas crash and burn. But I, for one, try to keep an open mind. For now, let me continue with my introduction to ETFs, but rest assured that I address this controversy (in Chapter 2 and throughout the rest of this book).

Another big controversy is whether you may be better off with an even newer style of ETFs — those that follow no indexes at all but rather are "actively" managed. I prefer index investing to active investing, but that's not to say that active investing, carefully pursued, has no role to play. (You can find more on that topic later in this chapter and throughout this book.)

Other ETFs — a distinct but growing minority — represent holdings in assets other than stocks, most notably, bonds and commodities (gold, silver, oil, and such). And then there are exchange-traded notes (ETNs), which allow you to venture even further into the world of alternative investments — or speculations — such as currency futures. (I discuss these products in Part 2.)

Preferring ETFs over individual stocks

Okay, why buy a basket of stocks rather than an individual stock? Quick answer: You'll sleep better.

A company I'll call ABC Pharmaceutical sees its stock shoot up by 68 percent because the firm just earned an important patent for a new diet pill; a month later, the stock falls by 84 percent because a study in the *New England Journal of Medicine* found that the new diet pill causes people to hallucinate and think they're Genghis Khan.

Compared to the world of individual stocks, the stock market as a whole is as smooth as a morning lake. Heck, a daily rise or fall in the Dow of more than a percent or two (well, maybe 2 percent or 3 percent these days) is generally considered a pretty big deal.

If you, like me, are not especially keen on roller coasters, you're advised to put your nest egg into not one stock, not two, but many. If you have a few million sitting around, hey, you'll have no problem diversifying — maybe individual stocks are for you. But for most of us commoners, the only way to effectively diversify is with ETFs or mutual funds.

Distinguishing ETFs from mutual funds

So, what's the difference between an ETF and a mutual fund? After all, mutual funds also represent baskets of stocks or bonds. The two, however, are not twins. They're not even siblings. Cousins are more like it. Here are some of the big differences between ETFs and mutual funds:

>> ETFs are bought and sold just like stocks (through a brokerage house, either by phone or online), and their prices change throughout the trading day. Mutual-fund orders can be made during the day, but the actual trading doesn't occur until after the markets close.

>> ETFs tend to represent indexes — market segments — and the managers of the ETFs tend to do very little trading of securities in the ETF. (The ETFs are *passively* managed.) Most mutual funds are actively managed.

>> Although they may require you to pay small trading fees, ETFs usually wind up costing you much less than mutual funds because the ongoing management fees are typically much lower, and there is never a *load* (an entrance and/or exit fee, sometimes an exorbitant one), as you find with many mutual funds.

>> Because of low portfolio turnover and also the way ETFs are structured, ETFs generally declare much less in taxable capital gains than mutual funds do.

Table 1-1 provides a quick look at some ways that investing in ETFs differs from investing in mutual funds and individual stocks.

TABLE 1-1 Comparing ETFs, Mutual Funds, and Individual Stocks

	ETFs	Mutual Funds	Individual Stocks
Are they priced, bought, and sold throughout the day?	Yes	No	Yes
Do they offer some investment diversification?	Yes	Yes	No
Is there a minimum investment?	No	Yes	No
Are they purchased through a broker or online brokerage?	Yes	Yes	Yes
Do you pay a fee or commission to make a trade?	Rarely	Sometimes	Rarely
Can that fee or commission be more than a few dollars?	No	Yes	No
Can you buy/sell options?	Sometimes	No	Sometimes
Are they indexed (passively managed)?	Typically	Atypically	No
Can you make money or lose money?	Yes	Yes	You bet

Why the Big Boys Prefer ETFs

When ETFs were first introduced, they were primarily of interest to institutional traders — insurance companies, hedge-fund people, banks — whose investment needs are often considerably more complicated than yours and mine. In this section, I explain why ETFs appeal to the largest investors.

Trading in large lots

Prior to the introduction of ETFs, a trader had no easy way to buy or sell instantaneously, in one fell swoop, hundreds of stocks or bonds. Because ETFs trade both during market hours and, in some cases, after market hours, they made that possible.

Institutional investors also found other things to like about ETFs. For example, ETFs are often used to put cash to productive use quickly or to fill gaps in a portfolio by allowing immediate exposure to an industry sector or geographic region.

Savoring the versatility

Unlike mutual funds, ETFs can also be purchased with limit, market, or stop-loss orders, taking away the uncertainty involved with placing a buy order for a mutual fund and not knowing what price you're going to get until several hours after the market closes. See the nearby sidebar "Your basic trading choices (for ETFs or stocks)" if you're not certain what limit, market, and stop-loss orders are.

And because many ETFs can be sold short, they provide an important means of risk management. If, for example, the stock market takes a dive, then *shorting* ETFs — selling them now at a locked-in price with an agreement to purchase them back (cheaper, you hope) later on — may help keep a portfolio afloat. For that reason, ETFs have become a darling of hedge-fund managers who offer the promise of investments that won't tank should the stock market tank.

YOUR BASIC TRADING CHOICES (FOR ETFs OR STOCKS)

Buying and selling an ETF is just like buying and selling a stock; there really is no difference. Although you can trade in all sorts of ways, the vast majority of trades fall into the following categories:

- **Market order:** This is as simple as it gets. You place an order with your broker or online to buy, say, 100 shares of a certain ETF. Your order goes to the stock exchange, and you get the best available price.

- **Limit order:** More exact than a market order, you place an order to buy, say, 100 shares of an ETF at $23 a share. That's the maximum price you'll pay. If no sellers are willing to sell at $23 a share, your order won't go through. If you place a limit order to sell at $23, you'll get your sale if someone is willing to pay that price. If not, there will be no sale. You can specify whether an order is

(continued)

(continued)

good for the day or until canceled (if you don't mind waiting to see if the market moves in your favor).

- **Stop-loss (or stop) order:** Designed to protect you should the price of your ETF or stock take a tumble, a stop-loss order automatically becomes a market order if and when the price falls below a certain point (say, 10 percent below the current price). Stop-loss orders are used to limit investors' exposure to a falling market, but they can (and often do) backfire, especially in very turbulent markets. Proceed with caution.

- **Short sale:** You sell shares of an ETF that you've borrowed from the broker. If the price of the ETF then falls, you can buy replacement shares at a lower price and pocket the difference. If, however, the price rises, you're stuck holding a security that is worth less than its market price, so you pay the difference, which can sometimes be huge.

For more information on different kinds of trading options, see the U.S. Securities and Exchange Commission (SEC) discussion at www. sec.gov/investor/alerts/trading101basics.pdf.

Why Individual Investors Are Learning to Love ETFs

Clients I've worked with are often amazed that I can put them into a financial product that will cost them a fraction in expenses compared to what they're currently paying. Low costs are probably what I love the most about ETFs. But I also love their tax-efficiency, transparency (you know what you're buying), and — now in their third decade of existence — good track record of success.

The cost advantage: How low can you go?

In the world of actively managed mutual funds (which is to say, most mutual funds), the average annual management fee, according to the Investment Company Institute and Morningstar, is 0.63 percent of the account balance. That may not sound like a lot, but don't be misled. A well-balanced portfolio with both stocks and bonds may return, say, 5 percent over time. In that case, paying 0.63 percent to a third party means that you've just lowered your total investment returns by one-eighth. In a bad year, when your investments earn, say, 0.63 percent, you've just lowered your investment returns to *zero*. And in a *very* bad year . . . you don't need me to do the math.

Active ETFs, although cheaper than active mutual funds, aren't all that much cheaper, averaging 0.51 percent a year (although a few are considerably higher than that).

WARNING

I'm astounded at what some funds charge. Whereas the average active fund charges between 0.51 percent (for ETFs) and 0.63 percent (for mutual funds), I've seen charges five times that amount. Crazy. Investing in such a fund is tossing money to the wind. Yet people do it. The chances of your winding up ahead after paying such high fees are next to nil. Paying a *load* (an entrance and/or exit fee) that can total as much as 6 percent is just as nutty. Yet people do it.

In the world of index funds, the expenses are much lower, with index mutual funds averaging 0.06 percent and ETFs averaging 0.17 percent, although many of the more traditional index ETFs cost no more than 0.06 percent a year in management fees, and as more competition has entered the market, even that price now seems high. A handful are now under 0.03 percent. And one purveyor, BNY Mellon, has actually introduced two ETFs with *no fees*.

No fees?

How can no fees make sense?

The multibillion-dollar BNY Mellon Bank didn't enter the ETF game until 2020, and it took the price-cutting war to a new level. The bank issued two ETFs with an expense ratio of *zero*. How can the company do that and expect to make money? It doesn't. "It's a courtesy to investors, and we're hoping that they'll look at our other ETFs," says a BNY Mellon official. Indeed, it got me looking at the BNY Mellon lineup, and I showcase a few of their other ETF offerings later in this book, all of which are very reasonably priced. However, there may be no more freebies in the pipeline, and to date, no other ETF purveyors have dropped their prices to zero, although a number of index mutual-fund purveyors have.

Keep in mind that price is just one of the characteristics — albeit a very important one — that you'll be looking at in deciding how to pick "best in class" when choosing an ETF.

Numerous studies have shown that low-cost funds have a huge advantage over higher-cost funds. One study by Morningstar looked at stock returns over a five-year period. In almost every category of stock mutual fund, low-cost funds beat the pants off high-cost funds. Do you think that by paying high fees you're getting better fund management? Hardly. The Morningstar study found, for example, that among mutual funds that hold large-blend stocks (*blend* meaning a combination of value and growth — an S&P 500 fund would be a blend fund, for example), the annualized gain was 8.75 percent for those funds in the costliest quartile of funds; the gain for the least-costly quartile was 9.89 percent.

Why ETFs are cheaper

The management companies that bring us ETFs, such as Black-Rock and Invesco, are presumably not doing so for their health. No, they're making a good profit. One reason they can offer ETFs so cheaply compared to mutual funds is that their expenses are much less. When you buy an ETF, you go through a brokerage house, not BlackRock or Invesco. That brokerage house (for example, Fidelity) does all the necessary paperwork and bookkeeping on the purchase. If you have any questions about your money, you'll likely call Fidelity, not BlackRock. So, unlike a mutual-fund company, which must maintain telephone operators, bookkeepers, and a mailroom, the providers of ETFs can operate almost entirely in cyberspace.

ETFs that are linked to indexes have to pay some kind of fee to S&P Dow Jones Indices or MSCI or whoever created the index. But that fee is *nothing* compared to the exorbitant salaries that mutual funds pay their dart throwers, er, stock pickers, er, market analysts.

An unfair race

Active mutual funds (the vast majority of mutual funds are active) really don't have much chance of beating passive index funds — whether mutual funds or ETFs — over the long run, at least not as a group. (There are individual exceptions, but it's virtually impossible to identify them before the fact.) Someone once described the contest as a race in which the active mutual funds are "running with lead boots." Why? In addition to the management fees that eat up a substantial part of any gains, there are also the trading costs. Yes, when mutual funds trade stocks or bonds, they pay a spread and a small cut to the stock exchange, just like you and I do. That cost is passed on to you, and it's on top of the annual management fees previously discussed.

An actively managed fund's annual turnover costs will vary, but one study several years ago found that they were typically running at about 0.8 percent. And active mutual-fund managers must constantly keep some cash on hand for all those trades. Having cash on hand costs money, too: The opportunity cost, like the turnover costs, can vary greatly from fund to fund, but a fund that keeps 20 percent of its assets in cash — and there are many that do — is going to see significant cash drag. After all, only 80 percent of its assets are really working for you.

So, you take the 0.63 percent average management fee, and the perhaps 0.8 percent hidden trading costs, and the cash drag or opportunity cost, and you can see where running with lead boots comes in. Add taxes to the equation, and although some actively managed mutual funds may do better than ETFs for a few years, over the long haul, I wouldn't bank on many of them coming out ahead.

Uncle Sam's loss, your gain

Alas, unless your money is in a tax-advantaged retirement account, making money in the markets means that you have to fork something over to Uncle Sam at year's end. That's true, of course, whether you invest in individual securities or funds. But before there were ETFs, individual securities had a big advantage over funds in that you were required to pay capital gains taxes only when you actually enjoyed a capital gain. With mutual funds, that isn't so. The fund itself may realize a capital gain by selling off an appreciated stock. You pay the capital gains tax regardless of whether you sell anything and regardless of whether the share price of the mutual fund increased or decreased since the time you bought it.

WARNING

There have been times (pick a bad year for the market — 2000, 2008 . . .) when many mutual-fund investors lost a considerable amount in the market, yet had to pay capital gains taxes at the end of the year. Talk about adding insult to injury! One study found that over the course of time, taxes have wiped out approximately two full percentage points in returns for investors in the highest tax brackets.

In the world of ETFs, such losses are very unlikely to happen. Because most ETFs are index based, they generally have little turnover to create capital gains. Perhaps even more important, ETFs are structured in a way that largely insulates shareholders from capital gains that result when mutual funds are forced to sell in order to free up cash to pay off shareholders who cash in their chips.

The structure of ETFs makes them different from mutual funds. Actually, ETFs are legally structured in three different ways: as exchange-traded open-end mutual funds, as exchange-traded unit investment trusts, and as exchange-traded grantor trusts. The differences are subtle, and I elaborate on them somewhat in Chapter 2. For now, I want to focus on one seminal difference between ETFs and mutual funds, which boils down to an extremely clever setup whereby ETF shares, which represent stock holdings, can be traded without any actual trading of stocks.

Think of the poker player who plays hand after hand, but thanks to the miracle of little plastic chips, they don't have to touch any cash.

In the world of ETFs, you don't have croupiers, but you have market makers. *Market makers* are people who work at the stock exchanges and create (like magic!) ETF shares. Each ETF share represents a portion of a portfolio of stocks, sort of like poker chips represent a pile of cash. As an ETF grows, so does the number of shares. Concurrently (once a day), new stocks are added to a portfolio that mirrors the ETF. Figure 1-1 may help you envision the structure of ETFs and what makes them such tax wonders.

When an ETF investor sells shares, those shares are bought by a market maker who turns around and sells them to another ETF investor. By contrast, with mutual funds, if one person sells, the mutual fund must sell off shares of the underlying stock to pay off the shareholder. If stocks sold in the mutual fund are being sold for more than the original purchase price, the shareholders left behind are stuck paying a capital gains tax. In some years, that amount can be substantial.

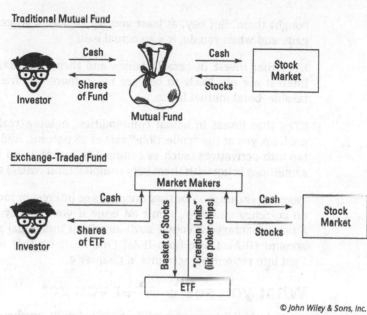

Traditional Mutual Fund

Investor — Cash → Mutual Fund
Mutual Fund — Shares of Fund → Investor
Mutual Fund — Cash → Stock Market
Stock Market — Stocks → Mutual Fund

Exchange-Traded Fund

Market Makers
Investor — Cash → Shares of ETF
Basket of Stocks
"Creation Units" (like poker chips)
Market Makers — Cash → Stock Market
Stock Market — Stocks → Market Makers
ETF

© John Wiley & Sons, Inc.

FIGURE 1-1: The secret to ETFs' tax-friendliness lies in their very structure.

In the world of ETFs, no such thing has happened or is likely to happen, at least not with the vast majority of ETFs, which are index funds. Because index funds trade infrequently, and because of ETFs' poker-chip structure, ETF investors rarely see a bill from Uncle Sam for any capital gains tax. That's not a guarantee that there will never be capital gains on any index ETF, but if there ever are, they're sure to be minor.

The actively managed ETFs — currently a small fraction of the ETF market, but almost certain to grow — may present a somewhat different story. They're going to be, no doubt, less tax-friendly than index ETFs but more tax-friendly than actively managed mutual funds. Exactly where will they fall on the spectrum? It may take another few years before we really know.

REMEMBER

Tax-efficient does not mean tax-free. Although you won't pay capital gains taxes, you will pay taxes on any dividends issued by your stock ETFs, and stock ETFs are just as likely to issue dividends as are mutual funds. In addition, if you sell your ETFs and they're in a taxable account, you have to pay capital gains tax (15 percent for most folks; 20 percent for those who make big bucks) if the ETFs have appreciated in value since the time you bought them. But hey, at least you get to decide when to take a gain, and when you do, it's an actual gain.

ETFs that invest in taxable bonds and throw off taxable-bond interest are not likely to be very much more tax-friendly than taxable-bond mutual funds.

ETFs that invest in actual commodities, holding real silver or gold, tax you at the "collectible" rate of 28 percent. And ETFs that tap into derivatives (such as commodity futures) and currencies sometimes bring with them very complex (and costly) tax issues.

Taxes on earnings — be they dividends or interest or money made on currency swaps — aren't an issue if your money is held in a tax-advantaged account, such as a Roth individual retirement account (IRA). I love Roth IRAs! Find more on that topic when I get into retirement accounts in Chapter 9.

What you see is what you get

A key to building a successful portfolio, right up there with low costs and tax-efficiency, is diversification, a subject I discuss more in Chapter 10. You can't diversify optimally unless you know exactly what's in your portfolio. In a rather infamous example, when tech stocks (some more than others) started to go belly-up in 2000, holders of Janus mutual funds got clobbered. That's because they learned after the fact that their three or four Janus mutual funds, which gave the illusion of diversification, were actually holding many of the same stocks.

Style drift: An epidemic

With a mutual fund, you often have little idea of what stocks the fund manager is holding. In fact, you may not even know what *kinds* of stocks they're holding — or even if they're holding stocks! I'm talking here about *style drift*, which occurs when a mutual-fund manager advertises their fund as aggressive, but over time it becomes conservative, and vice versa. I'm talking about mutual-fund managers who say they love large value but invest in large growth or small value.

One classic case of style drift cost investors in the popular Fidelity Magellan Fund a bundle. The year was 1996, and then fund manager Jeffrey Vinik reduced the stock holdings in his "stock" mutual fund to 70 percent. He had 30 percent of the fund's assets in either bonds or short-term securities. He was betting that the market was going to sour, and he was planning to fully invest in stocks after that happened. He was dead wrong. Instead, the market continued to soar, bonds took a dive, Fidelity Magellan seriously underperformed, and Vinik was out.

One study by the Association of Investment Management concluded that a full 40 percent of actively managed mutual funds are not what they say they are. Some funds bounce around in style so much that you, as an investor, have scant idea of where your money is actually invested.

ETFs are the cure

When you buy an index ETF, you get complete transparency. You know exactly what you're buying. No matter what the ETF, you can see in the prospectus or on the ETF provider's website (or on any number of independent financial websites) a complete picture of the ETF's holdings. See, for example, https://etf.fdh com or https://finance.yahoo.com. If I go to either website and type IYE (the ticker symbol for the iShares Dow Jones U.S. Energy Sector ETF) in the search box, I can see in an instant what my holdings are.

You simply can't get that information on most actively managed mutual funds. Or, if you can, the information is both stale and subject to change without notice.

Transparency also discourages dishonesty

REMEMBER

The scandals that have rocked the mutual-fund world over the years have left the world of ETFs untouched. There's not a whole lot of manipulation that a fund manager can do when their picks are tied to an index. And because ETFs trade throughout the day, with the price flashing across thousands of computer screens worldwide, there is no room to take advantage of the "stale" pricing that occurs after the markets close and mutual-fund orders are settled. All in all, ETF investors are much less likely ever to get bamboozled than are investors in active mutual funds.

How to Get the Professional Edge

I don't know about you, but when I, on rare occasions, go bowling and bowl a strike, I feel as if a miracle of biblical proportions has occurred. And then I turn on the television, stumble upon a professional bowling tournament, and see people for whom *not* bowling a strike is a rare occurrence. The difference between amateur and professional bowlers is huge. The difference between investment amateurs and investment professionals can be just as huge. But you can close much of that gap with ETFs.

By *investment professionals*, I'm not talking about stockbrokers or variable-annuity salespeople (or my barber, who always has a stock recommendation for me); I'm talking about the managers of foundations, endowments, and pension funds with $1 billion or more in invested assets. By *amateurs*, I'm talking about the average U.S. investor with a few assorted and sundry mutual funds in their 401(k).

Let's compare the two: During the 30-year period from 1990 through the end of 2020, the U.S. stock market, as measured by the S&P 500 Index, provided an annual rate of return of 10.7 percent. Yet the average stock-fund investor, according to a study by the Massachusetts-based research firm Dalbar, earned an annual rate of 6.24 percent over that same period. The Bloomberg-Barclays U.S. Aggregate Bond Index earned 5.86 percent a year over that same period, while the average bond-fund investor earned just 0.45 percent.

Why the pitiful returns? Although there are several reasons, here are three main ones:

>> Mutual-fund investors pay too much for their investments.

>> These investors jump into hot funds in hot sectors when they're hot and jump out when those funds or sectors turn cold. (In other words, they're constantly buying high and selling low.)

>> Small investors panic easily and all too often cash out when the going gets rough.

Professionals tend not to do those things. To give you an idea of the difference between amateurs and professionals, consider this: For the ten-year period ending December 31, 2020, the average small investor, per Dalbar, earned a 4.9 percent annual return on their investments. Compare that to, say, the endowments of MIT (11.4 percent), Yale (10.9 percent), or Dartmouth (10.4 percent).

Professional managers, you see, don't pay high expenses. They don't jump in and out of funds. They know that they need to diversify. They tend to buy indexes. They know exactly what they own. And they know that asset allocation, not stock picking, is what drives long-term investment results. In short, they do all the things that an ETF portfolio can do for you. So, do it. Well, maybe — but first, read the rest of this chapter!

Passive versus Active Investing: Your Choice

Surely, you've sensed by now my preference for index funds over actively managed funds. For the first years of their existence, all ETFs were index funds.

On March 25, 2008, Bear Stearns introduced an actively managed ETF: the Current Yield ETF. As fate would have it, Bear Stearns was just about to go under, and when it did, the first actively managed ETF went with it. Prophetic? Perhaps. In the years since, hundreds of actively managed ETFs have hit the street. Many have died. At the time of writing, there are 586, but they aren't enjoying enormous commercial success. At the time of writing, active ETFs, per Morningstar Direct, accounted for a very measly 2.8 percent of the nearly $7 trillion invested in ETFs.

According to Cerulli Associates, however, the majority (79 percent) of U.S. ETF issuers, as of end of year 2020, were either developing or planning to develop active ETFs.

I don't think the advent of actively managed ETFs is necessarily a bad thing, but I'm not frothing at the mouth to invest in actively managed ETFs, either. Let's look at a few of the pros and cons of index investing versus investing in actively managed funds, and then let's look at how the ETF wrapper throws a wrinkle into the equation.

The index advantage

The superior returns of index mutual funds and ETFs over actively managed funds have had much to do with the popularity of ETFs to date. As discussed, the vast majority of ETFs — 77 percent in terms of actual numbers, and nearly 98 percent in terms of assets — are index funds (which buy and hold a fixed collection of stocks or bonds). And, as index funds, they can be expected to outperform actively managed funds rather consistently. According to Standard & Poor's SPIVA Scorecard, 88 percent of large-cap core stock funds underperformed their benchmark index in the past five years. High-yield bond funds? Ninety-five percent underperformed. Flipping that around, only 5 percent to 12 percent of actively managed funds succeeded at beating the index funds.

REMEMBER

Here are some reasons why index funds (both mutual funds and ETFs) are hard to beat:

>> They typically carry much lower management fees, sales loads, or redemption charges.

>> Hidden costs — trading costs and spread costs — are much lower when turnover is low.

>> They don't have cash sitting around idle (as the manager waits for what they think is the right time to enter the market).

>> They're more — sometimes much more — tax-efficient.

>> They're more "transparent"; you know exactly what securities you're investing in.

WARNING

Perhaps the greatest testament to the success of index funds is how many allegedly actively managed funds are actually index funds in (a very expensive) disguise. I'm talking about closet index funds. According to a report in *Investment News*, a newspaper for financial advisors, the number of actively managed stock funds that are closet index funds has tripled over the past several years. As a result, many investors are paying high (active) management fees for investment results that could be achieved with low-cost ETFs.

According to a study done by Credit Suisse, of all the funds in the United States — both mutual funds and ETFs — 27 percent are true index funds, 58 percent are actively managed funds, and a full 15 percent are closet index funds, meaning they invest as an index fund would, but charge what an active fund would.

The allure of active management

Speaking in broad generalities, actively managed mutual funds have been no friend to the small investor. Their persistence remains a testament to people's ignorance of the facts and the enormous amount of money spent on (often deceptive) advertising and PR that give investors the false impression that buying this fund or that fund will lead to instant wealth. The media often plays into this nonsense with splashy headlines, designed to sell magazine copies or attract viewers, that promise to reveal which funds or managers are currently the best.

Still, active management can make sense — and that may be especially true when some of the best aspects of active management are brought to the ETF market and some of the best aspects of ETF investing are brought to active management.

Some managers actually do have the ability to "beat the markets," but they're few and far between, and the increased costs of active management often nullify any and all advantages these market-beaters have. If those costs can be minimized, and if you can find such a manager, you may wind up ahead of the game. Actively managed ETFs cost more than index ETFs, but they're cheaper than actively managed mutual funds.

Active management in ETF form may also be both more tax-efficient and more transparent than it is in mutual-fund form. *Transparent* means you get to see the manager's secret sauce. Active managers like to keep their secret sauce, well, secret. To date, this has been easier when the wrapper has been a mutual fund rather than an ETF. However, this may not continue to be the case, because the active managers have already gotten the okay from the SEC for partial intransparency and are busy petitioning the SEC to allow yet more smoke.

And finally, with some kinds of investments, such as commodities and micro-cap stocks, active management may simply make more sense in certain cases. (I talk about these scenarios in Part 2.)

Why the race is getting harder to measure . . . and what to do

Unfortunately, the old-style "active versus passive" studies that consistently gave passive (index) investing two thumbs up are getting harder and harder to do. What exactly qualifies as an index fund anymore, now that many ETFs are set up to track indexes that, in and of themselves, were created to outperform "the market" (traditional indexes)? And whereas index investing once promised a very solid cost saving, some of the newer ETFs, with their newfangled indexes, are charging more than some actively managed funds. Future studies are only likely to become muddier.

Here's my advice: Give a big benefit of the doubt to index funds as the ones that will serve you the best in the long run. If you want to go with an actively managed fund, follow these guidelines:

>> Keep your costs low.

>> Don't believe that a manager can beat the market unless that manager has done so consistently for years, and for reasons that you can understand.

>> Pick a fund company that you trust.

>> Don't go overboard! Mix an index fund or two in with your active fund(s).

>> All things being equal, you may want to choose an ETF over a mutual fund. But the last section of this chapter can help you to determine that. Ready?

Do ETFs Belong in Your Life?

Okay, so on the plus side of ETFs, you have ultra-low management expenses, super tax-efficiency, transparency, and a lot of fancy trading opportunities, such as shorting, if you're so inclined. What about the negatives? In the sections that follow, I walk you through some other facts about ETFs that you should consider before parting with your precious dollars.

Calculating commissions

I talk about commissions when I compare and contrast various brokerage houses in Chapter 2, but I want to give you a heads-up here: You may have to pay a commission every time you buy and sell an ETF. But as I'm writing these words, another brokerage house may have eliminated commissions altogether.

Trading commissions for stocks and ETFs (it's the same commission for either) have been dropping faster than the price of desktop computers. What once would have cost you a bundle, now — if you trade online, which you definitely should — is really pin money, perhaps a few dollars a trade, and increasingly, nothing at all. So, unless you're investing a very small amount of money, you don't need to worry about commissions anymore. They're the smallpox of Wall Street.

Moving money in a flash

The fact that ETFs can be traded throughout the day like stocks makes them, unlike mutual funds, fair game for day-traders and institutional wheeler-dealers. For the rest of us common folk, there isn't much about the way that ETFs are bought and sold that makes them especially valuable. Indeed, the ability to trade throughout the day may make you more apt to do so, perhaps selling or buying on impulse. As I discuss in detail in Chapter 11, impulsive investing, although it can get your endorphins pumping, is generally not a profitable way to proceed.

Understanding tracking error

At times, the return of an ETF may be greater or less than the index it follows. This situation is called *tracking error*. At times, an ETF may also sell at a price that is a tad higher or lower than what that price should be, given the prices of all the securities held by the ETF. This situation is called selling at a *premium* (when the price of the ETF rides above the value of the securities) or selling at a *discount* (when the price of the ETF drops below the value of the securities). Both foreign stock funds and bond funds are more likely to run off track, either experiencing tracking errors or selling at a premium or discount. But the better funds don't run off track to any alarming degree.

In Chapter 2, I offer a few trading tricks for minimizing "off-track" ETF investing, but for now, let me say that it isn't something to worry about if you're a buy-and-hold ETF investor — the kind of investor I want you to become.

Making a sometimes tricky choice

Throughout this book, I give you lots of detailed information about how to construct a portfolio that meets your needs. Here, I just want to whet your appetite with a couple of very basic examples of decisions you may be facing.

Say you have a choice between investing in an index mutual fund that charges 0.06 percent a year and an ETF that tracks the same index and charges the same amount. Or, say you're trying to choose between an actively managed mutual fund and an ETF with the very same manager managing the very same kind of investment, with the same costs. What should you invest in?

If your money is in a taxable account, and you're looking at stock index funds, go with the ETF, provided there are no commissions to pay; it may wind up being more tax-efficient. If you're looking at bond index funds, I'd say this decision is a flip of the coin. Managed funds? Same.

But say you have, oh, $5,000 to invest in your traditional IRA. (All traditional IRA money is taxed as income when you withdraw it in retirement, so the tax-efficiency of securities held within an IRA isn't an issue.) In this case, I'd say that the choice between the ETF and the mutual fund is nothing to sweat over. If all else is the same, I'd have a very slight preference for the ETF, if for no other reason than its portability. (See the nearby sidebar "The index mutual fund trap.")

And what if your brokerage still charges a commission? Avoid it by going with the mutual fund (provided the mutual fund doesn't cost you a commission). What if there's a difference in management fees between the two funds? Say, an ETF charges you a management fee of 0.1 percent a year, and a comparable index mutual fund charges 0.15 percent, but buying and selling the ETF will cost you $5 at either end. Now what should you do?

The math isn't difficult. The difference between 0.1 percent and 0.15 percent is 0.05 percent, and 0.05 percent of $5,000 is $2.50. It will take you two years to recoup your trading fee of $5. If you factor in the cost of selling (another $5), it will take you four years to recoup your trading costs. At that point, the ETF will be your lower-cost tortoise, and the mutual fund will be your higher-cost hare.

WARNING

If you have a trigger finger and you're the kind of person who is likely to jump to trade every time there's a blip in the market, you would be well advised to go with mutual funds (that don't impose short-term redemption fees). You're less likely to shoot yourself in the foot!

THE INDEX MUTUAL FUND TRAP

Some brokerage houses, such as Vanguard and Fidelity, offer wonderful low-cost index mutual funds. Fidelity even offers a small handful of no-cost index mutual funds. But a problem with them is that you either can't buy them at other financial "supermarkets" (such as Charles Schwab or T. Rowe Price), or you have to pay a substantial fee to get into them. So, building an entire portfolio of index mutual funds can be tough. If you want both Fidelity and Vanguard funds, you may be forced to pay high fees or open up separate accounts at different supermarkets, which means extra paperwork and hassle.

With ETFs, you can buy them anywhere, sell them anywhere, and keep them — even if they're ETFs from several different providers — all parked in the same brokerage house. I know of no major brokerage house that now charges more than a few dollars to make an online ETF trade.

IN THIS CHAPTER

» Setting up an account for your ETFs

» Meeting the brokerage houses

» Finding out who supplies ETFs to the brokers

» Introducing the indexers

» Distinguishing between the exchanges

Chapter 2

Introducing the ETF Players

I love to shop on Christmas Eve. It's the only time of the entire year when men — who have finally realized that they need to buy a gift, quickly — outnumber women at the mall. I see these hulking figures, some in bright-orange hunting jackets, walking the fluorescent-lit halls of the mall, looking themselves like scared prey.

Sometimes, when I suggest to a client that they buy a few exchange-traded funds (ETFs) for their portfolio, I see the same look of dire trepidation. I need to reassure them that buying ETFs isn't that difficult. In this chapter, I want to do the same for you.

This chapter is something of a shopper's guide to ETFs — a mall directory, if you will. I don't suggest which specific ETFs to buy (I will, I will — but that's for later chapters). Instead, I show you where to find the brokerage houses that allow you to buy and sell ETFs; the financial institutions that create ETFs; the indexes on which the financial institutions base their ETFs; and the exchanges where millions of ETF shares are bought, sold, and borrowed every day.

Creating an Account for Your ETFs

You — you personally — can't just buy a share of an ETF as you would buy, say, a sweater. You need someone to actually buy it for you and hold it for you. That someone is a broker, sometimes referred to as a *brokerage house* or a *broker-dealer*. Some broker-dealers, the really big ones, are sort of like financial department stores or supermarkets where you can buy ETFs, mutual funds, individual stocks and bonds, or fancier investment products like puts and calls. You'll recognize, I'm sure, the names of such financial department stores as Fidelity, Vanguard, and Charles Schwab.

REMEMBER

ETFs are usually traded just as stocks are traded. Same commissions (or lack of commissions). Mostly the same rules. Same hours (generally 9:30 a.m. to 4 p.m. Eastern time). Through your brokerage house, you can buy 1 share, 2 shares, or 10,000 shares. Recently, some have begun to allow for the purchase of partial shares. (Not that any ETF shares are selling for the high price of, say, a new iPhone.) I know this sounds silly, but it can make trading in ETFs a lot easier for those who are math-challenged. Where partial shares are allowed, you don't need to figure out how many shares you want to buy with your, say, $1,000. You can Invest the whole $1,000, and you may wind up with, oh, 9.75 or 12.34 shares, or some such number.

Here's one difference between ETFs and stocks: Although people today rarely do it, you can sometimes purchase stocks directly from a company, and you may even get a pretty certificate saying you own the stock. (I *think* some companies still do that!) Not so with ETFs. Call BlackRock or State Street and ask to buy a share of an ETF, and they'll tell you to go find yourself a broker. Ask for a certificate, and, well, don't even bother.

The first step, then, prior to beginning your ETF shopping expedition, is to find a brokerage house, preferably a financial department store where you can keep all your various investments. It makes life a lot easier to have everything in one place, to get one statement every month, and to see all your investments on one computer screen.

Answering a zillion questions

The first question you have to answer when opening an account is whether it will be a retirement account or a non-retirement account. If you want a retirement account, you need to specify what kind — individual retirement account (IRA)? Roth IRA? Simplified Employee Pension (SEP)? I cover the ins and outs of retirement accounts — and how ETFs can fit snugly into the picture — in Chapter 9. A non-retirement account is a simpler animal. You don't need to know any special tax rules, and your money isn't committed for any time period unless you happen to stick something like a certificate of deposit (CD) into the account.

The next question you have to answer is whether you want to open a *margin account* or a *cash account.* A margin account is somewhat similar to a checking account with overdraft protection. It means that you can borrow from the account or make purchases of securities (such as ETFs, but generally not mutual funds) without actually having any cash to pay for them on the spot.

You're also asked questions about beneficiaries and titling (or registration), such as whether you want your joint account set up with rights of survivorship. I'll just say one quick word about naming your beneficiaries: Be certain that who you name is who you want to receive your money when you die.

Beneficiary designations supersede your will. In other words, if your will says that all your ETFs go to your sister, and your beneficiary designation on your account names someone else, your sister loses; all the ETFs in your account will go to that other person.

Finally, you're asked all kinds of personal questions about your employment, your wealth, and your risk tolerance. Don't sweat them! Federal securities regulations require brokerage houses to know something about their clients. Honestly, I don't think anyone ever looks at the personal section of the forms. I've never heard any representative of any brokerage house so much as whisper any of the information included in those personal questions.

Placing an order to buy

After your account is in place, which should take only a few days, you're ready to buy your first ETF. Most brokerage houses give you a choice: Call in your order, or do it yourself online. Calling is typically much more expensive because it requires the direct assistance of an actual person. Being the savvy investor that you are, you're not going to throw away money, so place all your orders online! If you need help, a representative of the brokerage house will walk you through the process step-by-step — for free!

DON'T MARGIN YOUR HOUSE AWAY!

I once knew a woman whose husband handled all their finances. (More often than not, one spouse handles much, if not all, of the money matters. In this case, as it happens, it was the man who handled the money, even though the woman was quite capable.) Then they divorced. Divorcing couples usually split the family assets, but they also split the liabilities. This client had no idea until she divorced, that her husband had been playing with stocks and ETFs, buying them on margin. Suddenly, the woman inherited a rather enormous debt.

Buying on margin means that the brokerage house is lending you money, and charging you interest, so you can purchase securities. Ouch. One of the often touted "advantages" of ETFs is that you can buy them on margin — something you often can't do with mutual funds. Margin buying is a very dangerous business. The fact that you can buy an ETF on margin is *not* an advantage as I see it. The stock market is risky enough. Don't ever compound that risk by borrowing money to invest. You may wind up losing not only your nest egg but also your home. This client was able to save their home; not everyone is so lucky.

Two things about margin you should know:

- The brokerage house can usually change the rate of interest you're paying without notice.
- If your investments dip below a certain percentage of your margin loan, the brokerage house can sell your stocks and bonds right from under you.

Once again, it can be a dangerous business; margin only with great caution.

Keep in mind when trading ETFs that the trading fees charged by the brokerage house may nibble seriously into your holdings (although usually not all that much). Even if you work with a brokerage house that charges nothing for trading ETFs, there will still be a small cost called the *spread* that you don't readily see. The spread is where you may lose a penny or two or three to middlemen working behind the scenes of each trade. Spreads can nibble at your portfolio just as the more visible fees do.

Here's how to avoid getting nibbled:

>> **Don't trade often.** Buy and hold, more or less (see Chapter 11). Yes, I know that headlines from time to time declare that "buy and hold is dead." That's nonsense. Don't believe it. "Buy and hold," by the way, doesn't mean you *never* trade. But if you're making more than a few trades every few months, that's too much.

>> **Know your percentages.** In general, don't bother with ETFs if the trade is going to cost you anything more than 0.5 percent. In other words, if making the trade is going to cost you $5, you want to invest at least $1,000 at a pop. If you have only $900 to invest, or less, you're often better off purchasing a no-load mutual fund, preferably an index fund, or waiting until you've accumulated enough cash to make a larger investment. Alternatively, you may choose a no-commission ETF, even if it's slightly less attractive than the ETF you'd have to pay a commission for. You may swap for the better alternative down the road, especially if you're funding a retirement account where swapping will have no tax consequences.

>> **Be a savvy shopper.** Keep the cost of your individual trades to a minimum by shopping brokerage houses for the lowest fees, placing all your orders online, and arguing for the best deals. Yes, you can often negotiate with these people for better deals, especially if you have substantial bucks. Also, know that many brokerage houses offer special incentives for new clients: Move more than $100,000 in assets and get your first 50 trades for free, or that sort of thing. Always ask.

But wait just a moment!

Please don't be so enthralled by anything you read in this book that you rush out, open a brokerage account, and sell your existing mutual funds or stocks and bonds to buy ETFs. Rash investment decisions almost always wind up being mistakes. Note that whenever you sell a security, you may face serious tax consequences. (Vanguard offers a unique advantage here; see the nearby sidebar "The Vanguard edge.") If you decide to sell certain mutual funds, annuities, or life insurance policies, there may also be nasty surrender charges. If you're unsure whether selling your present holdings would make for a financial hit on the chin, talk to your accountant or financial planner.

Trading ETFs like a pro

REMEMBER

If you're familiar with trading stocks, you already know how to trade ETFs. If you aren't, don't sweat it. Although there are all kinds of fancy trades you could make, and I'll touch on a few later, I'm going to ask you now to familiarize yourself with only the two most basic kinds of trades:

THE VANGUARD EDGE

If you own a Vanguard mutual fund and you want to convert to the Vanguard ETF that tracks the same index, you may be able do so without any tax ramifications. The conversion is tax-free because you'll actually be exchanging one class of shares for another class of shares, all within the same fund. You can do this *only* with Vanguard ETFs. Vanguard actually has a U.S. patent that gives it a lock on this share structure. Most, but not all, Vanguard funds are eligible.

For example, if you own shares in the Vanguard Total Stock Market Index Fund Admiral Shares (ticker symbol: VTSAX), and you decide that you want to exchange them for the Vanguard Total Stock Market ETF (ticker symbol: VTI), you can do so and not worry about having to take any tax hit. So, should you do it? The expense ratio on the mutual fund is 0.04. The expense ratio on the ETF is 0.03. If you have, say, $20,000 in the account, moving from the mutual fund to the ETF will save you $2 a year in management fees.

Note that the tax-free transfer works only in one direction. If you have ETF shares that have appreciated in value, you can't convert them to mutual-fund shares without incurring a taxable gain (unless you hold them in a retirement account).

>> **Market orders:** A *market order* to buy tells the broker that you want to buy. Period. After the order is placed, you will have bought your ETF shares . . . at whatever price someone out there was willing to sell you those shares for.

>> **Limit orders:** A *limit order* to buy asks you to name a price above which you walk away and go home. No purchase will be made. (A limit order to sell asks you to name a price below which you will not sell. No sale will be made.)

Market orders are fairly easy. You should be just fine as long as you are buying a domestic ETF that isn't too exotic (the kind of ETFs I'll be recommending throughout this book); as long as you aren't trading when the market is going crazy; or as long as you aren't trading right when the market opens or closes (9:30 a.m. and 4 p.m. Eastern time on weekdays).

A limit order may be a better option if you're placing a purchase for an ETF where the "bid" and the "ask" price may differ by more than a few pennies (indicating the middlemen are out to get you), or where there may be more than a negligible difference between the market price of the ETF and the net asset value of the securities it's holding. This would include ETFs that trade not that many shares — especially on a day when the market seems jumpy. The risk with limit orders is that you may not get your price, and so the order may not go through.

TIP

To execute a limit order without risk that you'll miss out on your purchase, place the order slightly above the last sale. If your ETF's last sale was for $10 a share, you may offer $10.03. If you're buying 100 shares, you may have just blown a whole $3, but you'll have your purchase in hand.

Introducing the Shops

I've read that the motorcycle industry boasts the highest level of consumer loyalty in the United States. A Harley person would *never* be caught dead on a Yamaha. Not being a motorcyclist, I have no idea why that is. In the world of brokerage houses, after someone has a portfolio in place at a house such as Fidelity, Vanguard, or Charles Schwab, that client is often very hesitant to switch. I know *exactly* why that is: Moving your account can sometimes be a big, costly, and time-consuming hassle. So, whether you're a

Harley person or a Yamaha person, if you have money to invest, it behooves you to spend some serious time researching brokerage houses and choose the one that will work best for you. Perhaps I can help.

Here's what you want from any broker who is going to be holding your ETFs:

>> Reasonable fees

>> Good service, meaning they answer the phone without putting you through answering-system hell

>> A user-friendly website

>> Good advice, if you think you're going to need advice — reps that don't stand to earn a commission for steering you into high-priced products

>> A service center near you, if you like doing business with real people

>> Financial strength

Financial strength really isn't as important as the others because all brokerage houses carry insurance. Still, a brokerage house that collapses under you can be a problem, and it may take time to recoup your money. (See the nearby sidebar "Can you lose your ETFs if your brokerage house collapses?")

Comparing the prices at brokerage houses was once very difficult, with trading commissions varying depending on how much money you had in your portfolio. Fortunately, those days are almost over. The majority of brokerage houses — including every one of the largest — have, over just the past year or two, killed all trading commissions. (Don't worry, they make their money elsewhere!)

So, whereas trading costs were once all-important in choosing a brokerage house, that's no longer the case, although you do need to concern yourself with other, ancillary fees. And then there are several nonmonetary considerations to take into account, which I address on the following pages. I'll start with the biggest of the brokers: Vanguard, Fidelity, Charles Schwab, and E*TRADE.

CAN YOU LOSE YOUR ETFs IF YOUR BROKERAGE HOUSE COLLAPSES?

Brokerage houses, as part of their registration process with the federal government, are automatically insured through the Securities Investor Protection Corporation (SIPC). Each individual investor's securities are protected up to $500,000 should the brokerage house go belly-up. Almost all larger brokerage houses carry supplemental insurance that protects customers' account balances beyond the half-million that SIPC covers. TD Ameritrade, for example, has insurance through Lloyd's of London that provides each customer $149.5 million worth of protection for securities and another $2 million for cash.

For additional information on SIPC, check out its website at www.sipc.org. For information on a prospective broker's supplemental insurance, check the brokerage's website, or call and ask.

Vanguard

I mention Vanguard (www.vanguard.com) frequently in this book for a number of reasons. For one, I like Vanguard because of its leadership role in the world of index investing. Vanguard is also both an investment house that serves as a custodian of ETFs and a major provider of ETFs (second in the nation after BlackRock).

Previously, you could buy only Vanguard ETFs commission-free, but that has recently changed. Now *all* ETFs held at Vanguard can be bought and sold without a fee.

But that's become pretty standard these days. Here's what really shines about Vanguard:

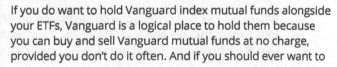

>> **Its broad array of top-rated index mutual funds:** I know, I know, this is a book about ETFs. But index mutual funds and ETFs are close cousins, and sometimes it makes sense to have both in a portfolio.

If you do want to hold Vanguard index mutual funds alongside your ETFs, Vanguard is a logical place to hold them because you can buy and sell Vanguard mutual funds at no charge, provided you don't do it often. And if you should ever want to switch from a mutual fund to an ETF, it's easy at Vanguard. (See the earlier sidebar, "The Vanguard edge.")

>> **The structure of the company:** Vanguard is owned "mutually" by its shareholders, unlike, say, Fidelity, which is privately owned, or just about all the other brokerage houses, which are publicly owned. The mutual ownership means that investors are shareholders in the company, and that means the Vanguard elite, although certainly well paid, have an obligation to serve your best interests. That gives me trust in the company.

Vanguard reps, by the way, don't ever work on commission. Yes, if you ask for advice, they may try to steer you toward Vanguard products, but not because they'll be taking a cut. Salespeople masquerading as "advisors" or "brokers" are rampant in the finance business. At Vanguard, you don't need to worry about that.

Fidelity

Fidelity (www.fidelity.com) is a giant in the field, a very competitive giant. Like Vanguard, Fidelity also has some excellent low-cost index mutual funds — as well as a handful of no-cost index mutual funds — of its own, which you may want to keep alongside your ETF portfolio. Unlike some other brokerages, Fidelity mutual funds have no minimums. (ETFs never have minimums, unless you consider one share a minimum.)

The Fidelity website has some really good tools — some of the best available — for analyzing your portfolio and researching new investments. Fidelity's reps are very knowledgeable and helpful, although post-COVID-19 phone wait times have been disappointingly long. But that problem, alas, affects the whole industry.

Charles Schwab

"Invest with Chuck" Schwab (www.schwab.com) was the nation's first discount broker, and they offer a lineup of sensible ETFs of their own creation, which trade free — along with other ETFs (since October 2019) — when you open an account with this brokerage house.

Whenever I've had occasion to do business with "Chuck's" staff, I found them friendly and knowledgeable. I just wish I could forgive Chuck for investing — and losing — so much of its clients' money in the mortgage crisis of 2008, and then admitting no wrong and making no restitution until being strong-armed by the court. (For those familiar with the case, I'm referring to Schwab's YieldPlus Fund debacle.)

Note: In 2019, Charles Schwab acquired the brokerage house TD Ameritrade (www.tdameritrade.com), and the scuttlebutt is that in 2023, all TD accounts will be integrated into Schwab.

E*TRADE

As the name implies, E*TRADE (https://us.etrade.com) was born in the digital age and has since become a major player, known especially for its easy-to-use mobile apps and on-the-fly trading tools, colorful graphics, and orientation toward younger investors.

As with the other biggies, commissions on ETFs have been obliterated.

Note: In 2020, E*TRADE was purchased by Morgan Stanley (www.morganstanley.com), so it is possible that E*TRADE may be changing its name in time.

Other brokerage houses

The houses I discuss in the previous sections aren't the only players in town. Here are a few more to consider.

>> **Ally** (www.ally.com): Primarily an online savings bank, Ally is also where you can house an ETF portfolio, as you can at many savings banks. But, as with many savings banks, not all the ETFs trade commission-free, and even those that do are subject to short-term trading costs. Ally has good rates on savings accounts and CDs, and if you have a chunk of your portfolio in these safe (but low-yielding) investments, and you want an ETF portfolio housed under the same roof, consider Ally.

>> **Interactive Brokers** (www.interactivebrokers.com): A very popular firm among international, institutional, and serious active traders, Interactive Brokers is also open to smaller, buy-and-hold investors. ETF trading is commission-free, but be aware that small accounts may be subject to

maintenance fees. If you're planning to retire abroad, especially to Europe, this firm is worth considering.

>> **T. Rowe Price** (www.troweprice.com): This Baltimore-based shop has several claims to fame, including its bend-over-backward friendliness to small investors and its plethora of really fine financial tools, especially for retirement planning, that are available to all customers at no cost. The service at this firm is excellent (reps tend to be very chummy). Trading ETFs? No commissions.

>> **TIAA** (www.tiaa.org): This is a good company, but I can't work with them directly because I'm not a teacher. This brokerage house works only with people who have chalk under their fingernails. (If you're married to such a person, you qualify, too.) There are some ETFs that trade with no commissions, and others that do.

Presenting the Suppliers

There are more than 1,000 mutual-fund providers. Many of these firms offer just one fund, and they sometimes give the impression that the entire business is run out of someone's garage. Not so with ETFs. Fewer providers exist (currently about 160 at the time of writing), and they tend to be larger companies. The top five providers — BlackRock, Vanguard, State Street, Invesco, and Charles Schwab — control 89 percent of the ETF market. Why is that? In large measure, it's because ETFs' management fees are so low that a company can't profit unless it enjoys the economies of scale and multiple income streams that come from offering a bevy of ETFs.

REMEMBER

I want to emphasize that while picking a single brokerage house to manage your accounts makes enormous sense, there is no reason that you can't own ETFs from different sources. Like your favorite professional sports team or clothing store, each supplier of ETFs has its own personality. A portfolio with a combination of BlackRock, Vanguard, and State Street ETFs can work just fine. In fact, I would recommend *not* wedding yourself to a single ETF supplier but being flexible and picking the best ETFs to meet your needs in each area of your portfolio.

Note that brokerage houses typically do not sell every available mutual fund. But I've never heard of a brokerage house limiting which ETFs it will sell.

TIP

When mixing and matching ETFs, I would just caution that you don't want holes in your portfolio, and you don't want overlap. Mixing and matching, say, a total U.S. stock fund from one ETF provider with a European stock fund of another provider would be just fine because there's virtually no chance for either overlap or gaps. However, I would recommend that in putting together, say, a U.S. value and a U.S. growth fund, or a U.S. large-cap and a U.S. small-cap fund, in the hopes of building a well-rounded portfolio, you may want to choose ETFs from the same ETF provider, using the same index providers (Russell, Morningstar, S&P, and so on). That's because each indexer uses slightly (and sometimes not so slightly) different definitions of *value, growth, large,* and *small.* So, mixing and matching funds from different providers may be less than ideal.

REMEMBER

One last preliminary note before I introduce the players: You'll recall that when I introduced you to the brokerage houses earlier in this chapter, I said that price is no longer key. That's because most brokerage houses have reduced their trading commissions to zero, and where there is a charge to trade an ETF, it is almost always miniscule. In choosing ETF providers — and, more important, individual ETFs — price *is* key. Every dollar you pay a fund provider in fees is probably, in the long run, one less dollar you're going to earn.

Table 2-1 offers a handy reference to the largest ETF providers, which I introduce you to in a moment. Note that I list the companies in order of the total assets each has in all its ETFs.

REMEMBER

A quick word for readers who live outside the United States: All ETFs (and mutual funds) sold in the United States must be approved by the U.S. Securities and Exchange Commission (SEC). Other countries have their equivalent governmental regulatory authorities. None of the ETFs listed in this section or in Part 2 are sold beyond the borders of the United States. Some of the ETF providers mentioned — particularly BlackRock and Vanguard — do sell ETFs in other countries, but not the same ETFs.

TABLE 2-1 Providers of ETFs

Company	Total Assets (in Trillions) at the Time of Writing	Number of ETFs at the Time of Writing	Claim to Fame
BlackRock iShares	$2.24	388	Biggest variety of funds
Vanguard	$1.76	80	Sensible, classic indexes
State Street Global Advisors	$0.90	130	Oldest and single-largest ETF
Invesco	$0.33	228	Quirky indexes
Charles Schwab	$0.24	26	Cheap, basic
First Trust	$0.12	174	Creative portfolios

BlackRock Financial Management iShares

With 338 ETFs for sale and $2.24 trillion in ETF assets (about a third of the U.S. ETF market) at the time of writing, iShares is the undisputed market leader. The firm behind iShares, BlackRock, Inc., merged in 2009 with Barclays Global Investors, the mega corporation that is now one of the largest investment banks in the world ($8.7+ trillion in assets under management at the time of writing). Through its iShares, BlackRock offers by far the broadest selection of any ETF provider. You can buy iShares that track the major S&P indexes for growth, value, large-cap, and small-cap stocks. Other iShares equity ETFs track the major Russell and Morningstar indexes. You can also find industry-sector iShares ETFs from technology and health care to financial services and software.

In the international arena, you can buy an iShares ETF to track either an intercontinental index, such as the MSCI EAFE (Europe, Australia, and the Far East), or much narrower markets, such as the Malaysian or Brazilian stock markets. iShares also offer a broad array of fixed-income (bond) ETFs, including 18 ETFs for U.S. government bonds alone, 15 for tax-free municipals, and others for corporate bonds and mortgage-backed securities of many different maturities and credit ratings.

Management fees vary from a low of 0.03 percent for its short-term Treasury Bond fund (ticker symbol: SGOV) and its plain-vanilla S&P 500 stock fund (ticker symbol: IVV). Most of the offerings cost in the range of 0.05 percent to 0.3 percent. Only the niche, more exotic offerings are what I would call really expensive. At the time of writing, the BlackRock Future Tech ETF (ticker symbol: BTEK) carries an expense ratio of 0.88, and the iShares India 50 ETF (ticker symbol: INDY) costs an eyebrow-raising 0.93 percent.

The single-country ETFs tend to run in the 0.6 ballpark, but BlackRock may be forced to cut that cost or lose market share to Franklin Templeton, which launched a very similar lineup of individual-country ETFs for a fraction of the price.

TIP

Generally, you won't go too wrong with BlackRock/iShares. The firm has done an outstanding job of tracking indexes and offering variety. It also has done a good job of maintaining tax-efficiency. I caution you, however, not to get sucked into the iShares candy store. Some of the ETFs track very small markets and market segments and clearly don't belong in most people's portfolios. I suggest that you think twice, for example, before making the iShares MSCI Peru ETF (ticker symbol: EPU) a major part of your portfolio. It's expensive at 0.59 percent a year, and the market capitalization of the entire Lima Stock Exchange — including every publicly owned corporation issuing stock — is about $97 billion. That may sound like a good sum, but it's less than half the size of PepsiCo, Inc., America's thirty-fifth largest company! For more information, visit www.ishares.com.

Vanguard ETFs

It goes without saying that these people know something about index investing. In 1976, Vanguard launched the first index-based mutual fund for the retail investor, the Vanguard Index Trust 500 Portfolio. (Wells Fargo already had an index fund, but it was available only to endowments and other institutions.) In 2001, Vanguard launched its first ETF. Why Vanguard wasn't exactly in the ETF vanguard is anyone's guess, but by the time Vanguard ETFs were introduced to the market, iShares (then under Barclays) had already taken a solid lead. But Vanguard ETFs are quickly moving up. As of this writing, 80 Vanguard ETFs hold $1.76 trillion in assets, making Vanguard the second-largest ETF provider.

Vanguard is the fastest-growing ETF provider due to its sensible methodologies and its low costs. How low is low cost? The lowest-cost Vanguard ETFs — the Vanguard S&P 500 ETF (ticker symbol: VOO) and the Vanguard Total Stock Market ETF (ticker symbol: VTI) — will set you back 0.03 percent in total management expenses per year. (That's 30 cents per $1,000 invested.) Even the *most* expensive of Vanguard's offerings, the Vanguard International High Dividend Yield Index Fund (ticker symbol: VYMI), costs only 0.27 percent at the time of writing — not at all outrageous.

TIP

I *love* Vanguard's low costs. Who wouldn't? Vanguard's lineup of ETFs, in line with Vanguard's corporate personality, is sensible and direct. In fact, Vanguard is perhaps the only major supplier of ETFs that offers nothing I would consider wacky or inappropriate for most investors' portfolios. In other words, Vanguard doesn't market something simply because it will sell. The company uses reasonable indexes, tracks them well, and takes the utmost care to avoid capital gains taxes and make certain that all dividends paid are "qualified" dividends subject to a lower tax rate. For more information, visit www.vanguard.com.

State Street Global Advisors SPDRs

State Street's flagship ETF, the first ETF on the U.S. market, is the SPDR S&P 500 (ticker symbol: SPY). It boasts more than $364 billion in net assets at the time of writing, considerably larger than any other ETF on the market. State Street Global Advisor's pet spider gives it a firm perch as the third-largest provider of ETFs, having recently fallen well behind number-two Vanguard. State Street's initial ETFs tended to follow more traditional indexes but have since branched out into some awfully niche areas. The more basic ETFs (the ones I prefer) carry reasonable fees and are varied enough to allow for a very well-diversified portfolio. All told, State Street's 130 U.S.-based ETFs hold about $900 billion in assets at the time of writing.

TIP

The management expenses — with most of the basic ETFs costing less than 0.2 percent a year — are generally reasonable. The SPDRs offer a very efficient way of investing in various industry sectors (if that's your thing), both at home and abroad. Some of the newer offerings are, like BlackRock's, awfully niche and a tad on the pricey side — although not nearly as niche and pricey as the ETF offerings of some of the smaller purveyors. For more information, visit www.ssga.com/us/en/intermediary/etfs.

WARNING

One drawback to State Street's offerings is the legal structure of some of its ETFs. The oldest ETFs, such as SPY, are set up as unit investment trusts rather than open-end funds as most of the newer ETFs are. That means the older funds can't reinvest dividends on a regular basis, creating a cash drag that can bring down long-term total returns by a smidgen. It's hard to actually measure the impact, but a recent glance at three S&P 500 ETFs — Vanguard's VOO, iShares's IVV, and SPY — show VOO's and IVV's one-year returns clocking in at one basis point (1/1,000) higher than SPY's. Not a huge deal.

Invesco

Invesco, formerly Invesco PowerShares, gobbled up ETF provider Guggenheim (which formerly gobbled up Rydex) to become number four in size and number two in number of fund offerings among ETF providers. The ETFs tend to be a bit pricier than those of the Big Three, and the methodologies may often be called "innovative" or "nutty," depending on your point of view. Invesco is perhaps the leader in so-called "smart beta" indexing, where the line between passive and active management can get a wee bit blurry.

That is to say that most of the ETFs do follow indexes, but the indexes themselves are designed to beat the market, where "the market" is defined as classic indexes, such as the S&P 500. These indexes choose securities, generally not based on the market-cap company, but on other criteria, such as low volatility, high volatility, momentum, sensitivity to interest rates, growth in revenue, and so on.

Some of the ETFs are based on multiple valuation criteria. That means potential high turnover and some added trading expenses. It also means that if you choose PowerShares ETFs to build your portfolio, you're no longer a true index investor, which (judging by historical data over the long haul) may put you at something of a disadvantage.

The company has been quite creative in its offerings, and allows you to slice and dice your portfolio in 228 ways.

Nothing about Invesco's alternative indexes scares me too much. The problem is which alternative indexes are going to beat the classical indexes? You don't know. And if you choose a whole bunch of the alternative indexes — momentum, low-volatility, high-revenue, and so on — you'll be buying the whole stock market but paying a boatload more than you would for any whole-stock-market ETF.

TIP

I have used one Invesco ETF, despite the relatively high expense ratio of 0.4 percent: the Invesco S&P 500 Equal Weight Consumer Staples ETF (ticker symbol: RHS). In Chapter 10, I discuss how I diversify a portfolio, which can include the mild overweighting of certain industry sectors, notably Consumer Staples. The problem with most Consumer Staples funds is that they offer only large-cap companies, whereas RHS gives you large, medium, and small. If the expense ratio were lower, I would use this fund more. For more information, visit www.invesco.com/us/en/Individual-investor.html. (Be sure to capitalize the *I* in the URL as I've done here — otherwise, the URL won't work.)

Table 2-2 shows the average expense ratio (weighted by assets under management) of all the ETFs issued by one purveyor. The six largest ETF providers tend to have relatively low costs, which is one reason why they're the largest. The data is provided by ETF Database.

TABLE 2-2   ## Expense Ratio Comparison

Company	Average Expense Ratio
Vanguard	0.06%
Charles Schwab	0.08%
BlackRock iShares	0.19%
State Street Global Advisors	0.23%
Invesco	0.3%
First Trust	0.65%

Charles Schwab

Brokerage giant Charles Schwab came into the ETF game late — in 2009 — but immediately caught market share by offering free trading of Schwab ETFs on the Schwab platform (you can now trade all ETFs free) and by offering ETFs with lower expense ratios than anyone else. At present, only Vanguard can match Schwab in terms of economy. And like Vanguard, Schwab has been prudent in its offerings.

Nothing flashy. Nothing off-the-wall. Of Schwab's 26 ETFs, 20 are plain-vanilla market-weighted offerings, such as the Schwab U.S. Large-Cap ETF (ticker symbol: SCHX) with an expense ratio of 0.03 percent, and the Schwab U.S. Aggregate Bond ETF (ticker symbol: SCHZ) with an expense ratio of 0.04 percent. Six of the ETFs are based on what Schwab on its website calls "fundamental" indexes: "a complement to traditional market-cap index and actively managed strategies, helping to create the potential for more attractive risk-adjusted portfolios."

The fundamental-index funds have expense ratios of 0.25 percent to 0.39 percent, so it will be hard for these passive-active funds to beat the much cheaper passive-index ETFs over the long haul. Not impossible, but hard.

TIP

I've become a recent Schwab convert, switching over my portfolios to sell off the iShares TIPS fund (ticker symbol: TIP) — TIPS stands for Treasury Inflation-Protected Securities — and buy the very, very similar Schwab U.S. TIPS ETF (ticker symbol: SCHP). The cost is 0.19 percent for the iShares but only 0.04 percent for the Schwab model. For more information, visit www.schwab.com.

First Trust

First Trust, which is sixth among the largest ETF providers, comes with only half the assets of Schwab (which is in the number-five spot). Like most of the smaller contenders, the management fees are higher. However, if you're looking for active management or truly different, unusual asset classes, First Trust may be the place to turn. Where else will you find such investments as the First Trust Merger Arbitrage ETF (ticker symbol: MARB) or the First Trust Hedged BuyWrite Income ETF (ticker symbol: FTLB)?

First Trust also offers structured-product ETFs, otherwise known as defined-outcome ETFs, which have just hit the market in the past year or so. I'm not a fan.

Buying a basic portfolio-building-block kind of ETF through First Trust just doesn't make any sense. The prices are too high. On the other hand, First Trust doesn't offer much in the way of basic. Most of its ETFs are one of a kind. As with any investment of this ilk, proceed with caution. For more information, visit www.ftportfolios.com.

Other suppliers

At present, there are 200 or so issuers of ETFs in addition to the six I talk about. These include some fairly strong brands that offer a bevy of ETFs at fairly reasonable prices, such as ProShares, WisdomTree, Van Eck Associates, Franklin Templeton, and Mirae Asset Global Investments.

The list includes some financial giants that got into the ETF game late, but with all the muscle they have, they may become major players. Fidelity, JPMorgan Chase, BNY Mellon, Dimensional, New York Life, and TIAA are examples.

Some of the real niche providers are the World Gold Council, ARK, Cambria, Innovator, Amplify Investments, and Sprott. Some are pretty small companies with only a handful of offerings — or one — and some of their novel ideas may pan out. Unfortunately, the small fries too often try to make up for the lack of economies of scale by throwing economy out the window and charging you as much as, or more than, you'd pay for an actively managed mutual fund, greatly diminishing your odds of seeing a healthy return. Many of the small providers will be gone in the years to come. On the other hand, some awfully overpriced and under-achieving mutual funds have been around for years.

Familiarizing Yourself with the Indexers

At the core of most ETFs is an index. The index is the blueprint on which the ETF is based. Some ETF providers use old, established indexes. Others create their own, often in conjunction with sea-soned indexers. (That association helps them get approval from the SEC.) As a rule, for an ETF to be any good, it has to be based on a solid index. On the other hand, a solid index doesn't guaran-tee a good ETF because other things, like costs and tax-efficiency, matter as well. That being said, I turn now to the five indexers that create and re-create the indexes on which most ETFs are based.

S&P Dow Jones Indices

Once known as Standard & Poor's, and today simply as S&P Global, or S&P, the company maintains hundreds of indexes, including the S&P 500 (the one you're most likely to see flashed across your TV on the business channel). Trillions in investors' assets are directly tied to S&P Dow Jones Indices — close to all other indexes combined.

More ETFs are based on S&P and Dow indexes than any other, by far. These include many of the offerings of BlackRock, Vanguard, Charles Schwab, State Street Global Investors, Invesco, ProShares, WisdomTree, and Direxion. For more information, visit www. spglobal.com.

MSCI

With indexes of all kinds — stocks, bonds, hedge funds, U.S. and international securities — MSCI (formerly Morgan Stanley Capital International), although not quite a household name, has been gaining ground as the indexer of choice for many ETF providers.

MSCI indexes are the backbone of many of the iShares global-industry funds and single-country ETFs. MSCI is also a preeminent provider of ESG benchmarks (see Chapter 6). For more information, visit www.msci.com.

FTSE/Russell

The largest 1,000 U.S. stocks make up the Russell 1000 index, although it remains relatively obscure because the Dow Industrial and the S&P 500 hog the spotlight when it comes to measuring large-cap performance. The next 2,000 largest stocks on the U.S. market are in the Russell 2000. And the Russell 1000 plus the Russell 2000 make up the Russell 3000. Those are Russell's more popular indexes, but it has plenty of others as well.

Many of the iShares domestic ETFs are based on FTSE/Russell indexes, as are a good number of Vanguard's U.S. offerings. ProShares and Direxion also use Russell indexes. For more information, visit www.ftserussell.com.

CRSP

CRSP (pronounced "crisp") stands for the Center for Research in Security Prices. For 60 years, CRSP, a baby of the University of Chicago Booth School of Business, has been creating indexes used mostly by academics. All that changed in 2012 when Vanguard dumped MSCI for a number of its U.S. index funds (both mutual funds and ETFs) and started to use CRSP. The changeover wasn't so much Vanguard preferring one indexer's indexes more than the others; the industry scuttlebutt is that the CRSP deal saved Vanguard a lot of money, part of which saving could presumably be passed on to investors. For more information, visit www.crsp.org.

Bloomberg

Lehman Brothers for years was the leading indexer in the world of fixed-income investments. The firm was acquired by Barclays Capital in 2008 (just as Barclays was leaving the ETF business). Thus, the long-famous Lehman Brothers Aggregate Bond Index, the closest thing the fixed-income world had to the S&P 500, was changed to the Barclays Capital Aggregate Bond Index. Then in 2016, the index was turned over to Bloomberg, L.P., which renamed it the Bloomberg Barclays Aggregate Bond Index, which in 2021 became the Bloomberg U.S. Aggregate Bond Index. *Whew!* This thing has had more incarnations than any character from Bollywood!

Although the Bloomberg Aggregate Bond Index is the firm's most famous product, there are dozens of other bond indexes, and they're used by BlackRock, Vanguard, and State Street. Just about any company that issues plain-vanilla bond funds uses Bloomberg indexes for its fixed-income ETFs. For more information, visit www.bloomberg.com.

Meeting the Middlemen

In the beginning, most ETFs were traded on the American Stock Exchange. In July 2005, however, iShares decided to move its primary listings for 81 of its ETFs to the New York Stock Exchange (NYSE), citing superior technology. Then, in 2008, the American Stock Exchange was gobbled up by the New York Stock Exchange, which today goes by the name NYSE Arca. Most ETFs today are listed on either the NYSE Arca or the Nasdaq, but a fair number are also traded on BATS, a stock exchange run by Cboe Global Markets.

TIP

Note that there is a difference between an ETF being *listed* on, say, the NYSE Arca, and an ETF being *traded* on the NYSE Arca. And an ETF or a stock that is listed (meaning more or less proffered for sale) on the NYSE Arca can trade on any number of exchanges simultaneously. In fact, the Securities Exchange Act of 1934 permits securities listed on any national securities exchange to be traded by all other such exchanges.

Does it matter to you on which exchange your ETF is listed or traded? No, not really, except to the extent that the stock exchanges love ETFs, and if you're an ETF investor, they will love *you*. The reason is fairly obvious: The stock exchanges make their money on, uh, exchanges of stocks. Mutual funds, per se, are not exchanged. ETFs are. And to promote ETFs, the stock exchanges offer some good information on their websites that you may want to check out.

>> **NYSE Arca** (www.nyse.com): Tracing its origins to 1792, the NYSE Arca today lists about 8,000 securities, has about 3,000 member companies, and trades billions of shares a day. About 80 percent of all ETFs are listed on the NYSE Arca. Most of the others are listed on the Nasdaq.

>> **Nasdaq** (www.nasdaq.com): No bricks and mortar here — the Nasdaq is a uniquely electronic exchange. The acronym Nasdaq, by the way, stands for National Association of Securities Dealers Automatic Quotation. If you go to www.nasdaq.com and click Market Activity and then ETFs, there's fun information at your fingertips, such as which ETFs are trading the most and which have seen the most price movement in the past day.

>> **BATS** (www.cboe.com): About 220 ETFs are traded on BATS, an outfit run by Cboe Global Markets, Inc. (Cboe). Once upon a time, Cboe stood for Chicago Board Options Exchange, and even though there are lots of securities that now trade on BATS, the emphasis is still on options. So, if you want to learn anything about options (on ETFs or other securities), the website offers a good education.

Meeting the Wannabe Middlemen

On January 24, 1848, James Marshall found gold at Sutter's Mill, touching off the California gold rush. About 150 years later, ETFs were the hottest investment product in the land, and so began the ETF rush. Everyone wants in on the game. So, we have our ETF providers, the brokerage houses where ETFs are bought and sold, the exchanges where they're listed, and the indexes on which they're based. Who else is there? Ah, the wannabe middlemen: They're about as necessary as forks in a soup kitchen, but rest assured that they'll continue to try to muscle in on the money.

Commissioned brokers

Most often they call themselves "financial planners," and some may actually do some financial planning. Many, however, are merely salespeople in poor disguise, marketing pricey and otherwise inferior investment products and living off the "load." The *load* — or entrance fee — to buying certain investment products, such as some mutual funds, most annuities, and virtually all life insurance products, can be ridiculously high. Thank goodness they don't exist in the world of ETFs — yet.

When first introduced, the PowerShares lineup of ETFs was designed to be sold through commissioned brokers at 2 percent a pop. The SEC killed the idea. But in time, the commissioned brokers may return to the world of ETFs, with their lobbyists in tow.

Separately managed accounts

Separately managed accounts (SMAs) have traditionally been aimed at the well-to-do. Instead of buying into mutual funds, the wealthy hire private managers with Persian rugs in their lobbies to do essentially what a mutual-fund manager does: Pick stocks. But now many SMAs are billing themselves as ETF gurus. Instead of picking stocks, they pick ETFs — at a price.

WARNING

ETF SMAs that promise to beat the market through exceptional ETF selection or market timing are unlikely to do any better than stock SMAs. Don't hold your breath waiting for these people to make you rich. Some SMA managers may be very good at what they do, but much of what they do can be learned in this book. If you want to hire someone to manage your ETFs, that's fine, but if they start talking about skimming 2 percent a year off your assets, heck, you'll very likely do better on your own (with this book in hand!). Trust me.

Annuities and life insurance products

WARNING

I've seen ads of late from variable annuity companies that feature ETFs in their portfolio. Great! That's better than high-priced mutual funds. But still, most variable annuities are way overpriced, carry nasty penalties for early withdrawal, and prove to be lousy investments. The same is true for many life insurance products other than simple term life. Investments in ETFs can make these products better, but that's a relative thing. As a rule, it's best to keep your investment products apart from your insurance products. And never buy an annuity unless you're absolutely sure you know what you're buying.

Funds of funds

WARNING

Question the purchase of any mutual fund that features ETFs among its top holdings. Or any ETF that is made up of other ETFs. Ask yourself if there's a good reason for you to be paying two layers of management fees. There are times when such layering makes sense. Such is the case with many "target date" or "life cycle" funds. But in all cases, if those two layers add up to, say, more than 0.5 percent, you need to *really* start to question your purchase.

2

Familiarizing Yourself with Different ETFs

Know what to expect from large- and small-growth stocks — the behemoths and the start-ups — so you can appropriately utilize both.

Satisfy your wanderlust (sorta) by delving into the world of international investing.

Discover how to specialize with sector and style investing.

Get the details you need to get into the bond game with exchange-traded funds (ETFs).

Go down further specialized ETF roads, like real estate investment trusts (REITs) and commodities.

IN THIS CHAPTER

» Sizing up the size factor in ETF investing

» Recognizing large-growth ETFs that may work well for you

» Evaluating value investing

» Taking note of ETFs that fill the large-value bill

Chapter **3**

ETFs for Large Growth and Large Value

Why do American suburbanites gingerly cultivate their daisies, yet go nuts swinging spades or spraying poison chemicals at their dandelions? Why is a second cup of coffee in a diner free, but a second cup of tea isn't? Some things in this world just don't make a lot of sense. Why, for example, would slower-growing companies (the dandelions of the corporate world) historically reward investors better than faster-growing (daisy) companies? Welcome to the shoulder-shrugging world of value investing.

I'm talking about companies you've probably heard of, yes, but they aren't nearly as glamorous as Microsoft or as exciting as Tesla. I'm talking about companies that usually ply their trade in older, slow-growing industries, like insurance, petroleum, and transportation. I'm talking about companies such as United-Health Group, Procter & Gamble, ExxonMobil, and Exelon Corporation (providing electricity and gas to customers in Illinois and Pennsylvania).

I see you yawning! But before you fall asleep, consider this: Since 1927, large-value stocks have enjoyed an annualized growth rate of roughly 12 percent, versus 10 percent for large-growth stocks — with roughly the same standard deviation (volatility). And thanks to exchange-traded funds (ETFs), investing in value has never been easier.

In this chapter, I explain not only the role that both large-growth and large-value stocks play in your portfolio, but I also run through considerations for utilizing them and good ETF options to consider.

Reviewing Large-Growth Basics

One approach to building a portfolio involves investing in different styles of stocks: large cap, mid cap, small cap, value, and growth. How did the whole business of style investing get started? Hard to say. Benjamin Graham, the "Dean of Wall Street," the "Father of Value Investing," who wrote several oft-quoted books in the 1930s and 1940s, didn't give investors the popular style grid that you see in Figure 3-1. But Mr. Graham certainly helped provide the tools of fundamental analysis whereby more contemporary brains could figure things out.

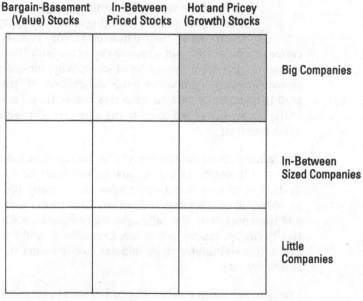

© John Wiley & Sons, Inc.

FIGURE 3-1: The place of large-growth stocks in the grid.

In the early 1980s, studies out of the University of Chicago began to quantify the differences between large caps and small caps, and in 1992, two economists named Eugene Fama and Kenneth French delivered the seminal paper on the differences between value and growth stocks.

What makes large cap large?

REMEMBER

Capitalization or *cap* refers to the combined value of all shares of a company's stock. The lines dividing large cap, mid cap, and small cap are sometimes blurry. The distinction is largely in the eyes of the beholder. If you took a poll, however, I think you would find that the following divisions are generally accepted:

>> **Large caps:** Companies with more than $10 billion in capitalization

>> **Mid caps:** Companies with $2 billion to $10 billion in capitalization

>> **Small caps:** Companies with $300 million to $2 billion in capitalization

Anything from $50 million to $300 million would usually be deemed a *micro cap*. And your local pizza shop, if it were to go public, might be called a *nano cap (con aglio)*. There are no nano-cap ETFs. For all the other categories, there are ETFs to your heart's content.

How does growth differ from value?

Many different criteria are used to determine whether a stock or basket of stocks (such as an ETF) qualifies as *growth* or *value*. (Later in this chapter, I list six ways to recognize value.) One popular measure is the price-to-book (P/B) ratio, which looks at the price of the stock in comparison to the book value, which is a company's total assets minus its liabilities. But perhaps the most important measure (if I were forced to pick one) would be the price-to-earnings (P/E) ratio, sometimes referred to as the *multiple.*

The P/E ratio is the price of a stock divided by its earnings per share. For example, suppose McDummy Corporation stock is currently selling for $40 a share. And suppose that the company earned $2 last year for every share of stock outstanding. McDummy's P/E ratio would be 20. (At the time of writing, the S&P 500 has a P/E of about 45, but that ratio changes frequently. Historically, the average is about 15.)

REMEMBER

The higher the P/E, the more investors have been willing to pay for the company's earnings. Or to put it in terms of growth and value:

>> **The higher the P/E, the more "growthy" the company:** Either the company is growing fast, or investors have high hopes (realistic or foolish) for future growth.

>> **The lower the P/E, the more "valuey" the company:** The business world doesn't see this company as a mover and shaker.

Each ETF carries a P/E reflecting the collective P/E of its holdings and giving you an indication of just how "growthy" or "valuey" that ETF is. A growth ETF is filled with companies that look like they're taking over the planet. A value ETF is filled with companies that seem to be meandering along but whose stock can be purchased for what looks like a bargain price.

Putting these terms to use

Today, most investment pros develop their portfolios with at least some consideration given to the cap size and growth or value orientation of their stock holdings. Why? Because study after study shows that, in fact, a portfolio's performance is inexorably linked to where that portfolio falls in the style grid in Figure 3-1. A mutual fund that holds all large-growth stocks, for example, will generally (but certainly not always) rise or fall with the rise or fall of that asset class.

Some research shows that perhaps 90 percent to 95 percent of a mutual fund's or ETF's performance may be attributable to its asset class alone. In other words, any large-cap growth fund will tend to perform similarly to other large-cap growth funds. Any small-cap value fund will tend to perform similarly to other small-cap value funds. And so on. That's why the financial press's weekly wrap-ups of top-performing funds will typically list a bunch of funds that mirror each other very closely. (That being the case, why not enjoy the low cost and tax-efficiency of the ETF or index mutual fund?)

Looking into Big and Brawny Stocks

Large-growth companies grab nearly all the headlines, for sure. The pundits are forever singing their praises — or trumpeting their faults when the growth trajectory starts to level off. Either way, you'll hear about it; the northeast corner of the style grid in Figure 3-1 includes the most recognizable names in the corporate world. If you're seeking employment, I strongly urge you to latch on to one of these companies; your future will likely be bright. But do large-growth stocks necessarily make the best investments?

Er, no.

Mulling over theories about large-growth stocks

According to Fama and French (who are still operating as a research duo), over the course of the last 94 years, large-growth stocks have seen an annualized return rate (not accounting for inflation) of about 10 percent. Not too bad. But that compares to 12 percent for large-value stocks, which don't, on the face of it, seem to be any more volatile. Theories abound as to why large-growth stocks haven't done as well as value stocks. Value stocks pay greater dividends, say some. Value stocks really *are* riskier; they just don't look it, argue others.

REMEMBER

The theory that makes the most sense, in my opinion, is that growth stocks are simply hampered by their own immense popularity. Because growth companies grab all the headlines, because investors *think* they must be the best investments, the large-growth stocks tend to get overpriced by the time you buy them. If people expect a stock to tank (in which case, the P/E will be much lower), value investors may jump in and make a profit even if the company doesn't grow at all — but merely doesn't tank!

Letting history serve as only a rough guide

So, given that large-value stocks historically have done better than large-growth stocks, and given (as I discuss in Chapter 4) that small caps historically have knocked the socks off large, does it still make sense to sink some of your investment dollars into large growth? Oh, yes, it does. The past is only an indication of what the future may bring. No one knows whether value stocks will continue to outshine large-growth stocks. In the past decade, in fact, large-growth stocks have outperformed both value and small-cap stocks — shooting far ahead of the pack in 2020 when COVID-19 hit, and everyone stopped going to stores and hung out on their computers all day. So far, there seems to be a reversal, back to more historical norms.

WARNING

Please don't accuse me of market timing! I'm not saying that, because a reversal seems to be in gear, you should dump growth for value or large cap for small cap, or any such thing. I have no idea what will happen over the coming months. But to a small and limited degree, a little timely *tactical* tilting, I feel, is an okay thing. That is, it may make some sense to tilt a portfolio *gently* toward whatever sectors seem to be sagging and away from sectors that have been blazing. If you do that subtly and regularly, and if you don't let emotions sway you — and if you watch out carefully for tax ramifications and trading costs — history shows that you may eke out some modest added return. (You can read more on tactical tilting in Chapter 11.)

TIP

Stocks of large companies — value and growth combined — should make up between 50 percent and 70 percent of your total domestic stock portfolio. The higher your risk tolerance, the closer you'll want to be to the lower end of that range. Whatever your allocation to domestic large-cap stocks, I recommend that you invest anywhere from 40 percent to 50 percent of that amount in growth. Take a tilt toward value, if you want, but don't tilt so far that you risk tipping over.

Digging into Large-Cap ETF Options Galore

The roster of ETFs on the market now includes roughly 1,700 stock funds, and most of them are going to include at least some large-cap U.S. growth stocks. In fact — and this may surprise you — if you look at a "total stock-market" fund, such as, say, the popular Vanguard Total Stock Market fund (ticker symbol: VTI), you'll find that a full 73 percent of it is made up of large-cap stocks. That's because it is, like the vast majority of ETFs, a fund based on a "market-weighted" index. And because large-cap stocks have lots of weight, you'll find that they tend to dominate most indexes.

These large-cap stocks that you'll find in VTI are value and growth stocks, as well as in-between (blend) stocks. If you have a very small portfolio, and you really want to keep things super simple, then VTI is a great ETF to hold. But for most investors, it would be wise to have large-cap stocks separate from small-cap stocks, and to have growth stocks separate from value stocks. That approach gives you the opportunity to rebalance once a year and, by so doing, keep a cap on risk, and possibly juice out a higher return. (You can find more on rebalancing in Chapter 11.) It also allows for fine-tuning your portfolio, to give it a value tilt, if you so desire, and to give your portfolio more than a sprinkling of small-cap stocks, which is exactly what you'll get in "total-market" funds.

Winnowing the field

In addition to finding large-cap growth stocks in total-market funds, you're also going to find them, of course, in funds that are specifically large-cap funds and in just about all industry-sector funds, be they technology, health-care, or consumer-discretionary ETFs. You'll also find large-cap growth in actively managed ETFs. But the ETFs I'm about to introduce you to are broad-based large-growth funds, covering all industry sectors. And they're index funds because, well, as I discuss in Part 1, index funds are really where you want to be — just ask any academic who has studied market performance and investor returns.

There are, of course, differences among index funds. I look for reasonable indexes with very low costs. And when I'm looking for growth, I want more "growthy" rather than less (a high P/E ratio is a good sign), and when I'm looking for large cap, I want *large*.

Large means that the portfolio has a high average market cap — higher than others in the pack. Unfortunately, different fund companies measure "average" in different ways, so it can be hard to compare apples to apples because fund companies can't agree on exactly what weight to give, say, Apple stock (among others) when it appears in the portfolio. So, rather than go to each ETF purveyor directly for the average market cap, I went to Morningstar Direct. If you're a math geek, know that Morningstar Direct uses a "geometric mean" for a stock fund's average cap size, whereas others may use an "arithmetic mean," or a median. If you're not a math geek, think of Morningstar's measure as a "center of gravity" that is found by looking not only at the raw size of the companies in the portfolio but also at the importance that each company has within the portfolio mix, so one company with a market cap of $100 gazillion-gazillion doesn't ridiculously inflate the average.

The best options for strictly large growth

For a focus on large growth (complemented elsewhere in the portfolio by large value, of course), the five options I list here all provide good exposure to the asset class.

Vanguard Growth ETF (ticker symbol: VUG)

Indexed to: CRSP U.S. Large Cap Growth Index (280 or so of the nation's largest growth stocks)

Expense ratio: 0.04 percent

Average market cap: $276.4 billion

P/E ratio: 42

Top five holdings: Apple, Microsoft, Amazon, Alphabet, Facebook

Russell's review: The price is right. The index makes sense. There's good diversification. The companies represented are certainly large, even though they could be a bit more "growthy." This ETF is certainly a very good option. There's also "The Vanguard edge" (see Chapter 2), which gives this fund another advantage for those who may already own the Vanguard Growth Index mutual fund.

Vanguard Mega Cap 300 Growth ETF (ticker symbol: MGK)

Indexed to: CRSP U.S. Mega Cap Growth Index (110 or so of the largest growth companies in the United States)

Expense ratio: 0.07 percent

Average market cap: $435.7 billion

P/E ratio: 40.5

Top five holdings: Apple, Microsoft, Amazon, Alphabet, Facebook

Russell's review: Bigger is better . . . sometimes. If you have small caps in your portfolio, this mega-cap fund will give you slightly better diversification than the Vanguard Growth ETF (VUG; see the preceding section), but this fund is also a tad less "growthy"

than VUG, so you'll get a bit less divergence from your large-value holdings. Nothing to sweat. Either fund, given Vanguard's low expenses and reasonable indexes, would make for a fine holding.

Schwab U.S. Large-Cap Growth ETF (ticker symbol: SCHG)

Indexed to: Dow Jones U.S. Large-Cap Growth Total Stock Market Index (230 or so of the largest and presumably fastest-growing U.S. firms)

Expense ratio: 0.04 percent

Average market cap: $335.8 billion

P/E ratio: 40

Top five holdings: Apple, Microsoft, Amazon, Facebook, Alphabet

Russell's review: For the sake of economy alone, this fund, like nearly all Schwab ETFs, makes a good option. The management fee is one of the lowest in the industry. Most important, the index is a good one, and you can expect Schwab to do a reasonable or better job of tracking the index.

iShares Morningstar Large-Cap Growth ETF (ticker symbol: ILCG)

Indexed to: Morningstar U.S. Large-Mid Cap Broad Growth Index (420 or so of the largest and most "growthy" U.S. companies)

Expense ratio: 0.04 percent

Average market cap: $231.2 billion

P/E ratio: 45.5

Top five holdings: Microsoft, Amazon, Apple, Facebook, Alphabet

Russell's review: This ETF offers more "growthiness" than its competitors, which is good. And the price is right. Morningstar indexes are crisp and distinct: Any company that appears in the growth index is not going to be popping up in the value index. Even though that crispness could lead to slightly higher turnover, I like it.

Nuveen ESG Large-Cap Growth ETF (ticker symbol: NULG)

Indexed to: This ETF provides passive exposure to the 105 or so companies that are in MSCI's TIAA USA Large-Cap Growth Index. If you don't know what ESG is, it stands for *environmental, social, and governance* (turn to Chapter 6 to learn more).

Expense ratio: 0.35 percent

Average market cap: $165.7 billion

P/E ratio: 47

Top five holdings: Microsoft, Alphabet, Tesla, NVIDIA Corporation, Visa

Russell's review: The average market cap is smaller than the other large-cap growth ETFs, and the expense ratio is higher — significantly higher. To date, however, Nuveen offers you the only option to invest in ETFs with style (value, growth, large, small), and to have a portfolio constructed with ESG considerations. Given that the portfolio holdings of this ETF differ appreciably from the other large-growth ETFs, you could see a significant difference in performance. Higher or lower? Probably, in the long run, higher. But that's due largely to the smaller average market cap, which brings with it greater volatility.

Growth ETFs I wouldn't go out of my way to own

WARNING

None of the following ETFs is horrible. But given the plethora of choices, barring very special circumstances, I would not recommend them.

>> **SPDR Dow Jones Industrial Average ETF Trust (ticker symbol: DIA):** Based on the index on which this ETF is based, I don't like it. The Dow Jones Industrial Average is an antiquated and somewhat arbitrary index of about 30 large companies that some committee pulled together by S&P Global thinks represents Corporate America. That isn't enough on which to build a portfolio.

>> **Invesco QQQ (ticker symbol: QQQ):** This ETF tracks the Nasdaq-100 Index, which includes the 100 largest nonfinancial companies listed on the Nasdaq Stock Market. Lots of

tech; definitely large and definitely growth; but rather random (it includes Apple and Microsoft, but not Amazon or Alphabet). Randomness in a portfolio is not a good thing.

>> **First Trust Large Cap Growth AlphaDEX (ticker symbol: FTC):** I see a net expense ratio of 0.6 percent, and I see lead boots that you're going to be running in if you buy this ETF. At the time of this writing, this fund has returned 13.58 percent annually over the past ten years. That compares to 16.5 percent for the S&P Growth Index. Surprise, surprise.

>> **Invesco Dynamic Large Cap Growth ETF (ticker symbol: PWB):** This ETF doesn't make me recoil in horror; you could do somewhat worse. But the high-by-ETF-standards expense ratio (0.56 percent) is something of a turnoff. And the "enhanced" index reminds me too much of active investing, which has a less-than-gleaming track record.

Checking Out Six Ways to Recognize Value

REMEMBER

Warren Buffett knows a value stock when he sees one. Do you? Different investment pros and different indexes (upon which ETFs are fashioned) may define *value* differently, but here are some of the most common criteria.

>> **P/E ratio:** As early as 1934, Benjamin Graham and David Dodd (in their book with the blockbuster title *Security Analysis*) suggested that investors should pay heavy consideration to the ratio of a stock's market price (P) to its earnings (E) per share. Sometimes called the *multiple,* this venerable ratio sheds light on how much the market is willing to cough up for a company's earning power. The lower the ratio, the more "valuey" the stock. (The P/E ratio as it relates to growth stocks is addressed earlier in this chapter.)

>> **P/B ratio:** Graham and Dodd also advised that the ratio of market price to book value (B) should be given at least "a fleeting glance." Many of today's investment gurus have awarded the P/B ratio the chief role in defining value versus growth. A ratio well below sea level is what floats a value investor's boat. *Book value* refers to the guesstimated value of a corporation's total assets, both tangible (factories,

inventory, and so on) and intangible (goodwill, patents, and so on), minus any liabilities.

>> **Dividend distributions:** You like dividends? Value stocks are the ones that pay them.

>> **The cover of *Forbes*:** Magazine covers are rarely adorned with photos of the CEOs of value companies. Growth companies receive broad exposure, but value companies tend to wallow in obscurity.

>> **Earnings growth:** Growth companies' earnings tend to impress, whereas you can expect value companies to have less than awe-inspiring earnings growth.

>> **The industry sector:** Growth stocks are typically found in high-flying industries, such as internet commerce, computers, wireless communications, and biotechnology. Value stocks are more often found in older-than-the-hills sectors, such as energy, banking, transportation, foodstuffs, and toiletries.

Take a gander at Figure 3-2. It shows where large-value stocks fit into the investment style grid.

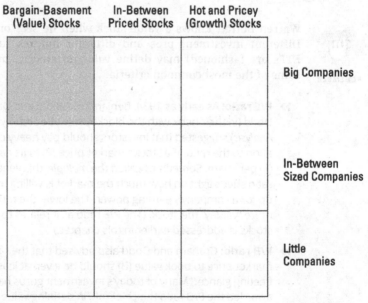

© John Wiley & Sons, Inc.

FIGURE 3-2: Large-value stocks occupy the northwest corner of the grid.

Searching for the Best Value Buys

Many academic types have looked at the so-called *value premium* and have tried to explain it. No one can agree on why value stocks have historically outperformed growth stocks. (A joke I remember from my college days: Put any three economists in a room, and you'll get at least five opinions.)

TECHNICAL STUFF

Some people say there is hidden risk in value investing that warrants greater returns. They explain that although the standard deviation for the two asset classes is about the same, value stocks tend to plummet at the worst economic times. This argument is not all that persuasive. During some serious market downturns, such as 2008 and again in 2020, value was hit harder than growth. But during other market downturns, such as the dot-com disaster of 2000 to 2002, value stocks proved much more buoyant than growth stocks. Others say that value stocks outperform growth stocks because of the greater dividends paid by value companies. Growth companies tend to plow their cash into acquisitions and new product development instead of issuing dividends to those pesky shareholders.

Here's the best explanation for the value premium, if you ask this humble author: Value stocks simply tend to be ignored by the market — or have been in the past — and, therefore, come relatively cheap. When value stocks do receive attention, it's usually negative. And studies show that investors tend to overreact to bad news. Such overreactions end up being reflected in a discounted price.

Taking the index route

Famous value investors like Warren Buffett make their money finding stocks that come at an especially discounted price. They recognize that companies making lackluster profits, and even sometimes companies bleeding money, can turn around (especially when Mr. Buffett sends in his team of whip-cracking consultants). When a lackluster company turns around, the stock that was formerly seen as a financial turd (that's a technical term) can suddenly turn into 14-karat gold. It's a formula that has worked well for the Oracle of Omaha.

Good luck making it work for you.

Unlike Warren Buffett, many or most value-stock pickers repeatedly take gambles on failing companies that continue to fail. I say the best way to invest in large value is to buy the index. There is no better way of doing that than through ETFs.

Making an ETF selection

The world of pure, index, large-cap, domestic value-stock ETFs includes at least 30 options from which to choose. The ETFs in the following sections offer good large-value indexes at reasonable prices.

I suggest that you read through the following descriptions and make the choice that you think is best for you. Whatever your allocation to domestic large-cap stocks, your allocation to value should be somewhere in the ballpark of 50 percent to 60 percent of that amount. In other words, I suggest that you tilt toward value, but don't go overboard.

The criteria you use in picking the best large-cap value ETF should include expense ratios, appropriateness of the index, and tax-efficiency (if you're investing in a taxable account). Note that the expense ratios, average cap sizes, P/E ratios, and top five holdings are all subject to change; you should definitely check for updated figures before investing.

You'll note that in choosing which funds I use and recommend, I don't often go out of my way to note past performance. Why is that? Isn't past performance important? Of course it is, but I'm recommending index funds, so keep in mind that managerial prowess (or bumbling) doesn't play into the game as it would if you were choosing an actively managed fund. Index funds attempt to track the performance of an index, and that index represents an asset class — in the case of this chapter, large-cap U.S. value stocks. What matters to me most is the long-term performance — and volatility — of the asset class.

What does it mean that one index fund outperforms another over the last three, five, or even ten years? Usually it's tied to the expense ratio: The higher the expenses, the lower the return. And where the differential isn't due to expenses, it's often due to the makeup of the index, which may offer either more "valuey" stocks or larger- or smaller-cap stocks. A value fund that did especially well over the past decade — a decade where growth uncharacteristically clobbered value — may simply offer less "valuey" stocks. If value stocks clobber growth in the next decade, these star index-fund performers will quickly lose their luster.

Vanguard Value Index ETF (ticker symbol: VTV)

Indexed to: CRSP U.S. Large Cap Value Index (340 or so of the nation's largest value stocks)

Expense ratio: 0.04 percent

Average market cap: $103.1 billion

P/E ratio: 21.9

TILTING TOWARD VALUE

Given the long-term outperformance of value over growth stocks, it's reasonable to tilt a portfolio toward value. I suggest a recipe of perhaps four to five parts growth to five to six parts value, but are there times when you may want to tilt more than others? In Chapter 11, I talk about *strategic asset allocation* — a fancy term for tilting a portfolio more or less, given certain market conditions.

In 2021, growth stocks had a freakishly good run, solidly outperforming value stocks for the past decade. The Russell 1000 Value Index, between 2010 and 2020, returned an annual 10.9 percent. The Russell 1000 Growth Index during the same decade has returned an annual 17.2 percent.

Growth stocks are now, vis-à-vis value stocks, about as expensive as they've ever been. For that reason, most professionals right now, including me, are thinking that value stocks are pretty likely to outperform growth over the next decade.

In other words, if ever there were a time to tilt, now may be it. But again, don't go wild, please. Perhaps 60 percent of your large-cap exposure may be to value. The value premium tends to be greatest among small caps, and there, I might lean more heavily toward value — perhaps as much as 70 percent. I wouldn't go higher than that, simply because the majority of financial professionals, including me, could be wrong. As Yogi Berra would say, "It's tough to make predictions, especially about the future."

Top five holdings: Berkshire Hathaway, JPMorgan Chase, Johnson & Johnson, UnitedHealth Group, Procter & Gamble

Russell's review: The price is right. The index makes sense. There's good diversification. The companies represented are certainly large. The ETF has been around since 2002. No one has more experience with indexing than Vanguard. This ETF is a very good option, although I'd like it even more if it were a tad more "valuey." (On the other hand, making it more "valuey" could increase turnover, which might increase costs and taxation.) All told, I like the VTV. I like it a lot. If you already own the Vanguard Value Index mutual fund and you're considering moving to ETFs, this fund would clearly be your choice.

Vanguard Mega Cap 300 Value Index ETF (ticker symbol: MGV)

Indexed to: CRSP U.S. Mega Cap Value Index (140 or so of the very largest U.S. stocks with value characteristics)

Expense ratio: 0.07 percent

Average market cap: $151.6 billion

P/E ratio: 21.9

Top five holdings: Berkshire Hathaway, JPMorgan Chase, Johnson & Johnson, UnitedHealth Group, Procter & Gamble

Russell's review: This fund offers exposure to larger companies than does the more popular VTV featured earlier. Is bigger better? Could be. If you have small caps in your portfolio (which you should!), this mega-cap fund will give you slightly less correlation than you'll get with VTV. As a stand-alone investment, however, I would expect that the very long-term returns on this fund will lag VTV, given that giant caps historically have lagged large caps. Given Vanguard's low expenses and reasonable indexes, either fund would make a fine holding.

iShares Morningstar Value ETF (ticker symbol: ILCV)

Indexed to: Morningstar U.S. Large-Mid Cap Broad Value Index (about 480 companies that qualify as value picks)

Expense ratio: 0.04 percent

Average market cap: $115.2 billion

P/E ratio: 25.9

Top five holdings: Apple, JPMorgan Chase, Johnson & Johnson, Berkshire Hathaway, The Walt Disney Company

Russell's review: I love the low price. It could be more "valuey," and it would be if not for the inclusion of Apple stock. I'm not sure what Apple stock is doing in a value index, but there it is. Morningstar indexers are clearly defining value a bit differently from the other indexers. As I mention earlier in this chapter, *value* can be identified using at least six different criteria.

Schwab U.S. Large-Cap Value ETF (ticker symbol: SCHV)

Indexed to: Dow Jones U.S. Large Cap Value Total Stock Market Index (made up of the more "valuey" half of the 1,000 or so stocks that comprise the Dow Jones U.S. Large Cap Stock Market Index)

Expense ratio: 0.04 percent

Average cap size: $80.8 billion

P/E ratio: 24.3

Top five holdings: Berkshire Hathaway, JPMorgan Chase, Johnson & Johnson, The Walt Disney Company, Proctor & Gamble

Russell's review: For the sake of economy alone, this fund, like all Schwab ETFs, is a good option. The management fee is one of the lowest in the industry. Most important, the index is a good one, and you can expect Schwab to do a reasonable or better job of tracking the index.

Nuveen ESG Large-Cap Value ETF (ticker symbol: NULV)

Indexed to: Provides passive exposure to the 140 or so companies that make up MSCI's TIAA ESG USA Large-Cap Value Index. If you don't know what ESG is, it stands for *environmental, social, and governance* (turn to Chapter 6 to read more).

Expense ratio: 0.35 percent

Average market cap: $74.9 billion

P/E ratio: 34.2

Top five holdings: Proctor & Gamble, The Coca-Cola Company, PepsiCo, Intel Corporation, Home Depot

Russell's review: The average market cap is smaller than the other large-cap growth ETFs, and the expense ratio is higher — significantly higher. To date, however, Nuveen offers you the only option to invest in ETFs with style (value, growth, large, small) and to have a portfolio constructed with ESG considerations. Given that the portfolio holdings of this ETF differ appreciably from the other large-growth ETFs, you could see a significant difference in performance. Higher or lower? Probably, in the long run, higher. But that's due largely to the smaller average market cap, which brings with it greater volatility.

Value ETFs I wouldn't go out of my way to own

WARNING

These ETFs aren't the worst things you could own. But given the strengths of some of the other offerings, I don't trade in these particular funds:

>> **Direxion Russell 1000 Value Over Growth ETF (ticker symbol: RWVG):** Expense ratio of 0.64 percent. Ugh. And this fund uses derivatives. And short stocks. *Ugh.*

>> **First Trust Large Cap Value AlphaDEX Fund (ticker symbol: FTA):** Expense ratio of 0.6 percent, which is only "cheap" compared to the aforementioned Direxion ETF! It doesn't use derivatives, but it does use a "tiered" indexing strategy that just sounds too much like a health insurance prescription plan.

>> **KFA Value Line Dynamic Core Equity Index ETF (ticker symbol: KVLE):** This fund has expenses of 0.58 percent annually and an unusual way of triaging value stocks from growth stocks. It was just born in 2020, so I'd give it quite a few years before investing. However, given the expenses, I doubt it will shine over the long haul. Expensive funds rarely do.

IN THIS CHAPTER

» Factoring small company stocks into your investment pie

» Recognizing ETFs that tap into the small-growth asset class

» Introducing micro caps

» Recognizing a small-value stock

» Earmarking ETFs that track small-value indexes

» Deciding whether to consider mid caps

Chapter 4

ETFs for Small Growth and Small Value

O nce upon a time in the kingdom of Redmond, there was a young company called Microsoft. It was a very small company with very big ideas, and it grew and grew and grew. Its founder and its original investors became very, very rich; bought very, very big houses; and lived happily ever after.

Oh, you've heard that story? Then you understand the appeal of small-growth companies. These are companies that typically have *market capitalization* (the market value of total outstanding stock) of about $300 million to $2 billion. They frequently boast a hot product or patent, often fall into the high-tech or biotech arena, and always seem to be on their way to stardom. Some of them make it, and along with them, their investors take a joy ride all the way to early retirement.

Unfortunately, for every Microsoft, there are a dozen (or two or three dozen) small companies that go belly-up long before their prime. For every investor who gambles on a small company stock and takes early retirement, a hundred others still drive their cars to work every Monday morning.

Look at the list of some of the top companies represented in the Vanguard Small-Cap Value ETF: Devon Energy Corp.; Index Corp.; VICI Properties, Inc.; L Brands, Inc.; Nuance Communications. These are not household names. Nor are they especially fast-growing companies. Nor are they industry leaders. Nor is there much excitement to be seen in companies such as Index Corp. — a corporation that designs, produces, and distributes positive displacement pumps and flow meters, compressors, and injectors. As you go farther down the list of holdings, you'll likely find some companies in financial distress. Others may be facing serious lawsuits, expiration of patents, or labor unrest. If you wanted to pick one of these companies to sink a wad of cash into, I would tell you that you're crazy.

But if you want to sink that cash into the entire small-value index, well, that's another matter altogether. Assuming you could handle some risk, I'd tell you to go for it. By all means. Your odds of making money are pretty darned good — at least if history is your guide.

This chapter shows you how small-growth and small-value stocks can fit into your exchange-traded fund (ETF) portfolio.

Getting Real about Small-Cap Investments

Take a ride with me through the world of small-cap growth stocks. First stop along the ride: Figure 4-1, where you can see how small growth fits into the investment style grid I introduce in Chapter 3.

REMEMBER

In the past century, small-cap stocks have outperformed large-cap stocks just as assuredly as bread has outsold sauerkraut. The volatility of small-cap stocks has also been greater, granted, but in terms of return per unit of risk (risk-adjusted rate of return), small caps are clearly winners. And so it would seem that investing in small caps is a pretty smart thing to do — and you should. But please know that not all small caps are created equal.

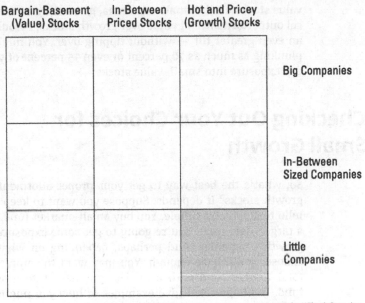

Bargain-Basement (Value) Stocks	In-Between Priced Stocks	Hot and Pricey (Growth) Stocks	
			Big Companies
			In-Between Sized Companies
			Little Companies

© John Wiley & Sons, Inc.

FIGURE 4-1: The shaded area is the portion of the investment grid represented by small-growth stocks.

As it happens, the true stars of the small-cap world have been small-cap *value* stocks rather than small-cap *growth* stocks. (Take a look at Chapter 3 if you aren't sure what I mean by these terms.) How slow-growing, often ailing companies have beat out their hot-to-trot cousins remains one of the great, unresolved mysteries of the investing world. But the numbers don't lie.

In fact, if you look at the numbers, you may be inclined to treat small-growth stocks as pariahs. Please don't. They belong in a well-diversified portfolio. Some years are clearly small-growth years. The best example is rather recent: About midway through 2021, small-cap growth stocks saw a three-year return of 19.4 percent annually, beating both small value and large value by a very wide margin (although trailing large growth). Who's to say that the long-term past wasn't a fluke and that small growth may actually go on to kick butt in the next three years?

TIP

In Chapter 3, I recommend that you may want to tilt your portfolio toward value. I suggest that, given value's outperformance of growth over the very long run, you may want to put 50 percent — or even as much as 60 percent — of your large-cap portfolio into value stocks. In the small-cap arena, given the enormous historical outperformance of value over growth stocks, I would allow for an even greater tilt — without tipping over. You might consider plunking as much as 70 percent or even 75 percent of your small-cap exposure into small-value stocks.

Checking Out Your Choices for Small Growth

So, what's the best way to get your proper allotment of small-growth stocks? It depends. Suppose you want to keep your portfolio really, really simple. You buy an all-market fund or perhaps a target-date fund. You're going to get some exposure to small-growth companies. And perhaps, depending on what fund you choose, you'll have enough. You may want to complement your total-market fund with a modest purchase Into a small-value fund. In Chapter 9, I give examples of how you might construct such a super-simple portfolio.

TIP

For most investors, however, at least those with more than a couple of thousand to invest, it will make sense to have a small-cap growth fund tucked into their portfolios.

You won't be surprised that I'm going to recommend index funds, just as I do for large-cap stocks and small-value stocks. The academic research (lots of it) says you'll wind up ahead.

Strictly small-cap growth funds

If you have enough assets to warrant splitting up small value and small growth, go for it, by all means. Following are what I consider to be the best small-growth options. Later in this chapter, I present small-value options to complement the funds presented here.

iShares Morningstar Small-Cap Growth ETF (ticker symbol: ISCG)

Indexed to: Approximately 1,290 companies from the Morningstar Small-Cap Growth Index

Expense ratio: 0.06 percent

Average market cap: $4.2 billion

P/E ratio: 31.2

Top five holdings: Rexford Industrial Realty, Inc.; Crocs, Inc.; Lattice Semiconductor Corporation; STAAR Surgical; First Financial Bankshares, Inc.

Russell's review: This is a low-cost and very well-diversified ETF. How diversified? The largest holding, Rexford Industrial Realty, Inc., represents just 0.42 percent of the portfolio. I like that Morningstar promises no crossover between growth and value. If you own this ETF along with the iShares Morningstar Small-Cap Value Index, you should get pleasantly limited correlation.

Vanguard Small-Cap Growth ETF (ticker symbol: VBK)

Indexed to: The CRSP U.S. Small Cap Growth Index, approximately 640 small-cap growth companies in the United States

Expense ratio: 0.07 percent

Average cap size: $6.5 billion

P/E ratio: 38.4

Top five holdings: Teledyne Technologies Incorporated; Entegris, Inc.; Bio-Techne Corporation; PTC, Inc.; Charles River Laboratories International, Inc.

Russell's review: Vanguard is charging about one-fifth what you'd spend for most small-growth ETFs. Add to that economy the wide diversification, tax-efficiency beyond compare, and a very definite growth exposure, and I really have no complaints. The Vanguard Small-Cap Growth ETF offers a very good way to tap into this asset class. If the average market cap were just a bit smaller, I think I'd be in love.

SPDR S&P 600 Small Cap Growth ETF (ticker symbol: SLYG)

Indexed to: Those stocks (about 330) that exhibit the strongest growth characteristics among the stocks represented by the S&P Small Cap 600 Index.

Expense ratio: 0.15 percent

Average market cap: $2.7 billion

P/E ratio: 21.9

Top five holdings: Omnicell, Inc.; GameStop Corp. (Class A); Saia, Inc.; NeoGenomics; Chart Industries, Inc.

Russell's review: S&P indexes are a bit too subjective for me to really love them, and the price of this fund, although low, is higher than some of the competitors' offerings. Still, there's no reason to hate this State Street Global Advisors offering. It isn't a bad fund, just not my favorite for the asset class.

iShares S&P Small-Cap 600 Growth ETF (ticker symbol: IJT)

Indexed to: Tracks the "growthier" stocks (about 350 or so) out of the S&P Small Cap 600 Growth Index

Expense ratio: 0.18 percent

Average cap size: $2.8 billion

P/E ratio: 24.1

Top five holdings: Omnicell, Inc.; GameStop Corp. (Class A); Saia, Inc.; NeoGenomics; Chart Industries, Inc.

Russell's review: This is essentially the very same fund as SLYG (see the preceding section), although it costs 0.18 percent rather than 0.15 percent. The iShares literature claims a slightly higher P/E ratio (which would be a good thing for a growth fund), but I wonder whether the different numbers are just a fluke. *Note:* The information I'm sharing about all these ETFs comes from the ETF purveyors' disclosure statements, with the exception of the average cap sizes, which come from Morningstar Direct.

Smaller than small: The micro caps

If you want to invest your money in companies that are smaller than small, you're going to be investing in micro caps. These companies are larger than the corner delicatessen, but sometimes not by much. In general, micro caps are publicly held companies with less than $300 million in outstanding stock. Micro caps, as you can imagine, are volatile little suckers, but as a group they offer impressive long-term performance. In terms of diversification, micro caps — in conservative quantity — could be a nice addition to your portfolio, although I wouldn't call them a necessity. Take note that micro-cap funds, even index ETFs, tend to charge considerably more in management fees than you'll pay for most funds.

TECHNICAL
STUFF

Micros move at a modestly different pace from other equity asset classes. The theory is that because micro caps are heavy borrowers, their performance is more tied to interest rates than the performance of larger-cap stocks is. (Lower interest rates would be good for these stocks; higher interest rates would not.) In fact, when interest rates dropped to all-time historical lows, micros did very well. The largest of the funds, the iShares Micro-Cap ETF, returned nearly 83 percent in the year prior to May 31, 2021, versus 56.3 percent for the iShares Core S&P 500 ETF.

Micro caps also tend to be more tied to the vicissitudes of the U.S. economy and less to the world economy than, say, the fortunes of Apple or McDonald's.

Given the high risk of owning any individual micro-cap stock, it makes sense to work micro caps into your portfolio in fund form, despite the management fees, instead of trying to pick individual companies. To date, a handful of micro-cap ETFs have been introduced. They differ from one another to a much greater extent than do the larger-cap ETFs. Notice that the top five holdings of each ETF are completely different; you don't find Microsoft and Apple in every list, as you do with large-cap growth funds.

Despite the differences, all the funds that I discuss next have seen rather lackluster performance since their inception. The iShares Micro-Cap ETF (ticker symbol: IWC) had a blockbuster year at the time of writing, but in the ten years prior to May 31, 2021, the fund saw average annual returns of 12.1 percent versus the far less volatile iShares Core S&P 500 ETF, which returned 14.3 percent.

WARNING

It may be possible that micro caps are a particular kind of asset class (commodities would be another) where index ETFs may be less than the ideal vehicle. The performance may have something to do with the illiquidity of micro caps (it's not always easy to buy and sell shares on the open market). Time will tell. In the meantime, proceed with caution, and if you want to invest in any of these funds, do so with only a modest percentage of your portfolio.

iShares Micro-Cap ETF (ticker symbol: IWC)

Indexed to: 1,300 of the smallest publicly traded companies, culled from the Russell 3000 (small-cap) Index, plus the next 1,000 smallest issuers on the stock market, as determined by Russell

Expense ratio: 0.6 percent

Average cap size: $825 million

P/E ratio: 17.2

Top five holdings: GameStop Corp. (Class A); Digital Turbine; Intellia Therapeutics, Inc.; Overstock.com; Magnite, Inc.

Russell's review: There aren't a lot of choices in this field, so I'm glad this is one of them. I'm not crazy about paying 0.6 percent, which is high for an ETF. *Note:* More than one-quarter of the stocks held in this fund are health-care company stocks.

First Trust Dow Jones Select MicroCap Index Fund (ticker symbol: FDM)

Indexed to: Dow Jones Select Micro-Cap Index, which contains about 150 of the smallest stocks listed on the New York Stock Exchange and the Nasdaq

Expense ratio: 0.6 percent

Average market cap: $664 million

P/E ratio: 12.9

Top five holdings: Silvergate Capital Corp. (Class A); Clean Energy Fuels Corp.; Enova International, Inc.; U.S. Concrete, Inc.; Dime Community Bancshares, Inc.

Russell's review: The expense ratio is the same as the competitors, and the average cap size is not much different. All in all, everything else looks okay, but this fund offers less diversification. In fact, there's a lot of industry concentration — at last glance, nearly one-third of the stocks are financials; financials and industrials together make up more than half. For that reason, I'd go with the iShares Micro-Cap ETF before I'd go with this one.

AdvisorShares Dorsey Wright Micro-Cap ETF (ticker symbol: DWMC)

Indexed to: This is *not* an index fund, but an actively managed fund. The managers choose the micro-cap stocks they believe are going to perform the best. Usually, active management fails to outperform the indexes. In micro caps, however, active management *may* make sense.

Expense ratio: 1.32 (This expense ratio is much on par with the expense ratios of the handful of actively managed micro-cap mutual funds that preexisted DWMC.)

Average market cap: $637 million

P/E ratio: 9.9

Top five holdings: XPEL, Inc.; Calix, Inc.; Danaos Corporation; Kornit Digital Ltd.; Surgery Partners, Inc.

Russell's review: It's hard for me, an indexing proponent, to even think about recommending a fund that charges 1.32 percent in annual fees and invests wherever the managers want, but micro caps may be a different kind of beast. Since the inception of the fund, on July 10, 2018, until May 31, 2021, the fund returned 15.27 percent, versus the Russell Microcap Index, which returned 13.12 percent. A fluke? It could take years to tell. If the expense ratio were lowered, it would up the odds of this fund's continued outperformance.

Opting for Small Value: Diminutive Dazzlers

Don't let "small value" fool you. If you can stomach a bit of risk, these stocks can more than pull their weight. Don't take my word for it; consult history. On the way there, see Figure 4-2, which shows where small value fits into the investment style grid I introduce in Chapter 3. And then follow me as I explain the importance of small-value stocks in a poised-for-performance ETF portfolio.

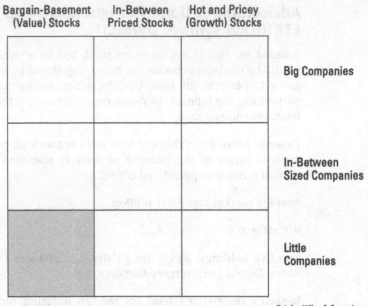

	Bargain-Basement (Value) Stocks	In-Between Priced Stocks	Hot and Pricey (Growth) Stocks	
				Big Companies
				In-Between Sized Companies
				Little Companies

© John Wiley & Sons, Inc.

FIGURE 4-2: Small-value stocks occupy the southwest corner of the investment style grid.

Small-value stocks collectively have returned more to investors than have large-value stocks or any kind of growth stocks. In fact, the difference in returns has been somewhat staggering: I'm talking about an annualized return of about 14 percent over the past nine or so decades for small value, versus 12 percent for large value, 10 percent for large growth, and 9 percent for small growth. Compounded over time, the outperformance of small-value stocks has been *huge*.

Latching on for fun and profit

To be sure, small-value stocks are risky little suckers. Even the entire index (available to you in neat ETF form) is more volatile than any conservative investor may feel comfortable with. But as part — a very handsome part — of a diversified portfolio, a small-value ETF can be a beautiful thing indeed.

If you knew the past were going to repeat, such as it did in the movie *Groundhog Day*, there'd be no reason to have anything but small value in your portfolio. But of course, you don't know that the past will repeat. Bill Murray's radio alarm clock may not go off at sunrise. And the small-value premium, like Bill Murray's hairline, may start to seriously recede. Still, the outperformance of small value has historically been so much greater than that of small growth that I favor a good tilt in the direction of value.

Keeping your balance

TIP

Whatever your total allocation to domestic small-cap stocks (see Chapter 9 for advice), I recommend that anywhere from 60 percent to 75 percent of that amount be allocated to small value. But no more than that, please. If the value premium disappears or becomes a value discount, I don't want you left holding the bag. And even if small value continues to outperform, having both small value and small growth (along with their bigger cousins, all of which tend to rise and fall in different cycles) will help smooth out some of the inevitable volatility of holding stocks.

There aren't nearly the number of small-cap value ETFs as there are large-cap funds, but still, you have choices. The best choices among small-value ETFs include offerings from iShares and Vanguard. I also review an option from Invesco, which isn't terrible.

iShares Morningstar Small-Cap Value Index (ticker symbol: ISCV)

Indexed to: Morningstar's Small-Cap Value Index (about 1,300 companies of modest size and modest stock price)

Expense ratio: 0.06 percent

Average cap size: $4 billion

P/E ratio: 16.4

Top five holdings: AMC Entertainment Holdings, Inc.; Ovintiv, Inc.; Apartment Income REIT Corp.; Tenet Healthcare Corp.; Cimarex Energy Co.

Russell's review: My only complaint with the Morningstar indexes is that they tend to be a bit too concentrated, at least in the large-cap arena where a company like Microsoft can hold too much sway. (At the time of writing, Microsoft comprises almost 10 percent of the large-growth index.) In the Morningstar small-cap indexes, that isn't a problem. The largest holding here, AMC

Entertainment, gets only a 1.5 percent allocation, which is fine and dandy. The expense ratio is the lowest in this category. And I like that Morningstar promises no crossover between growth and value. If you own this ETF along with the iShares Morningstar Small-Cap Growth Index, you should get pleasantly modest correlation. (In lay terms, if one fund gets slammed, the other may not.)

Vanguard Small-Cap Value ETF (ticker symbol: VBR)

Indexed to: The CRSP U.S. Small Cap Value Index (about 930 small-value domestic companies)

Expense ratio: 0.07 percent

Average cap size: $5.7 billion

P/E ratio: 20.2

Top five holdings: Index Corp.; VICI Properties, Inc.; Devon Energy Corp.; L Brands, Inc.; Williams-Sonoma, Inc.

Russell's review: This ETF has low cost, wide diversification, tax-efficiency beyond compare, and a very definite value bias — what's not to like? Um . . . the average market cap is larger than I would find ideal. For that reason, I'd say the Vanguard Small-Cap Value ETF offers a very good way to tap into this asset class, but I can't call it great.

iShares S&P Small-Cap 600 Value Index (ticker symbol: IJS)

Indexed to: 550 of the S&P Small-Cap 600 Value Index companies

Expense ratio: 0.18 percent

Average cap size: $2 billion

P/E ratio: 20.1

Top five holdings: GameStop Corp. (Class A); Macy's, Inc.; PDC Energy, Inc.; Resideo Technologies, Inc.; Signet Jewelers Ltd.

Russell's review: S&P indexes are a bit too subjective for me to want to marry them. Case in point is that the largest holding in this portfolio is GameStop. Yup, that's the same GameStop that appears as a major holding in the iShares S&P Small Cap 600 Growth Index ETF (covered earlier in this chapter). I find that confusing, and, as a rule, I don't go out of my way to own investments that confuse.

Invesco S&P 600 SmallCap Pure Value (ticker symbol: RZV)

Indexed to: S&P SmallCap 600 Pure Value Index (approximately 150 of the smallest and most "valuey" S&P 600 companies)

Expense ratio: 0.35 percent

Average cap size: $1.2 billion

P/E ratio: 20.2

Top five holdings: Genworth Financial, Inc.; Customers Bancorp, Inc.; EZCORP, Inc.; Boston Private Financial Holdings, Inc.; Hanmi Financial Corporation

Russell's review: The price is higher than others in this category, and the promise of "purity" is a bit murky, especially if that quest for purity leads to high turnover, which can bleed profitability. The average market cap is quite small. When cap size gets too small (and small caps start looking like micro caps), liquidity becomes an issue, and index funds can sometimes get hurt.

What about the Mid Caps?

In a word, my take on mid-cap ETFs is: *Why?* Yes, there are years when mid-cap stocks — investments in companies with roughly $2 billion to $10 billion in outstanding stock — have performed especially well. There are years where mid caps have done better than either large- or small-cap stocks. But there aren't many such years. It's a rarity.

REMEMBER

If you look at the risk/return profile of mid caps over many years, you find that it generally falls right where you would expect it to fall: smack-dab in between large and small cap. Owning both a large-cap ETF and a small-cap ETF, therefore, will give you an average return very similar to mid caps but with considerably less volatility because large- and small-cap stocks tend to move up and down at different times.

Other investment pros may disagree, but I really don't see the point of shopping for mid-cap ETFs, even though there are many mid-cap offerings. Keep in mind, too, that most large-cap and small-cap funds are rather fluid: You'll get some mid-cap exposure from both. Many sector funds — including real estate, materials, and utilities — are also chock-full of mid caps (see Chapter 6).

Chapter **5**

Around the World: Global and International ETFs

A s of mid-2011, the ten-year annualized return of the U.S. stock market stood at about 4 percent. In sharp contrast, stocks of the world's emerging-market nations clocked in with a rather astounding 16 percent per year for the previous decade. Developed nations in the Pacific Rim (Japan, Australia, Singapore) more or less matched the United States for the decade. European stocks (including the United Kingdom), despite some sharp losses due largely to a debt mess in Greece and Portugal, showed an average return of about 6 percent.

Americans couldn't get enough foreign stock, and their equity portfolios got up to about 30 percent foreign. But, as is nearly always the case, after all the money poured into this hot sector, the sector cooled. Since 2011, the U.S. stock market has way outperformed foreign markets. In the decade that followed — mid-2011 to mid-2021 — the U.S. stock market saw annual growth of nearly 14 percent, whereas developed overseas markets grew only about 6 percent, and emerging-market nations grew just a bit more than 3 percent.

Sure enough, American investors' love affair with foreign stocks has started to wane. And the percent of Americans' portfolios devoted to non-U.S. stocks has shrunk again.

I'm going to suggest that you take careful note that U.S. investments sometimes do better than foreign investments, and sometimes they don't, and no one can say what the next decade will bring. Regardless, you *do* want to have your portfolio both at home and away. Not to chase returns — there really is no good reason to think that in the very long run, U.S. stocks will outperform foreign stocks, or the other way around — but to diversify your portfolio and smooth out your returns over time. Fortunately, global diversification is easy with exchange-traded funds (ETFs). In this chapter, I explain the whys and the hows of investing abroad.

Studying the Ups and Downs of Markets around the World

For what it's worth, I think you can expect that foreign stocks overall may do better than U.S. stocks in the coming decade. (If you want the nitty-gritty of my reasoning, you'll find it later in this chapter.) But I certainly wouldn't bet the farm on international stocks outperforming U.S. stocks — or underperforming them either, for that matter. If there is one thing I know for sure, it's that markets are unpredictable.

In all likelihood, international stocks as a whole will have their day. U.S. stocks will then come up from behind. Then international stocks will have their day again. And then U.S. stocks will get the jump. This type of horse race has been going on since, oh, long before *Mr. Ed* was on the air. Over a 45.5-year period, outperformance by U.S. stocks versus non-U.S. stocks has been followed quite regularly by years of underperformance. What will next year bring? No one can say.

The reason to invest abroad isn't primarily to try to outperform the Joneses, or the LeBlancs, or the Yamashitas. Instead, the purpose is to diversify your portfolio so as to capture overall stock-market gains while tempering risk. You reduce risk whenever you own two or more asset classes that move up and down at different times. Stocks of different geographic regions tend to do exactly that.

Oh, by the way, the terms *foreign* and *international* are used interchangeably to refer to stocks of companies outside the United States. The word *global* refers to stocks of companies based anywhere in the world, including the United States.

Low correlation is the name of the game

Why, you may ask, do you need European and Japanese stocks when you already have all the lovely diversification discussed in previous chapters (large, small, value, and growth stocks, and a good mix of industries)? (See Chapter 3 if you need a reminder of what these terms mean.) The answer is quite simple: You get better diversification when you diversify across borders.

I'll use several iShares ETFs to illustrate my point. Suppose you have a wad of money invested in the iShares S&P 500 Growth Index fund (ticker symbol: IVW), and you want to diversify:

>> If you combine IVW with its large-value counterpart, the iShares S&P 500 Value Index Fund (ticker symbol: IVE), you find that your two investments have a three-year correlation of 0.87. In other words, over the past three years, the funds have had a tendency to move in the same direction 87 percent of the time. Only 13 percent of the time have they tended to move in opposite directions.

>> If you mix IVW into the same portfolio with the iShares S&P Small Cap 600 Growth Index Fund (ticker symbol: IJT), you find that your two investments have tended to move up and down together by the same degree as IVW and IVE — 87 percent of the time.

>> If you combine IVW with the iShares S&P Small Cap 600 Value Index Fund (ticker symbol: IJS), your investments tend to move north or south at the same time 80 percent of the time. Not bad. But not great.

Now consider adding some Japanese stock to your original portfolio of large-growth stocks. The iShares MSCI Japan Index Fund (ticker symbol: EWJ) has tended to move in sync with large U.S. growth stocks only about 76 percent of the time. And the ETF that tracks the FTSE China 25 Index (ticker symbol: FXI) has moved in the same direction as large-cap U.S. growth stocks only 65 percent of the time. There's clearly more zig and zag when you cross oceans to invest, and that's what makes international investing a must for a well-balanced portfolio.

The increasing interdependence of the world's markets wrought by globalization may cause these correlation numbers to rise over time. Indeed, investors saw in 2008 that in a global financial crisis, and again in 2020 with a global health crisis, stock markets around the world will suffer. The trend toward rising correlations has led some pundits to make the claim that diversification is dead. Sorry, those pundits are wrong. In down times, yes, stocks of different colors, here and abroad, tend to turn a depressing shade of gray together. When investors are nervous in New York, they're often nervous in Berlin. And Sydney. And Cape Town. That's been true for years. The great apple-cart-turnovers of 2008 and 2020 were particular cases in point. But in both cases, it still paid to be diversified, because U.S. and foreign stocks recovered at very different rates.

REMEMBER

Diversification lowers, but does not eliminate, stock-market risk. Never did. Never will. Your portfolio, in addition to being well diversified, should also have some components, such as cash and bonds, that are less volatile than stocks.

Note what happened to Japan

To just "stay home" on the stock side of your portfolio would be to exhibit the very same conceit seen among Japanese investors in 1990. If you recall, that's when the dynamic and seemingly all-powerful rising sun slipped and then sank. Japanese investors, holding domestically stuffed portfolios, bid sayonara to two-thirds of their wealth, which, more than two decades later, they had yet to fully recapture. By year-end 2010, a basket of large-company Japanese stocks purchased in 1989 would have returned a very sad −1.3 percent a year over two full decades. In the following decade (2011–2021), Japanese stocks inched forward.

If you had bought the iShares MSCI Japan ETF at its inception in March 1996, your average annual return as of mid-2021 would have been a very disappointing 1.7 percent.

Ouch. It could also happen here. Or worse.

Finding Your Best Mix of Domestic and International

TIP

The U.S. stock market is by far the largest in the world. Still, even after a decade of solidly outperforming foreign markets, the total capitalization of the U.S. market is but 55 percent of the world stock market. Huge, yes, but far from everything. A market-weighted global portfolio would have you owning 45 percent foreign. Should you invest that much of your stock portfolio in foreign ETFs? My answer is *yes*, absolutely. I would say the same at any point in time, but especially as I'm writing this paragraph: With valuations (such as P/E ratios) much more attractive abroad than at home, I want a big heaping of foreign stock exposure — without going overboard. Everything in moderation.

Why putting three-quarters of your portfolio in foreign stocks is too much

WARNING

I see five distinct reasons to avoid overloading your portfolio with foreign stocks:

>> **Currency volatility:** When you invest abroad, you're usually investing in stocks that are denominated in other currencies. Because your foreign ETFs are denominated in euros, yen, or pounds, they tend to be more volatile than the markets they represent. In other words, if European stock markets fall and the dollar rises (vis-à-vis the euro) on the same day, your European ETF will fall doubly hard. If, however, the dollar falls on a day when the sun is shining on European stocks, your European ETF will soar.

Over the long run, individual currencies tend to go up and down. Although it could happen, it's unlikely that the dollar (or euro) would permanently rise or fall to such a degree that it would seriously affect your nest egg. In the short term, however, such currency fluctuations can be a bit nauseating. *Note:* There are currency-hedged stock ETFs that can mitigate currency risk, but hedging adds to a fund's expenses.

>> **Inflation issues:** Another risk with going whole hog for foreign-stock ETFs is that, to a certain extent, your fortunes are tied to those of your home economy. Stocks tend to do best in a heated economy. But in a heated economy, you also tend to see inflation. Because of that correlation between general price inflation and stock inflation, stock investors are generally able to stay ahead of the inflation game. If you were to invest all your money in, say, the United Kingdom, and if the economy here took off while the economy there sat idly on the launch pad, you could potentially be rocketed into a Dickensian kind of poverty.

>> **Higher fees for foreign ETFs:** There was once a huge difference in costs between foreign and domestic stock funds. This is far less true today. Still, domestic stock funds tend to cost a wee bit less than foreign. The Vanguard Total Stock Market ETF (ticker symbol: VTI), for example, comes with an expense ratio of 0.03 percent. The iShares Core S&P Total U.S. Stock Market ETF (ticker symbol: ITOT) has the same low, low cost ratio as Vanguard's ETF. Schwab's U.S. Broad Market ETF (ticker symbol: SCHB) — yet again the same. All can be had for a measly 0.03 percent. Compare this to the Vanguard Total International Stock ETF (ticker symbol: VXUS) and iShares's (ticker symbol: IXUS) and Schwab's (ticker symbol: SCHF) similar all-international ETFs: 0.08 percent, 0.09 percent, and 0.06 percent, respectively.

>> **Lower correlation with homegrown options:** Certain kinds of stock funds in the United States offer similar low correlation to the rest of the U.S. market as do international stock funds, and I suggest leaving room in your portfolio for some of those funds. (I discuss some of these industry-sector funds in Chapter 6.) You may also want to make room for market-neutral funds. And, of course, you want to leave plenty of room for the king of stock diversifiers: bonds (see Chapter 7).

A WORD ON FOREIGN TAXES

If you're buying both a foreign ETF and a domestic ETF, with one going into a taxable account and the other going into your individual retirement account (IRA), Roth IRA, or other tax-deferred retirement plan, choose the foreign fund for the taxable account and plug the domestic fund into your tax-deferred account. That's because many foreign countries will slap you with a withholding tax on your dividends, which you can write off only in a taxable account. Typically, such a tax may be 15 percent. (If you invest, say, $30,000 in a foreign fund with a dividend yield of 3 percent, you'll be losing $135 a year to foreign taxes.) If the foreign ETF is in a non-retirement account, your brokerage house will likely supply you with a year-end statement noting the foreign tax paid. You can then write that amount off in full against your U.S. taxes (see line 43 of your friendly IRS Form 1040). If the foreign fund is held in your retirement account, however, you get no year-end statement or write-off — you eat the loss.

>> **A double tax hit:** Foreign governments almost always hit you up for taxes on any dividends paid by stocks of companies in their countries. You don't pay this tax directly, but it's taken from your fund holdings. If your funds are held in certain accounts, Uncle Sam may want your money, too, and you wind up taking a double tax hit. This is a relatively minor reason not to go overboard when sailing overseas. (Specifics on this tax, and how to avoid getting double-whammied, are in the nearby sidebar "A word on foreign taxes.")

Why putting one-quarter of your portfolio in foreign stocks is insufficient

Some well-publicized research indicates that a portfolio made up of about 80 percent domestic stocks and about 20 percent foreign stocks is optimal for maximizing return and minimizing risk. But almost all that research defines *domestic stock* as the S&P 500 and *foreign stock* as the MSCI EAFE (an index of mostly large companies in the developed world — *MSCI* stands for Morgan Stanley Capital International, and *EAFE* stands for Europe, Australasia, and Far East).

This analysis takes little account of the fact that you aren't limiting yourself to the S&P 500 or to the MSCI EAFE. In the real world, you have the option of adding many asset classes to your portfolio of U.S. stocks. And among your international holdings, you can include developed-world stocks in Europe, Australia, and Japan; emerging-market stocks in China, India, and elsewhere; and foreign stocks in any and all flavors of large, small, value, and growth.

Many investment pros know well — and several have even told me — that they favor a much larger international position than they publicly advocate. Some may be afraid of seeming unpatriotic. Much more prevalent is a certain lemming-over-the-cliff/cover-my-behind mentality. If I, as your financial advisor, suggest a portfolio that resembles the S&P 500 and your portfolio tanks, you'll feel a bit peeved but you won't hate me. That's because all your friends' and neighbors' portfolios will have sunk as well. If I give you a portfolio that's 50 percent foreign, and if foreign stocks have a bad year, you'll compare your portfolio to your friends' and neighbors' portfolios, and you may hate me. You may even sue me.

I wouldn't want that. Neither would most investment professionals. So, most of them err on the side of caution and give their clients portfolios that are more S&P 500 and less foreign — for their own protection, and not in the pursuit of their clients' best interests.

With that said, I've seen some huge players in the investment world, such as Vanguard, slowly raise the allocation of foreign stocks in their recommended portfolios, about doubling it over the past 20 years. If you buy shares today of the all-in-one Vanguard Institutional Target Retirement 2040 Fund, 40 percent of your stock allocation will be non-U.S.

Why ETFs are a great tool for international investing

TIP

By mixing and matching your domestic stock funds with 40 percent to 50 percent international, you'll find your investment sweet spot. In Chapter 9, I pull together sample portfolios that use this methodology. Time and time again, I've run the numbers through the most sophisticated professional portfolio analysis software available, and time and time again, 40 percent to 50 percent foreign is where I find the highest returns per unit of risk. And, yes, this range has worked very well in the real world, too.

Although I try not to make forecasts because the markets are so incredibly unpredictable, I will say that if you had to err on the side of either U.S. or foreign stock investment, I would err on the side of too much foreign. The world economic and political climate is telling me that the U.S. stock market may be on relatively shakier ground. I could give you a long list of reasons that includes an aging population, the health-care crisis, and the extent to which the United States is becoming a nation of haves and have-nots (historically great inequality leads to great dissension and upheaval), but the biggest reason is, as I allude to earlier, valuations.

The U.S. stock market is expensive by almost any measure. Foreign markets are much less pricey. How strong a predictor are such valuations? One study by Vanguard found that about 40 percent of the stock market's return in any given decade may be attributable to valuations at the start of the decade. So, valuations are not foolproof as a predictor, but they're too good a predictor to be ignored. *Note:* Valuations have little to no predictive value in the shorter run. *Anything* can happen to stock prices over the next year, regardless of valuations.

As for me, I eat my own international cooking: I have fully half of my own stock portfolio in foreign stocks — the vast majority of it held in ETFs.

Knowing That Not All Foreign Stocks Are Created Equal

TIP

At present, you have more than 300 global and international stock ETFs from which to choose. (Once again, *global* ETFs hold U.S. as well as international stocks; *international* or *foreign* ETFs hold purely non-U.S. stocks.) I'd like you to consider the following half dozen factors when deciding which ones to invest in:

>> **What's the correlation?** Certain economies are more closely linked to the U.S. economy than others, and the behavior of their stock markets reflects that. Canada, for

example, offers limited diversification. Western Europe offers a bit more. For the least amount of correlation among developed nations, you want Japan (the world's second-largest stock market) or emerging-market nations like Russia, Brazil, India, and China.

>> **How large is the home market?** Although you can invest in individual countries, I generally wouldn't recommend it. Oh, I suppose you could slice and dice your portfolio to include 50 or so ETFs that represent individual countries (from Belgium to Austria, and Singapore to Spain, and, more recently, Vietnam to Poland), but that's going to be an awfully hard portfolio to manage. So, why do it? Choose large regions in which to invest. (The only exceptions might be Japan and the United Kingdom, which have such large stock markets that they each qualify, in my mind, as a region.)

>> **Think style.** Consider giving your international holdings a value lean, and endeavor to get small-cap exposure as well as large, just as you do with your domestic holdings. You can also divvy up your foreign portfolio into industry groupings. (I discuss this strategy in Chapter 6.) I generally prefer style diversification to sector diversification, but using both together is warranted.

>> **Consider your risk tolerance.** Developed countries (United Kingdom, France, Japan) tend to have less volatile stock markets than do emerging-market nations (such as those of Latin America, the Middle East, China, Russia, or India). You want both types of investments in your portfolio, but if you're inclined to invest in one much more than the other, know what you're getting into.

>> **What's the bounce factor?** As with any other kind of investment, you can pretty safely assume that risk and return will have a close relationship over many years. Emerging-market ETFs will likely be more volatile but, over the long run, more rewarding than ETFs that track the stock markets of developed nations. *Note:* Don't assume that countries with fast-growing economies will necessarily be the most profitable investments.

>> **Look to P/E ratios.** How expensive is the stock compared to the earnings you're buying? You may ask yourself this question when buying a company stock, and it's just as valid a question when buying a nation's or a region's stocks.

In general, a lower P/E ratio is more indicative of promising returns than is a high P/E ratio. (See Chapter 3 for a reminder of how to calculate a P/E ratio.) CAPE (also known as the Shiller P/E or PE 10 Ratio), stands for *cyclically adjusted price-to-earnings-ratio,* and it looks at the P/E over ten years, adjusted for inflation. Think of it as P/E 2.0. It has proven to be an even better (although far from foolproof) indicator of future stock-market returns than P/E 1.0.

According to Bloomberg Indices, at the time of writing, the CAPE for the U.S. stock market is about 38, versus 23 for Europe, 24 for Japan, 19 for Korea, 17 for Spain, and 11 for Russia.

You want your portfolio to include U.S., European, Pacific, and emerging-market stocks, but if you're going to overweight any particular area, you may want to consider the relative P/E ratios, among other factors. Do keep in mind that certain countries, like Russia, have had lower multiples for a very long time, given political instability, lack of proper corporate governance, and so on. You may look at a country's current ratios — not only as they compare to those of other nations, but also how they compare to that nation's own historical averages.

Choosing the Best International ETFs for Your Portfolio

Although I'm (obviously) a huge fan of international investing and also a big fan of ETFs, I must admit that forming an optimal international portfolio is not the easiest thing in the world to do. For one thing, there's too much to choose from! You clearly don't want a portfolio of large-growth, large-value, small-growth, and small-value stocks in four separate ETFs (as I recommend for the U.S. holding) for every country in the world. That would make for one very cumbersome and unwieldly portfolio!

So, you need to create a well-diversified, low-cost, tax-efficient foreign portfolio with some kind of lean toward value and small cap. How to do that?

The strategy that makes the most sense to me is to split up your wisely chosen international ETFs into two large categories: developed markets and emerging markets. For most portfolios, a reasonable split of foreign stock holdings would be something in the neighborhood of 75/25, with 75 percent going to developed nations (England, France, Germany, Japan, Canada) and 25 percent going to emerging-market nations (Brazil, Russia, Turkey, South Africa, Mexico, and a host of countries where the entire value of all outstanding stock may be less than that of any S&P 500 company). Keep in mind that I'm talking about 75 percent and 25 percent of roughly half your stock portfolio, with the other half invested in the good old U.S. of A.

In this section, I suggest some of the ETFs you might consider first and foremost.

Choosing from a number of brands

By and large, the ETFs I discuss here belong to a handful of ETF families: Vanguard, BlackRock (iShares), Schwab, Dimensional, and Cambria. Yes, there are other global and international ETFs from which to choose, and I discuss some of your other options in Chapter 6, where I turn to global stocks divvied up by industry sector. As for global stocks that fit into a regional- or style-based portfolio, those mentioned in this section are among your best bets.

For more information on any of the international ETFs I discuss next, keep the following contact information handy:

>> **BlackRock iShares:** www.ishares.com

>> **Cambria:** www.cambriafunds.com

>> **Charles Schwab:** www.schwab.com

>> **Dimensional:** www.dimensional.com

>> **Vanguard:** www.vanguard.com

Examining ETFs that cover the planet

If you have a small portfolio and a strong desire to keep your investment management simple, you may be best off mixing and matching a total-market U.S. fund (see Chapter 3) with a total international fund.

Be forewarned that a good number of ETFs that may seem "total international" are not. The Schwab International Equity ETF, for example, is a fine fund, but only if you want to limit your international exposure to developed nations. To get both developed and emerging-market stocks, you're better off with the Vanguard Total International Stock ETF (ticker symbol: VXUS) or the iShares Core MSCI Total International Stock ETF (ticker symbol: IXUS). Both of these funds give you instant exposure to everything in the world of stocks, minus U.S. investments. Both ETFs are ultra low cost (0.08 for Vanguard; 0.09 for iShares), well diversified, and tax-efficient. The two funds are, in fact, *very* similar.

If you *really* want to keep things simple, you can buy a single ETF that tracks an index of all stocks everywhere, U.S. and foreign. That one fund would be either the Vanguard Total World Stock ETF (ticker symbol: VT), with an expense ratio of 0.08 percent, or the SPDR Portfolio MSCI Global Stock Market ETF (ticker symbol: SPGM), with an expense ratio of 0.09 percent. Both are perfectly fine options. These index ETFs, like practically all others, are self-adjusting. That is, if your goal is to own a single global fund that reflects each country's percentage of the global economy, as that percentage grows or shrinks, so will its representation in these ETFs. Easy!

If you have a portfolio larger than a few hundred dollars, and you're paying nothing in commissions to trade, and you're okay with adjusting its alignment (via rebalancing) once a year or so, I suggest that you keep your stocks and bonds in separate funds and that you break down your stock holdings into U.S. and non-U.S. Then, just as I advise for your domestic stocks, assign your foreign holdings to at least two categories: developed-nation stocks and emerging-market stocks.

If you've read Chapters 3 and 4, you know that my preferred way to split your U.S. stock holdings is by style: large growth, large value, small growth, and small value. On the international side, you could do the same, but I don't think you need to. Dividing both developing national and emerging markets into four categories each can be done, but it's a bit cumbersome at rebalancing time to deal with so many funds. And, especially where emerging markets are concerned, small-cap and value options tend to be expensive.

TIP

Instead, I suggest a broad developed-markets fund, a broad emerging-markets fund, and two other foreign funds to give the portfolio a value lean and an extra heaping of small cap. Note that most "total-market" funds are market weighted, so you'll be getting mostly large-cap exposure, which is why you'll want to add some small cap as a separate dish.

Oh, you could also slice the overseas pie into regions: European, Pacific, and emerging markets. This option would be fine, although you'd be lacking in Canadian stocks. Or you could buy an international value, an international growth, and an international small-cap ETF. This would be fine, as well, although your expense ratio would be higher than with the strategy I'm recommending.

Let's take a closer look at that strategy in the next sections, and some of the ETFs you might employ.

Digging into developed-market ETFs

By *developed markets*, we investment people generally mean Western Europe, the Pacific Rim (Japan, Australia, New Zealand), and Canada — in other words, the richer countries of the world. Sometimes, depending on the indexer, you might also encounter South Korea, Taiwan, South Africa, and Israel.

Want to tap into the developed-nations market in one fell swoop? Consider the following ETFs.

SPDR Portfolio Developed World ex-US ETF (ticker symbol: SPDW)

Indexed to: S&P Developed Ex-U.S. BMI Index. BMI stands for Broad Market Index. Broad? Enough. This fund has 2,320 holdings.

Expense ratio: 0.04 percent

Top five country holdings: Japan, United Kingdom, France, Canada, Germany

Russell's review: With the lowest expense ratio in the category, heck yeah, I like it. The diversification isn't quite that of Vanguard's equivalent (see the next section), but there is enough breadth that you don't need to worry about overconcentration. The single largest holding is Samsung Electronics, taking up just 1.59 percent of the portfolio.

Vanguard FTSE Developed Markets ETF (ticker symbol: VEA)

Indexed to: FTSE Developed All Cap ex-U.S. Index of 4,035 stocks

Expense ratio: 0.05 percent

Top five country holdings: Japan, United Kingdom, France, Canada, Germany

Russell's review: As with all Vanguard funds, you get solid basics here at a very reasonable cost. And few funds are as well diversified as this one. The single largest holding is Nestlé S.A., with just 1.41 percent of the portfolio. Samsung Electronics is second, with 1.35 percent of the portfolio.

Dimensional Core Equity Market ETF (ticker symbol: DFAI)

Indexed to: Dimensional's own recipe, which qualifies this fund as "actively managed," even though you likely won't see more turnover with this fund than with a typical index fund. The expense ratio is also more like an index fund than an actively managed fund.

Expense ratio: 0.18 percent

Top five country holdings: Japan, United Kingdom, Canada, France, Germany

Russell's review: Dimensional launched a handful of ETFs, including this one, in 2020. Dimensional has been in the mutual-fund business for many years, and its claim to fame is that it incorporates a value lean and provides greater exposure to small cap than the establishment indexes. This makes beautiful sense. And if you go with this fund (despite the higher expense ratio), you may not need the value and small-cap ETFs I recommend later — provided you pair this fund with Dimensional's Core Emerging Market ETF (ticker symbol: DFAU). But know that DFAU has an expense ratio of 0.36 percent, significantly more than some other good emerging-market funds.

Evaluating emerging-market stock ETFs

When economists feel optimistic, they call them "emerging-market" nations. But these same countries are also sometimes referred to as the Third World or, even more to the point, "poor countries." I'm talking about China, Taiwan, Mexico, Russia, India, Brazil, and South Africa, among others. In 2013, Greece, given a huge drop in average income, had the dubious honor of being the first developed nation to be downgraded to emerging-market status by a major indexer (MSCI).

All together, the emerging-market nations make up 6 billion people, or about 85 percent of the world's population, but only about 41 percent of global gross domestic product (GDP), and 13 percent of global equity market capitalization.

Much of the fortunes of emerging-market nations, especially those of sub-Saharan Africa and South America, are tied to commodity production. But commodity prices fluctuate greatly. And political unrest (often due to the fact that commodity production is controlled by very few), corruption, and overpopulation, as well as serious environmental challenges, plague many of these countries.

On the other hand, emerging-market stock prices — vis-à-vis U.S. stock prices, and even those of developed nations — seem underpriced at the moment. Many emerging economies seem especially strong. And — perhaps most important — these countries have young populations. Children tend to grow up to be workers, consumers, and perhaps even investors. Future growth of the economies seems almost assured. This should pan out to mean some profitability to shareholders in emerging-market stocks and ETFs.

Here are some excellent ETF options for capturing the performance of emerging markets.

Vanguard MSCI Emerging Market ETF (ticker symbol: VWO)

Indexed to: The FTSE Emerging Markets All Cap China A Inclusion Index. You're looking at 5,200 stocks.

Expense ratio: 0.1 percent

Top five country holdings: China, Taiwan, India, Brazil, South Africa

Russell's review: A good way to capture the potential growth of emerging-market stocks is through VWO. The cost is the lowest in the pack, and the diversity of investments is more than adequate. My only problem is that China represents nearly 41 percent of the portfolio. That's in line with the market weighting of Chinese-company stocks compared to the rest of the nations. Still, I wouldn't mind at all if Vanguard were to limit any one country's representation to, oh, maybe 30 percent of the total portfolio.

iShares Core MSCI Emerging Markets (ticker symbol: IEMG)

Indexed to: MSCI Emerging Markets Investable Market Index. This features 2,515 holdings.

Expense ratio: 0.11 percent

Top five country holdings: China, Taiwan, South Korea, India, Brazil

Russell's review: Good fund. Good company. Good index. In fact, because China makes up less than 35 percent of the total portfolio, versus Vanguard's 41 percent, I might give the edge to this ETF, despite the slightly higher (very slightly higher) expense ratio and more limited company diversification. But it would be a close call.

Dimensional Emerging Core Equity Market ETF (ticker symbol: DFAE)

Indexed to: Dimensional's own propriety index. It has thrown in 4,100 holdings and given the portfolio a value and small-cap lean.

Expense ratio: 0.35 percent

Top five country holdings: China, Taiwan, South Korea, India, Brazil

Russell's review: It's significantly more expensive than some other emerging-market options, but this fund does offer advantages. One is the value and small-cap lean, making this fund perhaps the best-in-class if you're only going to have one developed-market ETF and one emerging-market ETF and not supplement them with separate international value and small-cap ETFs. In the very long run, those leans would give this fund a distinct advantage in terms of performance. Also, this fund gives Chinese stocks 34 percent of the total capitalization, which is high, but not as high as the other emerging-market ETFs.

Adding value to your international portfolio

Studies show that the same *value premium* — the tendency for value stocks to outperform growth stocks — that seemingly exists here in the United States can be found around the world. Therefore, I suggest a mild tilt toward value in your international stock portfolio, just as I recommend for your domestic portfolio.

TIP

You can easily accomplish this tilt by adding the iShares MSCI International Value Factor ETF (ticker symbol: IVLU) to your core international fund. I might, for example, create an international portfolio by mixing IVLU with the core Vanguard Total International Stock ETF (ticker symbol: VXUS). I might suggest 85 percent VXUS (which offers both value and growth, developed and emerging nations) with 15 percent IVLU.

Or, if you've already decided to split your international stocks by region — Europe, Pacific, emerging markets — then adding a bit of IVLU can give you the value lean you seek.

iShares MSCI International Value Factor ETF (ticker symbol: IVLU)

Indexed to: MSCI World ex USA Enhanced Value Index

Expense ratio: 0.3 percent

Top five country holdings: Japan, United Kingdom, France, Germany, Switzerland

Russell's review: There aren't a lot of ETF offerings in international value, so I'm grateful this fund exists. The cost is reasonable. The index is good and "valuey" (that's where the "enhanced" comes in). You're only getting developed-world stocks, no emerging markets, but that's okay as long as your total international exposure is balanced. If you want to add value on both the developed-market and emerging-market sides of your international portfolio, you'll have to go for now with a mutual fund, rather than an ETF. Vanguard's International Value Fund (ticker symbol: VTRIX) is a good option.

Cambria Global Value ETF (ticker symbol: GVAL)

Indexed to: This is not an index fund but an actively managed fund with a strategy that attempts to concentrate and thicken the value premium by selecting the most undervalued companies in those countries that themselves seem undervalued.

Expense ratio: 0.59 percent

Top five country holdings: Poland, Austria, Italy, Columbia, Greece

Russell's review: I know, I know. I say I don't like actively managed funds, and I don't like high expense ratios, but this fund's strategy is just too compelling to ignore. As I'm writing these words, the fund has returned 6.5 percent annually for the past five years. That's not very good. But these past five years have been awfully crappy years for both international and value stocks. When international and value come back into vogue, this fund could really shine. If Cambria were to lower the expense ratio, I could get really enthusiastic.

Surveying small-cap international: Yes, you want it

Small-cap international stocks have even less correlation to the U.S. stock market than larger foreign stocks. The reason is simple: If the U.S. economy takes a swan dive, it will seriously hurt conglomerates — Nestlé, Toyota, and Samsung Electronics, for example — that serve the U.S. market, regardless of where their corporate headquarters are located. A fall in the U.S. economy and U.S. stock market is less likely to affect smaller foreign corporations that sell mostly within their national borders. A midsize bank in Tokyo that makes its profits selling mortgages may be entirely immune to any goings-on on Wall Street.

TIP

Regardless of the investment vehicle you choose, I suggest that a good chunk of your international stock holdings — perhaps as much as 50 percent, if you can stomach the volatility — go to small-cap holdings. The two ETFs I'd like you to consider are from Vanguard and iShares. Note that there are considerable differences between the two.

Vanguard FTSE All-World ex-U.S. Small Cap Index (ticker symbol: VSS)

Indexed to: The FTSE All-World Small Cap Ex-U.S. Index, which tracks more than 4,100 small-cap company stocks in both developed nations (77 percent of the stocks) and emerging markets (23 percent)

Expense ratio: 0.11 percent

Top five country holdings: Canada, Japan, United Kingdom, Taiwan, China

Russell's review: For exposure to small-cap international stocks, you aren't going to find a less expensive or more diversified fund.

iShares International Developed Small Cap Value Factor ETF (ticker symbol: ISVL)

Indexed to: FTSE Developed ex U.S. ex Korea Small Cap Focused Value Index

Expense ratio: 0.3 percent

Top five country holdings: Canada, Japan, United Kingdom, Sweden, Australia

Russell's review: I have long lamented, and have been quite surprised, that it took the ETF industry until 2021 to provide investors with a small-cap, truly international (both developed-world and emerging-market) value fund. And finally, here it is! If you've taken my advice and built your international portfolio with one core developed-market fund and one core emerging-market fund, then adding ISVL can, in and of itself, give you the added exposure to both small cap *and* value that academic research says is likely to sharply increase your returns over the long haul. Downside: The expense ratio, while certainly reasonable, is higher than the Vanguard small-cap offering.

IN THIS CHAPTER

» Weighing the pros and cons of sector and style investing

» Listing the ETFs that work best for sector investing

» Choosing the best options for your portfolio

» Unearthing some facts about socially responsible investing

» Determining the potential payoff of dividend and other funds

Chapter **6**

Sector Investing and Different Specialized Stocks

Despite the firm convictions of zealots on both sides, style investing (large, small, growth, value) and sector investing (technology, utilities, health care, energy) are not matter and antimatter. They can, and sometimes do, exist very peacefully side by side.

In this chapter, I present the nuts and bolts of sector investing: how it can function alone, or in conjunction with style investing, to provide diversity on both the domestic and the international sides of your portfolio (or overlapping the two). However you decide to slice the pie (whether by style or by sector — or both), using exchange-traded funds (ETFs) as building blocks makes for an excellent strategy.

I also introduce a few stock ETFs that don't fit into any of the categories I discuss in previous chapters. They're neither growth nor value, large nor small. They aren't industry-sector funds, nor are they international. If ETFs were ice cream, the funds presented here wouldn't represent chocolate and vanilla, but rather, the outliers on the Baskin-Robbins menu: PB 'n J, Cotton Candy, No Sugar Added Pineapple Coconut, Pink Bubblegum, and Wild 'n Reckless Sherbet (a swirl of green apple, blue raspberry, and fruit punch).

Selecting Stocks by Sector, not Style

As of this writing, there are 471 industry-sector ETFs, per Morningstar Direct. You can find a fund to mirror each of the major industry sectors of both the U.S. and foreign economies: energy, basic materials, financial services, consumer goods, and so on.

REMEMBER

No standard methodology exists for breaking up the U.S. industry into sectors; MSCI does it one way, and FTSE Russell does it a slightly different way. Some ETFs mirror subsections of the economy, such as semiconductors (a subset of information technology) and biotechnology (a subset of health care). In some cases, subsectors of the economy you may not even know exist — such as nanotech, cloud computing, and water resources — are represented with ETFs. And in other instances, you can find ETFs that represent sub-subsections and sub-sub-subsections of the economy, such as cybersecurity, telemedicine, video games, and, of course, the latest darling of Johnny-come-lately ETFs, cannabis.

A good number of newer ETFs allow you to invest in industry sectors in foreign countries or in *global* industries (which is to say U.S. and foreign countries together).

Information technology is number one on the global chart, as it is on the U.S. chart. But health care moves from the number-two spot on the U.S. chart down to number five on the global chart. (Only in the United States does a trip to the dermatologist boost the national economy!)

WARNING

Here is living proof that you can, if you so wish, slice and dice a portfolio to ultimate death: You can actually find some ETFs that allow you to buy into a particular industry within a particular country, such as the KraneShares CSI China Internet ETF (ticker symbol: KWEB). These are similar to the sub-sub-subsector ETFs

I discuss earlier. Betting on slivers of the economy is almost as risky as betting on individual stocks. And day-traders these days are just as likely to use ETFs (often the sub-sub-subsectors) as if they were individual stocks. Sadly, most day-traders, whether they favor ETFs or stocks, are going broke, even as I'm typing these words. Please, invest broadly and trade infrequently. You'll be glad you did.

Calculating your optimal sector mix

If you're going to go the sector route and build your entire stock portfolio, or a good part of it, out of industry-sector ETFs, make sure you're able to have allocations to all or most major sectors of the economy.

Some advisors would tell you to keep your allocations roughly proportionate to each sector's share of the broad market. I think that's decent advice, with just a bit of caution. Had you taken that approach in 1999, your portfolio would've been chocked to the top with technology, given the gross overpricing of the sector at that point. (And you would've taken a bath the following year.) I'd suggest that no matter what sectors are hot at the moment, no single sector should ever make up more than 20 percent of your stock portfolio.

If you've read Chapter 5, you may recall that I noted that single-country and especially small single-country ETFs are not something I go out of my way to own. One reason is that a smaller country's economy can be dominated by one or two industries, making its markets especially volatile.

Perhaps start by roughly allocating your sector-based portfolio according to the market cap of each sector and then tweak from there — based not on crystal-ball predictions of the future but on the unique characteristics of each sector. What do I mean? Read on.

Seeking risk adjustment with high- and low-volatility sectors

Some industry sectors have historically evidenced greater return and greater risk. (Return and risk tend to go hand in hand, as I discuss in Chapter 10.) The same rules that apply to style investing apply to sector investing. Know how much volatility you can stomach, and then — and only then — build your portfolio in tune with your risk tolerance.

Keep in mind that *any* single sector — even utilities, the least volatile of all — will tend to be more volatile than the entire market because there is little diversification. Don't overindulge!

Finally, keep in mind that your allocation between bonds and stocks will almost certainly have much more bearing on your overall level of risk and return than will your mix of stocks. In Chapter 7, I introduce bonds and discuss how an ETF investor should hold them.

Knowing where the style grid comes through

There is nothing wrong with dividing a stock portfolio into industry sectors, but please don't be hasty in scrapping style investing. I really believe that if you're going to pick one strategy over the other, the edge goes to style investing. For one thing, I know that it works. Style investing helps to diffuse (but certainly not eliminate) risk. Scads of data show that.

In addition, style investing allows you to take advantage of years of other data that indicate you can goose returns without raising your risk, or raising it by much, by leaning your portfolio toward value and small cap (see Chapters 3 and 4). When you invest in industry sectors through ETFs, you're most often investing the vast majority of your funds in large caps, and you're usually splitting growth and value evenly. That approach may limit your investment success.

Another reason ETF investors shouldn't scrap style investing: Style ETFs are the cheaper choice. For whatever reason — yes, another one of those eternal mysteries that keeps me awake at night — style ETFs tend to cost much less than industry-sector ETFs. According to Morningstar Direct, the average sector equity fund will cost you 0.52 percent in management fees. Style funds are generally much less.

And one final reason to prefer style to sector for the core of your portfolio: You'll require fewer funds. With large growth, large value, small growth, and small value, you can pretty much capture the entire stock market. With sector funds, you need nearly a dozen funds to achieve the same effect. Each sector fund offers minimal diversification because the price movements of companies in the same industry sector tend to be closely correlated.

Seeking low correlations for added diversification

Some sectors, or industry subsectors, even though they're part of the stock market, tend to move out of lockstep with the rest of the market. By way of example, consider real estate investment trusts (REITs). Chapter 8 has the scoop on them.

Another sector that fills the bill is energy. For example, consider that in 2002, when the total U.S. stock market tanked by almost 11 percent, REITs were up 31 percent. The year 2005 was pretty lackluster for the total stock market, yet energy stocks were up 31 percent. In the past three years, *all* U.S. sectors have done very well, except for energy, with a return of −28 percent annually.

TIP

If you decide to build your portfolio around industry-sector funds, I urge you, at the very least, to dip into the style funds to give yourself the value or small-cap tilt that I discuss in Chapters 3 and 4. That's especially true if you use SPDRs to build your sector portfolio. This fund group is especially weighted toward large cap. In Chapter 9, I offer a few sample portfolios to illustrate workable allocations.

Surveying Sector Choices by the Dozen

After you decide which industry sectors you want to invest in, you need to choose among ETFs. BlackRock's iShares, Vanguard, Fidelity, State Street Global Advisors SPDRs, and other fund managers all offer good-sized menus of sector funds, both domestic and international.

TIP

Begin your sector selection here:

>> **Do you want representation in large industry sectors (health care, technology, utilities)?** Your options include Vanguard ETFs, BlackRock's iShares, State Street Global Advisors SPDRs, and Fidelity, as well as some slightly innovative funds from Invesco.

>> **Do you want to zero in on narrower industry niches (insurance, oil service, nanotech, autonomous technology, and robotics)?** Consider Invesco, iShares, VanEck, ARK

Invest, and Global X. You can also choose State Street Global Advisors (non–Select Sector) SPDRs.

>> **Are you looking for sometimes ridiculously narrow industry niches (aluminum) or sectors within sectors within individual foreign countries?** You should look at Global X, KraneShares, and Direxion ETFs. Ark Invest has one, too, if Israeli tech is your thing.

>> **Do you want to keep your expense ratios to a minimum?** Fidelity and Vanguard are the cheapest.

Investing for a Better World

How's the temperature where you are? A bit extreme? Global climate disruption is but one of the world's problems that has helped jostle millions of investors worldwide to move their money into investments that promise to provide more than just financial returns. These investments offer a chance to help combat climate change, end child labor, improve corporate-board diversity, and make the planet a cleaner, kinder, safer, more equitable place in myriad ways.

How many millions have been so jostled? Millions of millions. More than $35 trillion so far has been plunked into investments whose managers employ some kind of moral compass, according to the Global Sustainable Investment Alliance. Those trillions represent about 36 percent of all investment assets, and this figure has been rising fast. That grand sum represents money invested through endowments, trusts, institutional portfolios, mutual funds — and, growing perhaps fastest of all, ETFs.

There are now about 150 ETFs that focus specifically on sustainable investing, with combined assets of just about $100 billion. That's up from 91 ETFs that together held a mere $54 billion just one year earlier, according to Morningstar Direct.

What are "sustainable investing" and "ESG"?

Once upon a time, today's sustainable or *environmental, social, and governance* (ESG) funds were generally referred to as *socially responsible investing* (SRI). But times change, and with them, the terminology investors use. The term *SRI* is barely used today. Instead, you'll hear about a fund that invests sustainably — with an eye toward creating a better planet and a healthier society — or you'll hear about ESG funds.

ESG, among those savvy in the field, actually describes an approach to measuring sustainability. Within the ESG framework, issuers of stocks and bonds are rated according to three criteria:

>> **Environment:** Companies get points for complying with governmental environmental regulations and operating in a manner that doesn't contribute to climate change, deforestation, and pollution of air, water, and soil.

>> **Social:** Better companies promote fair labor practices, employee diversity, safe working conditions, and the health and well-being of the public. Better companies' workers are paid living wages and given decent health benefits.

>> **Governance:** The best corporations don't employ heavy-handed lobbying or bribe government officials. They diversify their boards and use transparent accounting methods. Those in charge work in the best interests of shareholders, employees, and customers.

Sustainable investing is sometimes filled with ambiguity

Is everyone in agreement as to the criteria that cause one company to have a high ESG rating and another company to have a low ESG rating? No. The world is still looking for objective measures, and in the meantime, corporate leadership and investment-fund managers have a lot of — perhaps too much — latitude in defining sustainability. And there is all too often a difference in what the managers of sustainable funds are doing and what their investors think they're doing.

Detractors of sustainable investing and ESG methodology (more accurately, methodologies) say that this lack of uniformity and the occasional profiteer ("greenwasher") are reasons to avoid sustainable investing. That is just silly. Just because *Car and Driver* and *Consumer Reports* don't necessarily agree on whether Toyota or Subaru produce the better sedan doesn't mean that you shun Toyota and Subaru or that you don't seek guidance from experts on the best car to purchase.

Sustainable investing is a great concept. And if you wonder if you can do well financially by doing good, I'm here to say, "Yes, yes, you can."

Are companies with better ESG ratings more profitable?

Keeping in mind that ESG ratings and definitions differ, can the argument nonetheless be made that companies that really care about the world around them do, indeed, have more robust bottom lines? It would make sense that companies that think sustainably have greater long-term vision, aren't making stupid decisions for short-term profits, and display sensibilities to others and the planet that could build long-term loyalty among workers and customers, with an end result of greater profitability. And studies show this is the case.

TECHNICAL
STUFF

Researchers at the NYU Stern Center for Sustainable Business, in cooperation with Rockefeller Asset Management, recently compiled 1,000 studies on the subject. They found that 58 percent of the studies showed a positive relationship between ESG and corporate financial performance, whereas only a handful (8 percent) showed an inverse relationship. (The remainder of the studies were either neutral or mixed.) The longer the time frame, the more likely that companies with a focus on ESG tended to be profitable.

Is ESG investing creating a better world?

ESG is a methodology or methodologies by which fund managers rank companies from great to good to mediocre to poor to horrible world citizens. Such ranking is often the first task of the manager of an ETF that promises you can do good by doing well. But ETFs that call themselves sustainable or ESG use differing methods to promote ethical and ecological goals.

Just as artists use different tools and different materials to create paintings and sculptures, fund managers use different strategies to invest so as to create financial return and return for the planet. These tools and materials are often integrated (you'll hear the term *ESG integration*) but may also be used solo. They include the following.

>> **Exclusions:** Let's use ESG ratings to identify companies that do the world more harm than good and then avoid investing in them.

>> **Positive screening:** Let's again use ESG ratings, but this time, to invest only or primarily in companies doing right, or at least that are "best in class" among companies in the same industry.

>> **Active ownership:** Let's arm-bend company leadership to become better world citizens, perhaps by raising a ruckus at shareholder meetings.

>> **Thematic investing:** Let's invest in industries like solar and wind power, recycling, and public transportation.

>> **Impact investing:** Let's find specific ventures or projects to promote. Impact investing is often used by ETFs that invest in *green bonds* (bonds used to raise money for ecologically minded projects).

REMEMBER

To date, sustainable ETFs have used exclusions more than any other strategy, but that seems to be changing, as more fund managers and investors realize that that strategy alone is suboptimal, and to have the most positive effects on the world and investment returns, it may pay to use several strategies. I feel confident in saying that, in the aggregate, these strategies have succeeded in making positive world change.

The ESG movement has undoubtedly had an impact on corporate America, notably by pushing certain auto, oil, chemical, and utility companies to reduce pollutants. Other victories include a nationwide ban on mercury thermometers and commitments from various corporations to start reducing greenhouse gas emissions, start recycling programs, and end discrimination against employees based on their sexual orientation.

And with $100 billion invested in ETFs that focus on sustainability — and growing fast — the pressure exerted by ETFs to create a better world will certainly grow.

Will investing in ESG funds make you rich?

The oldest ESG ETF is the iShares MSCI USA ESG Select ETF (ticker symbol: SUSA), which was started on January 24, 2005. Since its inception, the fund has returned a healthy 10.2 percent a year. In the past five years, the fund has returned 19.3 percent, while the total U.S. stock market has returned 18 percent. And moving along the spectrum, SUSA thoroughly trounces USA Mutuals' VICE mutual fund (ticker symbol: VICEX), which actually seeks to invest in socially *irresponsible* companies! (No, you won't find VICEX included in any of my sample portfolios presented in this book. Invest in sin on your own!) That fund has returned a meager 4.6 percent over the past five years.

Do these comparative returns mean you're always going to do better with ESG funds? No.

Lately, almost *all* ESG funds have clobbered *all* non-ESG funds, never mind this one ridiculous anti-ESG fund. It isn't because the ESG funds are ESG funds per se. It's largely because ESG funds, as a rule, underweight energy companies (which have tanked in past years) and overweight tech (which has soared in past years).

REMEMBER

ESG is *not* an asset class. ESG funds may have stock portfolios, bond portfolios, domestic portfolios, and foreign portfolios. All of these are asset classes and will generally play a much bigger role in the risk and return of a fund than whether it's an ESG fund or just a plain-vanilla ETF.

In the very long run, ESG funds of a certain asset class probably won't do much better or worse than non-ESG funds of the same asset class. That's because markets tend to be efficient. In other words, if highly rated ESG companies were to consistently outperform non-ESG companies (as studies indicate may well happen), then investors' money would steadily pour into the ESG companies, and their stock prices would rise. Hence, paying more for the stocks would temper stock performance. This is why stocks in growth companies, which are overall healthier and more profitable than value companies, don't outperform in the long haul.

Fence-sitters, make a decision

So, should you go out of your way to invest in ESG funds? For years, this was a tough question for me. Many ESG funds in years past simply charged too much. Or I didn't feel that they were necessarily managed in a way as to maximize return while minimizing risk. One especially annoying feature of broad ESG bond funds in the past was their tendency to charge investors a hefty fee for screening the corporations, while the fund actually carried mostly Treasury bonds.

But that has all changed in the past several years. Most ESG funds today cost roughly the same as their non-ESG counterparts. Some are even cheaper! And they're managed (passively or actively) by the best in the business.

According to a Morgan Stanley report from 2019, "[r]esearch conducted on the performance of nearly 11,000 mutual funds from 2004 to 2018 show[ed] that there is no financial trade-off in the returns of sustainable funds compared to traditional funds." (They used mutual funds and not ETFs because, back in 2004, there were so few ETFs.) The Morgan Stanley report not only found comparable performance between ESG and non-ESG funds, but also concluded that the ESG funds were slightly less volatile and less likely to tank when markets turned south. Other studies have noted the same slight advantage in stability.

So, if you can invest in a way that could make the world a better place, and your portfolio isn't going to suffer for it, and may actually benefit by slightly reducing risk, why not do so? And that's why, throughout this book, where I recommend ETFs, you often find ESG ETFs.

Which sustainable ETFs are best for your portfolio?

Keep in mind, once again, that sustainability and ESG criteria are *not* asset classes. All ETFs, regardless of whether they have a focus on ESG, are nothing but baskets of securities, usually stocks or bonds. So, the first question for you, if you want to "ESG-ize" your portfolio, is, "What kind of investment do I want?" Stocks? Bonds? Domestic? Foreign? Large cap? Small cap? I address these questions in the other chapters of Part 2.

TIP

After you've decided what asset class or classes you want to invest in, you can shop for an ESG fund that offers that asset class. Of course, you'll want a fund that is likely to earn you a good return. Start by looking for low costs. And, of course, you want to know that your money is making a difference. Here's where ESG funds, and the strategies they use, can vary enormously.

The most popular strategy used by ESG funds to date, as I mention earlier in this chapter, has been exclusions — avoiding investments in companies, and sometimes industries, such as tobacco and pornography, where the benefits to society are dubious, to say the least. Some of these funds have done a better job than others. Some, quite honestly, have been awfully lax in their screenings. Companies have been given gold stars not for having taken any positive actions, but merely for having made vague promises to do so. Some ESG strategies used by some ETF managers exclude only 10 percent of the U.S. stock-issuing corporations.

Even more troubling, some of the ETF purveyors promoting ESG funds actually have pretty terrible records where it comes to using their voting power to promote ESG initiatives, and these include the two largest providers of ETFs: iShares (BlackRock) and Vanguard. "These companies are powerful, and could make a huge difference, but they haven't been," says Jon Hale, director of ESG strategies for Morningstar.

Research done by Hale, along with Morningstar's Jackie Cook, based on 2020 proxy voting, found that both of these ETF giants voted against ESG proxies far more than they voted for them. "It isn't that fund managers love polluters," says Hale, "it's just that they vote most often in favor of whatever the board suggests." And it has long been known that executives of U.S. companies, in part because of how they're compensated, focus too much on short-term profits and not on bigger or more long-term issues.

But that, says, Hale, is destined to change. "BlackRock especially has heeded the criticism [that came from Hale's study], and they're starting to do better," says Hale. In fact, I opened up *The Wall Street Journal* on August 13, 2021, while drinking my morning coffee, and read that BlackRock, in the first half of 2021, backed 64 percent of environmental proposals, up from 11 percent in 2020.

"And Vanguard?" I asked Hale. Nothing but silence on the other end of the phone line. As a lifelong fan of Vanguard, I must say that this deeply disappointed me.

TIP

ETF purveyors that already had good track records in 2020, as reported in Hale's study, include Nuveen and Xtrackers (Deutsche Bank).

REMEMBER

Hale says it can be difficult to uncover a fund manager's proxy voting record, but it isn't impossible. Funds have to file how they voted with the Securities and Exchange Commission (SEC), and they generally post these documents somewhere on their websites. Morningstar Direct, a pay service, can also provide this information. As for other measures that an ETF is taking to promote a better world, you'll want to read up on them carefully. Every ESG fund's sponsor has a website with loads of information, including the holdings of the fund and specific strategies the managers are using to promote a better world.

TIP

There are about 150 ETFs that focus on sustainable investing. Many are discussed throughout this book. Even when choosing an ETF that doesn't focus specifically on sustainable investing, you can often find an ESG rating online (from various ratings groups) to help guide you in your choices.

Dividend Funds: The Search for Steady Money

The check is in the mail. When you know it's true (it isn't always), there are perhaps no sweeter words in the English language. To many investors, the thought of regular cash payments is a definite turn-on. Always willing to oblige, the financial industry of late has been churning out "high-dividend" funds — both mutual funds and ETFs — like there's no tomorrow.

The idea behind these funds is simple enough: They attempt to cobble together the stocks of companies that are issuing high dividends, have high-dividend growth rates, or promise future high dividends.

The oldest (launched March 11, 2003) and still one of the largest ETF dividends is the iShares Dow Jones Select Dividend Index Fund (ticker symbol: DVY). If you really want a fund that pays high dividends, neither that fund nor any of the funds listed here would be bad options:

>> Schwab U.S. Dividend Equity ETF (ticker symbol: SCHD)

>> Vanguard Dividend Appreciation ETF (ticker symbol: VIG)

>> Vanguard High Dividend Yield ETF (ticker symbol: VYM)

>> SPDR S&P Dividend ETF (ticker symbol: SDY)

>> First Trust Morningstar Dividend Leaders Index Fund (ticker symbol: FDL)

>> iShares Core Dividend Growth ETF (ticker symbol: DGRO)

And if you really want to invest in high-dividend-paying international stocks, the following ETFs wouldn't be so bad, either:

>> Schwab International Dividend Equity ETF (ticker symbol: SCHY)

>> Vanguard International High Dividend Yield (ticker symbol: VYMI)

>> First Trust S&P International Dividend Aristocrats ETF (ticker symbol: FID)

>> SPDR S&P International Dividend Equity ETF (ticker symbol: DWX)

If you want to fine-tune your dividends and have them come from, say, small-cap stocks, mid-cap stocks, or even emerging-market small caps, you can find these and much more among the ETF high-dividend-paying offerings from WisdomTree. They offer not only the U.S. SmallCap Dividend Fund (ticker symbol: DEM), the U.S. MidCap Dividend Fund (ticker symbol: DON), and the Emerging Markets SmallCap Dividend Fund (ticker symbol: DGS), but also a Europe SmallCap Dividend Fund (ticker symbol: DFE), a Japan SmallCap Dividend Fund (ticker symbol: DFJ), and even an International Dividend ex-Financials Fund (ticker symbol: DOO).

And if you want even more fine-tuning of where your dividends come from, try Invesco. It has the plain-vanilla-ish Invesco Dividend Achievers ETF (ticker symbol: PFM), the Invesco International Dividend Achievers ETF (ticker symbol: PID), the Invesco Dow Jones Industrial Average ETF (ticker symbol: DJD), and the Invesco S&P 500 High Dividend Low Volatility ETF (ticker symbol: SPHD).

There are also high-dividend ETFs of various shapes and sizes offered by ProShares, VanEck, and FlexShares. These tend to be narrower and more exotic.

All-In-One ETFs: For the Ultimate Lazy Portfolio

There's a lot of academic research, shared throughout this book, that provides reasons for you to construct a portfolio with stocks and bonds from around the world, allocated to your portfolio in a way that makes sense for you personally. This means building your portfolio with the right amount of aggressiveness (stocks) and the right amount of protectiveness (bonds and cash). It also means constructing your portfolio in such a way as to maximize return while minimizing risk. Decades of good data allow you to do that.

The optimal mix for you is unlikely to be the same optimal mix as it might be for, say, your parents, or for Joe on your Twitter feed, or for your dermatologist. Nor may the optimal mix for you necessarily be an exact replica of a market-weighted, total-world portfolio.

But for those who love simplicity and who are willing to accept what may be less than optimal, ETFs offer a way to build a portfolio with very, very few moving parts.

Buying into the world's stock markets in a flash

TIP

If you want instant exposure to the largest possible number of stocks, including U.S. and all sorts of foreign stocks (from both developed and emerging-market countries), your best options come from Vanguard and State Street SPDRs. Either of the following ETFs will give you an excellent representation of the world's stocks at a very reasonable cost:

>> Vanguard Total World Stock ETF (ticker symbol: VT)

>> SPDR Portfolio MSCI Global Stock Market ETF (ticker symbol: SPGM)

Both ETFs are based on market-weighted indexes, which means that you'll be getting a lot more large cap than you will small cap. It also means, given the run-up in capitalization of tech in the past several years, that your portfolio may have a lean toward growth. (Value stocks actually outperform growth in the long haul.) And given the recent outperformance and rise in capitalization of large U.S. companies — more like a handful of large U.S. companies (Apple, Microsoft, Amazon, Alphabet, and Facebook) — these all-world portfolios are now about 58 percent to 59 percent concentrated in but one country. Sure, it's a great country — with the Grand Canyon, Walt Disney World, and Bruce Springsteen — but it's still just one country. And as I know from years of tracking stock-market performance, U.S. stocks outperform foreign, and then foreign stocks outperform U.S, and then . . . ad infinitum.

Putting the world's bond markets at your fingertips

If you buy into an all-world stock ETF, such as one of the two introduced in the previous section, you'll want, if you're smart, to marry it to an all-world bond ETF. As I think I've made clear throughout this book, a portfolio with only stocks or only bonds is like a bicycle with but one wheel — you may move forward, but the going won't be easy, and you can easily topple over.

I present two good bond options here:

>> **Vanguard Total World Bond ETF (ticker symbol: BNDW):** It's super low-cost, with incredible diversification, and with more bonds than there are words in the Declaration of Independence and the Constitution combined. Nothing not to like.

>> **iShares Global Green Bond ETF (ticker symbol: BGRN):** It costs a bit more, but you get to promote a cleaner world. It's one of my favorite ESG funds. (See "Investing for a Better World," earlier in this chapter, for more about ESG funds.)

Both of these funds, like nearly all aggregate bond funds, offer a mix of federal government, agency, and private bonds. But these are all taxable bonds — no tax-free munis — so these babies are best kept nestled in tax-advantaged accounts, such as an individual retirement account (IRA).

Russell's average review for the average reader on an average day

"For every complex problem," said H. L. Mencken, "there is an answer that is clear, simple — and wrong." Certainly, finding the optimal portfolio is a complex problem. The all-in-one ETFs and mutual funds that I discuss in this chapter provide an answer that is clear, simple — and usually wrong. Oh, I suppose if you were the average 50-year-old, with the average amount of money, looking to work an average number of years, expecting to die at the average age, and you were willing to take on an average amount of risk, well, if you were all those things and planned on remaining forever average, an all-in-one fund might make sense for you.

But if you are anything other than perfectly average, I urge you to move on to Part 3 whenever you feel ready. Take a look at my model portfolios and craft an ETF portfolio that makes sense for *you*.

IN THIS CHAPTER

» Examining the rationale behind bond investing

» Recognizing different kinds of bonds

» Appreciating the risks that bond investing entails

» Knowing how much to allocate to your bond portfolio

Chapter **7**

For Your Interest: Bond ETFs

Plain and simple, there is no time-honored diversification tool for your portfolio that even comes close to bonds. They're as good as gold — even better than gold when you look at the long-term returns. Bonds are what may have saved your grandparents from selling pencils on the street following the stock-market crash of 1929.

The one thing that grandpa and grandma never had — but you do — is the ability to invest in bond exchange-traded funds (ETFs). Like stock ETFs, most bond ETFs are inexpensive, transparent (you know exactly what you're investing in), and highly liquid (you can sell them in a flash). Like individual bonds or bond mutual funds, bond ETFs can also be used to produce a reliable flow of cash in the form of interest payments, making them especially popular among grandparent types of any generation.

Throughout this chapter, I discuss a few things about bond investing in general. Then, without knowing the intimate particulars of your individual economics, I try my best to help you decide if bond ETFs belong in your portfolio, and, if so, which ones. I also address that all-important and highly controversial question of how to achieve an optimal mix of stocks and bonds.

REMEMBER

The single most important investment decision you'll ever make may occur when you determine the split between stocks and bonds in your portfolio. No pressure.

Tracing the Track Record of Bonds

Bonds, more or less in their present form, have been used as financial instruments since the Middle Ages. A bond, you see, is really nothing more than an IOU Jane lends money to Joe. Joe agrees to pay Jane back at a certain date. Joe also agrees to add a bit of money on top of the principal that he returns to Jane. That's a bond. The money thrown in on top of the principal is called interest. It's that simple. Then, as now, bonds of varying risk existed. Then, as now, risks and returns were highly correlated.

In other words, Jane won't lend Joe money unless Joe is trustworthy. If Jane suspects that there is any chance that Joe can't or won't repay, either she won't lend him the money or she'll demand higher compensation (more interest).

For the most part, bonds in the aggregate have been, and continue to be, less volatile than stocks, and their returns over time tend to be less. From 1926 to 2020, the average annualized nominal return of the S&P 500 (a broad index of U.S. stocks) has been around 10.7 percent, whereas the return of long-term U.S. government bonds has been approximately 5.6 percent.

These numbers may lead you to look at bonds and say to yourself, "Why bother?" Well, in fact, there's good reason to bother. Read on before you decide to forsake this all-important asset class.

Portfolio protection when you need it most

When determining the attractiveness of bonds, you need to look not only at historical return, but also at volatility: Long-term U.S. government bonds (which tend, like all long-term bonds, to be rather volatile) in their worst year *ever* (2009) returned −14.9 percent. In their second-worst year ever (1967), they returned −9.2 percent. Those are big moves but still a walk in the park compared to the worst stock-market years of 1931 (−43.3 percent), 1937 (−35 percent), 1974 (−26.5 percent), and 2008 (−37 percent).

During the Great Depression years, bonds may have saved your grandma and grandpa from destitution. The annualized real return of the S&P 500 from 1930 to 1932 was −20 percent. The annualized real return of long-term U.S. government bonds during the same three years was 14.9 percent.

There are two reasons that U.S. government bonds (and other high-quality bonds) often do well in the roughest economic times:

>> People flock to them for safety, raising demand.

>> Interest rates often (not always, but often) drop during tough economic times. Interest rates and bond prices have an inverse relationship. When interest rates fall, already-issued bonds (carrying older, relatively high coupon rates) shoot up in price.

REMEMBER

As in the past, bonds may similarly spare your hide should the upcoming years prove disastrous for Wall Street. (You never know.) Whereas international stocks and certain industry sectors, like energy and real estate, have limited correlation to the broad U.S. stock-market, bonds (not U.S. junk bonds, but most others) actually have a slight *negative* correlation to stocks. In other words, when the bear market is at its growliest, the complicated labyrinth of economic factors that typically coincide with that situation — lower inflation (possible deflation), lower interest rates — can bode quite well for fixed income. They certainly have done so in the past.

History may or may not repeat

Of course, as investment experts say again and again (although few people listen), historical returns are only mildly indicative of what will happen in the future; they're merely reference points. Despite all the crystal balls, tea leaves, and CNBC commentators in the world, the experts simply don't know what the future will bring.

REMEMBER

Although the vast majority of financial professionals use the past century as pretty much their sole reference point, some point out that in the 19th century, stocks and bonds actually had more similar — nearly equal, in fact — rates of return. And perhaps that may be true for the 21st century as well. Time will tell. In the meantime, given all this uncertainty, it would be most prudent to have both stocks and bonds represented in your portfolio.

Tapping into Bonds in Various Ways

Like stocks, bonds can be bought individually, or you can invest in any of hundreds of bond mutual funds or about 250 bond ETFs. The primary reason for picking a bond fund over individual bonds is the same reason you might pick a stock fund over individual stocks: diversification.

Sure, you have to pay to get your bonds in fund form, but the management fees on bond ETFs tend to be very low. Heck, there's even one broad market bond ETF that can be had at *no* expense. Conversely, the cost to trade individual bonds can be quite high. That's especially true of municipal bonds.

I'm not saying that you shouldn't consider ever buying individual bonds. Doing so may make sense, provided that you know how to get a good price on an individual bond (if not, please read my book on that topic, *Bond Investing For Dummies* [Wiley]) and provided that you're buying a bond with little default risk (such as a Treasury bond). But for the most part, investors do better with low-cost, indexed bond funds.

REMEMBER

Like stocks, bonds can (and should, if your portfolio is large enough) be broken up into different categories. Instead of U.S. and international, large, small, value, and growth (the way stocks are often broken up), bond categories may include U.S. government (both conventional and inflation-adjusted), corporate, international, and municipal bonds — all of varying maturity dates and credit ratings. Unless you've got many millions to invest, you simply can't effectively own enough individual bonds to tap into each and every fixed-income class.

Finding strength in numbers

To be honest, diversification in bonds, though important, isn't quite as crucial as diversification in stocks. If you own high-quality U.S. government bonds (as long as they aren't terribly long term) and you own a bevy of bonds from the most financially secure corporations, you're very unlikely to lose a whole lot of your principal, as you can with any stock. But diversification offers more benefits than just protecting principal. There's also much to be said for smoothing out returns and moderating risk.

Bond returns from one category of bonds to another can vary greatly, especially in the short run. In 2008, for example, high-yield corporate bonds, as represented by the SPDR Barclays Capital High Yield Bond ETF (ticker symbol: JNK), saw a return of −24.7 percent. That same year, U.S. Treasury bonds, as represented by the iShares Barclays 7–10 Year Treasury Bond ETF (ticker symbol: IEF), returned 17.9 percent. But the very next year, 2009, was a terrible year for Treasurys; IEF sagged −6.56 percent and JNK shot up 37.65 percent.

REMEMBER

By owning a handful of bond funds, you can effectively diversify across the map. You can have Treasurys of varying maturities, corporate bonds of varying creditworthiness, international bonds of varying continents and currencies, and municipal bonds from across the nation. As you see throughout the rest of this chapter, I urge investors primarily to seek safety in bonds. If you're looking for high returns, go to stocks. The purpose of bonds, as far as I'm concerned, is to provide ballast to a portfolio.

The purposes served by bond funds are to make your bond investing easy, help you to diversify, and keep your costs low. Just as in the world of stock funds, all bond funds are not created equal. Some Treasury funds are better than others. Some corporate bond funds are better than others. Ditto for funds holding municipal bonds and foreign bonds.

Considering bond investment costs

Low costs are even more essential when investing in bonds than they are when investing in stocks. That's always been the case, but especially when interest rates are low, and you must keep your costs low. When (historically, at least over the past century) you're looking at maybe earning 2.7 percent above inflation, paying 1.3 percent a year for some bond broker or fund company to manage your bond portfolio will cut your profits nearly in half — very likely more than half if you're paying taxes on the interest. Do you really care to do that?

As I write these words, interest rates are very low, which means that real interest rates (factoring in inflation, however low) for most bonds are considerably less than 2.7 percent. That fact means paying attention to the cost of your bond funds is more essential than ever.

The most economical bond funds are index funds, and you have a number of excellent index bond ETFs to choose from. Those I highlight in this chapter include some of the cheapest funds on the planet, which is a reason to like them.

TIP

Although I'm a big proponent of ETFs, I must tell you that the ETF tax edge in the fixed-income arena isn't nearly as sharp as it is in stocks. The tax-efficiency of a bond index mutual fund and a bond ETF are just about the same. The wonderful structure of ETFs that I discuss in Chapter 1 simply doesn't matter all that much when it comes to bonds. Bonds pay interest — that's how you make money with bonds — and they rarely see any substantial capital gains. To the extent that they do have capital gains, however, ETFs may have an edge over mutual funds. But that's generally not going to be any big deal.

Determining the Optimal Fixed-Income Allocation

Okay, now that I've given you a few reasons to want to invest in bonds, it's time to tackle the really tough question: How much of your portfolio should you allocate to bonds? The common thinking on the subject — and I'm not above common thinking, especially when it's right on the mark — is that a portfolio becomes more conservative as its percentage allocation to bonds increases and as its percentage allocation to stocks decreases.

Of course, that doesn't answer the $64,000 question (or however much that question would now be worth with inflation factored in): Just how conservative do you want your portfolio to be? Different financial planners use different approaches to arrive at an answer to this question. I feel confident that my approach is best (otherwise, I wouldn't use it); in the interest of brevity, let me present it in the simplest terms.

The balance between stocks and bonds is usually expressed as "[% stocks]/[% bonds]," so a 60/40 portfolio means 60 percent stocks and 40 percent bonds. The optimal balance for any given person depends on many factors: age, size of portfolio, income stream, financial responsibilities, economic safety net, and emotional tolerance for risk.

In general, I like to see working investors hold three to six months of living expenses in cash (money-market accounts or internet savings accounts) or near-cash (very short-term bond funds or short-term certificates of deposit [CDs]). Nonworking investors living largely off their portfolios should set aside much more, perhaps one to two years of living expenses. Beyond that, most people's portfolios, whether those people are working or not, should be allocated to stocks (including real estate investment trusts [REITs], which I discuss in Chapter 8), intermediate-term bonds, and perhaps a few alternative investments, such as market-neutral funds and perhaps a sprinkling of commodities (including precious metals).

TIP

In determining an optimal split, I would first ask you to pick a date when you think you may need to start withdrawing money from your nest egg. How much do you anticipate needing to withdraw? Maybe $30,000 a year? Or $40,000? If you haven't given this question much thought, please do! Start with your current income. Subtract what you believe you'll be getting in Social Security payments or other pension income. The difference is what you would need to pull from your portfolio to replicate your current income. But most retirees find they need perhaps 80 percent to 90 percent of their working-days income to live comfortably. (When you're retired, you'll likely put less in the gas tank, buy fewer lunches out, have lower wardrobe expenses, and pay lower taxes, and hopefully, your house will be paid for.)

Come up with a rough number of how much you're going to need to take from your nest egg each year. Whatever the number is, multiply it by 10. That amount, ideally, is what I'd like to see you have in your bond portfolio, at a minimum, on the day you retire. In other words, if you think you'll need to pull $30,000 a year from your portfolio, I'd like to see you have at least $30,000 in cash and about $300,000 ($30,000 × 10) in bonds. That's regardless of how much you have in stocks — and, with the assumptions outlined earlier, you should have at least an equal amount in stocks.

REMEMBER

If you're still in your twenties or thirties and you want to keep the vast lion's share of your portfolio in stocks, fine. But as you get older and start to think about quitting your day job, begin to increase your bond allocation with the aim of getting to your retirement date with at least ten times your anticipated post-retirement withdrawals in bonds. Most people (who aren't rich) should have roughly one year's income in cash and the rest in a 50/50 (stock/bond) portfolio, more or less, on retirement day.

With at least one year's living expenses in cash and ten years of living expenses in bonds, you can live off the nonstock side of your portfolio for a good amount of time if the stock market goes into a swoon. (You then hope that the stock market recovers.)

TIP

If my rule seems too complex, you can always go with an even rougher rule that has appeared in countless articles. It says you should subtract your age from 110, and that's what you should have, more or less, in stocks, with the rest in bonds. So, a 50-year-old should have 60 percent (110 − 50) in stocks and 40 percent in bonds. A 60-year-old would want a portfolio of about 50 percent (110 − 60) stocks and 50 percent bonds. And so on and so on. This rough rule — even rougher than mine! — may not be bad, assuming that you're of average wealth, you're going to retire at the average age, you'll live the average life expectancy, and you expect that the markets will see roughly average performance!

Your Basic Bonds: Treasurys, Agency Bonds, and Corporates

At the time of this writing, there are about 250 bond ETFs. (This number doesn't include leveraged and inverse bond ETFs, which you should steer away from.) The bond ETFs worth considering are issued largely by iShares, State Street SPDRs, Vanguard, JPMorgan, Schwab, Fidelity, Invesco, and BNY Mellon Bank.

In this section, I present some of my favorites, among the Treasury, U.S. agency, and corporate bond offerings. Later in this chapter, I introduce you to some faves in the municipal and foreign bond categories.

TIP

Please note that with the discussion of each bond ETF, I include the *current yield:* how much each share is paying as a percentage of your investment on the day I'm writing this chapter. I do so only to give you a flavor of how the yields differ among the funds. Current yields on a bond or bond fund, especially a long-term bond or bond fund, can change dramatically from week to week. So, too, can the difference in yields between short- and long-term bonds (known as the *yield curve*). You can check the current yield of any bond fund, as well as the yield curve, on the sites of the ETF providers themselves or on general investing sites such as www. bloomberg.com, www.treasury.gov, or (for the best compilation of aggregate yields on all kinds of bonds) www.fidelity.com.

Note: Several different kinds of bond yield exist. (For detailed information, I once again refer you to my book *Bond Investing For Dummies* [Wiley].) For the sake of consistency, the bond yield I refer to throughout the rest of this chapter is the "SEC 30-Day Yield."

Tapping the Treasurys: Uncle Sam's IOUs

If the creator/issuer of a bond is a national government, the issue is called a *sovereign bond*. The vast majority of sovereign bonds sold in the United States are Uncle Sam's own Treasurys. Treasury bonds' claim to fame is the allegedly absolute assuredness that you'll get your principal back if you hold a bond to maturity. The United States government guarantees it. For that reason, Treasurys are sometimes called "risk-free."

Treasury bond ETFs come in short-term, intermediate-term, and long-term varieties, depending on the average maturity date of the bonds in the ETF's portfolio. In general, the longer the term, the higher the interest rate but the greater the volatility. Note that interest paid on Treasurys — including Treasury ETFs — is federally taxable but not taxed by the states. As it happens, bonds issued by state and local governments in the United States, known as *municipal bonds*, are not taxed by the federal government.

Treasurys, regardless of whether they're short or long term, also come in two broad groupings: conventional and inflation-adjusted. I introduce conventional Treasurys first, and then inflation-adjusted Treasurys. Conventional bonds pay a higher interest rate than inflation-adjusted bonds. But inflation-adjusted bonds get to see their principal bumped up twice a year to match the Consumer Price Index (CPI).

Here are some of your best choices for conventional Treasury ETFs:

>> Schwab Short-Term U.S. Treasury ETF (ticker symbol: SCHO)

>> Vanguard Short-Term Treasury ETF (ticker symbol: VGSH)

>> Schwab Intermediate-Term U.S. Treasury (ticker symbol: SCHR)

- » Vanguard Intermediate-Term Treasury Index ETF (ticker symbol: VGIT)

- » Schwab Long-Term U.S. Treasury ETF (ticker symbol: SCHQ)

- » Vanguard Long-Term Treasury ETF (ticker symbol: VGLT)

TIP

If you don't see the word *inflation* or *TIPS* (short for Treasury Inflation-Protected Securities) in the name of a fund, you can assume that the fund is holding conventional Treasurys.

Bread at $15 a loaf? Getting inflation protection in a flash

Technically, TIPS are Treasurys, but few investment pros ever refer to them as Treasurys. Most refer to them simply as TIPS. I discuss them separately from the other Treasury obligations here because they play a distinctly different role in your portfolio.

The deal with TIPS is this: They pay you only a nominal amount of interest (at the time of writing, even long-term TIPS are paying about one-third of 1 percent), but they also kick in an adjustment for inflation. So, for example, if inflation is running at 3 percent, all things being equal, your long-term TIPS will return 3 percent, plus whatever nominal interest is on top of that.

TIP

If you want to know what the rate of inflation is going to be over the next few years, I can't tell you, but I can tell you what rate of inflation the bond market expects. That would be the difference between conventional Treasury bonds and TIPS. If, for example, a ten-year conventional Treasury bond were paying 3 percent and the ten-year TIPS were paying 0.5 percent, the difference (2.5 percent) would be the rate of inflation that bond buyers collectively expect to see.

Here are some ETFs to consider:

- » Schwab U.S. TIPS ETF (ticker symbol: SCHP)

- » Vanguard Short-Term Inflation-Protected Securities Index Fund (ticker symbol: VTIP)

Treasurys' cousins: U.S. agency bonds

The better part of mortgage-backed bonds are issued by the likes of the Government National Mortgage Association (Ginnie

Mae or GNMA) and the Federal National Mortgage Association (Fannie Mae or FNMA), collectively known as government agencies. Even though not all of Washington's agencies are technically part of the government, most of them — and the bonds they issue — have not only mortgages to buoy them but also the full faith and backing of the U.S. government.

And so these bonds, and the ETFs that offer these bonds, are generally considered very safe — almost as safe as Treasurys. Because of the nature of the bonds, they aren't as interest-rate sensitive as Treasurys. And because they're considered a tad less safe and also not as liquid (not a concern for buy-and-hold investors), they tend to pay slightly more over time than Treasurys. As I'm writing these words, the yield on agency bonds is about 1 percent, versus 0.9 percent for intermediate-term Treasurys. They're often that close.

So, why bother with agency bonds? Well, they also serve as a good diversifier within a bond portfolio. They sometimes see their prices rise or remain stable when other bond prices are falling, and vice versa. I do not consider them a necessity, although I certainly have used them with clients who have conservative portfolios and, therefore, a lot of bonds. They also tend to be less interest-rate sensitive than Treasurys.

If you want agency bonds in your portfolio, I recommend without reservation the Vanguard Mortgage-Backed Securities ETF (ticker symbol: VMBS).

Indexed to: The Bloomberg Barclays Capital U.S. MBS Float Adjusted Index

Expense ratio: 0.05 percent

Current yield: 1.03 percent

Average duration: 4.9 years

Russell's review: You can find a dozen ETFs just like this one issued by other providers. But given the great similarity between all these funds, I say go with the least expensive, and that, at least for now, is the Vanguard fund. *Float adjusted,* by the way, simply means that the index only counts shares available to investors and excludes closely held shares that don't trade on the open market.

In terms of the risk and return of an ETF, I'd say it's of minimal importance.

Banking on business: Corporate bond ETFs

Logically enough, corporations issue bonds called *corporate bonds*, and you can buy a dizzying array of them with varying maturities, yields, and ratings, either individually or in fund form. There are many dozens of corporate bond ETFs. And with corporate bonds — even more than government bonds because diversifying to curtail risk is crucial — it makes a whole lot of sense to buy them in fund form. With fees lately dropping like hail, ETFs provide a very potent way to access this important asset class.

TIP

In the area of corporate bonds, credit ratings are very important. Know that the average bond rating of, say, Vanguard's Intermediate-Term Corporate Bond ETF (ticker symbol: VCIT), is between Baa and A, which means, more or less, that the bonds are issued by companies that are fairly solvent. But you're "earning" the higher return over Vanguard's Intermediate-Term Treasury ETF (ticker symbol: VGIT) by taking a risk that, in the case of a recession, some of the issuers might go belly-up, and your ETF shares could see a price drop.

WARNING

If you don't know how the ratings agencies rank a certain bond or bond fund, just look at the bonds or fund's yield: Generally, the higher the yield, the lower the credit quality. The highest-yielding bonds are called, appropriately enough, *high-yield bonds,* which is more or less synonymous with *junk bonds.* I generally avoid junk bonds for the simple reason that they, unlike "investment-grade" bonds, do not offer a safe harbor if your stocks tumble. When stocks go south, junk bonds almost always do as well. So, what's the point? You might as well invest in stocks, where the long-term returns are going to be higher than with any bonds, including the highest-yielding bonds.

Here are some ETFs to consider:

>> Vanguard Intermediate-Term Corporate Bond ETF (ticker symbol: VCIT)

>> Vanguard ESG U.S. Corporate Bond ETF (ticker symbol: VCEB)

>> Vanguard Short-Term Corporate Bond Index (ticker symbol: VCSH)

>> iShares ESG Aware 1–5 Year USD Corporate Bond ETF (ticker symbol: SUSB)

The whole shebang: Investing in the entire U.S. bond market

The broadest fixed-income ETFs are all-around good bets, especially for more modestly sized portfolios. Note that these bonds use a total bond market approach, which means about two-thirds government bonds and one-third corporate. These funds also make the most sense for investors with lots of room in their tax-advantaged retirement accounts. If you have to stick your bonds in a taxable account, you're probably better off separating your Treasury bonds and your corporate bonds. Reason: You get a small tax break on Treasury bond interest, in that you don't have to pay state income tax. If, however, your Treasury bonds are buried in an aggregate fund, such as these, you have to pay state income tax on the interest. Dem's da rules.

Note that the terms *aggregate bond, total bond,* and *core bond* can be a bit misleading in that they represent bonds issued by the federal government (Treasury and agencies) and by corporations, but as a rule, they do not include tax-free municipal bonds, which make up a good chunk of the true total bond market but are considered an entirely separate genus from taxable bonds. They also do not include TIPS — that, too, is considered a different beast, kept aside from other "conventional" bonds.

Here are some ETFs to consider:

>> BNY Mellon Core Bond ETF (ticker symbol: BKAG)

>> Vanguard Total Bond Market (ticker symbol: BND)

>> Vanguard Short-Term Bond (ticker symbol: BSV)

Moving Beyond Basics into Municipal and Foreign Bonds

Every investor needs bonds. Not every investor needs municipal bonds or foreign bonds. But for higher-income investors who find themselves in the northern tax zones, municipal bonds, which pay interest exempt from federal income tax (and possibly state and local income tax as well), can make enormous sense. For those with larger bond portfolios, the added diversification of foreign bonds is something to consider very seriously.

Municipals for mostly tax-free income

Historically, municipal bonds have yielded about 80 percent of what Treasury bonds of similar maturity yield. As I write these words, the two kinds of bonds have yielded about the same recently — mostly due to Treasurys paying less and less. But that's on a before-tax basis. After taxes, you'll likely do better with munis, even if you're not in the highest tax bracket. If you *are* in the highest tax bracket, you'll likely do *much* better with munis — assuming the munis you buy don't default.

In fact, munis rarely do default. And the broad diversification offered by certain municipal ETFs makes any serious loss of principal due to defaults even less likely (but not impossible, by any means). Still, muni ETFs are riskier than Treasurys and riskier than agency bonds. You don't want your entire portfolio in munis.

TIP

To figure out the tax-equivalent yield on a muni or muni fund, you may want to visit one of the gazillion tax-equivalent yield calculators on the internet. One of my faves is on www.dinkytown. net. Click Investment Calculators and then click Municipal Bond Tax Equivalent Yield (or just go straight to www.dinkytown.net/ java/municipal-bond-tax-equivalent-yield.html). You'll figure it out from there.

TIP

If you live in a state with high income taxes, such as New York or California, and you're in a high tax bracket, you may want to investigate state-specific muni funds. When you buy muni funds that are specific to your home state, you exempt yourself from having to pay not only federal income tax on the interest, but often state income tax and potentially local income tax as well. At present, you'll only find a handful of state-specific muni ETFs, all designed for wealthier-than-average New Yorkers or Californians. (Both these states have high taxes, and they offer the largest potential number of investors.) I expect that over time, more state-specific munis will hit the stage, but for now, if you live in a state such as Colorado, Connecticut, Georgia, New Jersey, or Pennsylvania, you may have to go with a mutual fund if you want these tax-free darlings.

Here are some ETFs to consider:

>> Vanguard Tax-Exempt Bond ETF (ticker symbol: VTEB)

>> iShares National Muni Bond ETF (ticker symbol: MUB)

Foreign bonds for fixed-income diversification

Over the long haul, U.S. and foreign bonds of similar default risk and maturity will likely yield about the same returns. But in the short run, substantial differences can exist in the yields and total returns of U.S. versus foreign bonds.

TIP

Note that as is the case with U.S. bonds, international bonds can be of the conventional type or inflation-adjusted. Whereas I believe strongly that U.S. inflation-protected bonds deserve an allotment in most portfolios, foreign inflation-protected bonds just don't make as much sense (unless you plan to retire abroad or take a lot of senior world cruises). Nevertheless, for the sake of added diversification, if you want to add a small dose of inflation-adjusted foreign bonds to your portfolio, I won't object.

Foreign bonds, just like U.S. bonds, can also be issued by governments or corporations. Unless you choose to have an exceptionally large allocation to foreign bonds, I feel the best foreign bond funds for most American investors would include a mix: corporation bonds for higher yield, and government bonds (provided the government is solid, like that of Germany or Sweden versus, say, Venezuela) for security.

And finally, foreign bonds, unlike U.S. bonds, can come either currency hedged or currency unhedged. I prefer hedged.

Here are some ETFs to consider:

>> Vanguard Total International Bond (ticker symbol: BNDX)

>> iShares International Treasury Bond ETF (ticker symbol: IGOV)

>> SPDR FTSE International Government Inflation-Protected Bond ETF (ticker symbol: WIP)

>> Invesco International Corporate Bond ETF (ticker symbol: PICB)

Emerging-market bonds: High risk, high return

I don't like U.S. high-yield ("junk") bonds. They tend to be highly volatile, and they tend to move up and down with the stock market. In other words, they don't provide much of the diversification power or soft cushion that bonds are famous for. Foreign junk bonds are a little different. These bonds, issued by the governments of countries that may not be entirely stable, may be just as volatile as bonds issued by unstable U.S. corporations, but they don't necessarily go up and down with the U.S. stock market (although they certainly may at times — and did in 2008).

For reasons of diversification, investors with fairly good-sized portfolios may want to consider allocating a modest part of their portfolios to emerging-market debt. In my portfolio, I've allocated 4 percent of the total to this asset class. Note that I'm not referring to "my bond portfolio" but to "my portfolio." I actually think of my holdings in emerging-market debt as more of a stock-like investment than a true bond investment. After all, you're likely to see stock-like volatility and long-term stock-like returns with these investments.

Here are some ETFs to consider:

>> Vanguard Emerging Markets Government Bond (ticker symbol: VWOB)

>> SPDR Bloomberg Barclays Emerging Markets USD Bond ETF (ticker symbol: EMHC)

>> iShares J.P. Morgan USD Emerging Markets Bond Fund (ticker symbol: EMB)

IN THIS CHAPTER

» Understanding what makes a REIT a REIT

» Knowing how much to invest

» Weighing commodities as investments

» Digging for gold and silver, drilling for oil

» Taking a chance with active ETFs

Chapter **8**

REITs, Commodities, and Active ETFs

I
n the 2000s, building an entire, optimally diversified portfolio out of exchange-traded funds (ETFs) was just about impossible — sort of like trying to paint a landscape with no blues or yellows. There were holes, and many of them. You could not, for example, buy an ETF that gave you exposure to tax-free municipal bonds. Or international bonds. Only one ETF at that time allowed you to tap into international small-cap stocks. And none allowed for investing in international real estate investment trusts (REITs).

Back then, when there were but 300 ETFs from which to choose, and many of those tracked the same kinds of investments (such as large-cap U.S. stocks), you had to look elsewhere if you wanted to invest in certain asset classes. Today, the landscape is quite different. Among the thousands of available ETFs, you have blues, yellows, greens . . . an entire palette from which to compose a very well-diversified portfolio. In fact, you have more than enough. Now, not only can you track just about any conceivable stock, bond, or commodity index with passive ETFs, but also you have actively managed ETFs to consider.

In this chapter, I run you through some of those options and the ways they can help you pretty up your portfolio (or not).

Real Estate Investment Trusts

The value of commercial real estate — just about anywhere in the nation — softened right along with the housing market. But again, unless you bought just prior to the decline that began its serious fall in 2006, any investment in commercial property — or residential, for that matter — has probably done well. In fact, if you happen to own some commercial property, perhaps through a REIT, you've likely made out very well in recent years.

In a nutshell, *REITs* (rhymes with *beets*), are companies that hold portfolios of properties, such as shopping malls, office buildings, hotels, amusement parks, cellphone towers, or timberland. Or they may hold certain real estate–related assets, such as commercial mortgages. More than 160 REITs in the United States are publicly held, and their stocks trade on the open market just like most other stocks.

Via dozens of mutual funds, you can buy into a collection of REITs at one time. Through about 30 or so ETFs, you can similarly buy a bevy of REITs. And that may not be a bad idea. For the 42 years that ended in December 2020, the Dow Jones U.S. Select REIT Index enjoyed an average annual return of 11.4 percent. That isn't quite the 12 percent that the S&P 500 has returned during the same time span, but it is still a healthy return by anyone's measure. And more recently, REITs have clobbered the S&P 500, returning about 20 percent during the first half of 2021 versus less than 14 percent for the S&P 500.

REMEMBER

At the same time, REITs over the years have displayed a significant degree of noncorrelation. That is to say, REITs sometimes go up when the general market goes down, and vice versa. The end result, if you have both REIT and non-REIT stocks, is a portfolio with smoother returns.

Considering REITs' five distinguishing characteristics

Why, you may ask, didn't I merely include REITs in Chapter 6 with the other industry-sector ETFs? Good question! I have *five* reasons. Any one alone probably wouldn't justify giving REITs a chapter of their very own. All five together do, however. The first three reasons explain why REITs deserve some special status in the world of investments. The last two reasons are perhaps less compelling than the first three, but I include them in the interest of completeness.

Limited correlation to the broad markets

An index of U.S. REITs (such as the Dow Jones U.S. Select REIT Index) has evidenced a correlation of about 0.6 with the S&P 500 over the past 20 years. That means the price of an S&P 500 index fund and the share price of a REIT index fund have tended to move in opposite directions roughly 40 percent of the time. The REIT index has practically no correlation to bonds.

Will REITs continue to work their magic? Their correlation with the broad market has been increasing; undoubtedly REITs are becoming somewhat the victims of their own success. As they've become more mainstream investments, they've come to act more like other equities. Years ago, practically no one held REITs in their portfolios. Nowadays, according to one poll, fully two-thirds of professional money managers are using them.

REMEMBER

But as I write these words, and for the next few years, I believe you can expect continued positive returns and limited correlation — albeit on a lesser scale on both fronts. Therefore, REITs will still help to diversify a portfolio.

Unusually high dividends

REITs typically deliver annual dividend yields significantly higher than even the highest dividend-paying non-REIT stocks and almost three times that of the average stock. (Many stocks, of course, pay no dividends.) At the time of this writing, the Schwab U.S. REIT ETF (ticker symbol: SCHH) is offering a dividend yield of 2.86 percent versus the Schwab U.S. Mid-Cap ETF (ticker symbol: SCHM), which offers a dividend yield of 1.05 percent. I use the mid-cap fund because it makes for the best apples-to-apples comparison — most REITs are mid-cap stocks.

So, the cash usually keeps flowing regardless of whether a particular REIT's share price rises or falls, just as long as the REIT is pulling in some money. That's because REITs, which get special tax status, are required by law to pay out 90 percent of their income as dividends to shareholders. Cool, huh?

Still, REITs, like other stocks, can also be expected to see growth (and sometimes shrinkage) in share prices. Historically, about one-third of the total return of REIT stocks has come from capital appreciation.

You may have noted that I compared the dividend yield of REITs to the dividend yield of non-REIT mid-cap stocks, and that I did not compare the dividend yield of REITs to the interest on bonds (nor would I ever!). REITs and non-REIT stocks are similar in that they both represent equity, and as such, you can reasonably expect high long-term return with lots of volatility. Bonds are *not* similar in any way. With bonds, you can expect lower long-term return but with much less volatility.

WARNING

Suffice it to say that bonds are a different animal and should not be measured against any kind of equity investment. Do *not* sell your bonds to buy REITs because the yield on REITs is higher. I emphasize this because now with bond yields so pathetically low, I've seen articles, some in respectable publications, that ballyhoo REITs as a substitute for bonds. This is like suggesting that people bored with their docile house cat can trade it in for a mountain lion. Bad move.

Different taxation of dividends

REMEMBER

Because REITs are blessed in that they don't have to pay income taxes, their dividends are usually fully taxable to shareholders as ordinary income. In other words, whatever dividends you get will be taxed at year-end according to your income tax bracket. Few, if any, REIT dividends will be considered "qualified dividends" by the Internal Revenue Service (IRS), so you won't pay the special 15 percent dividend tax rate that most people pay on their stock dividends. For that reason, your accountant will undoubtedly urge you to handle your REITs a bit carefully. I also urge you to do so. Unless you're in a very low tax bracket, you should keep your REITs in a tax-advantaged account, such as your individual retirement account (IRA).

Special status among financial pros

The vast majority of wealth advisors — whether they primarily use style investing, sector investing, or astrology charts and tea leaves — recognize REITs as a separate asset class and tend to include them in most people's portfolios. Is that distinction logical and just? Yes, but I've asked myself this question: If REITs deserve that distinction of honor, what about some other industry sectors, such as energy? After all, energy has lately shown less correlation to the S&P 500 than REITs have. Doesn't energy deserve its own slice of the portfolio pie?

Well, one possible reason why REITs, and not energy stocks, are seen as a separate asset class (in addition to the reasons I explain in the previous sections) may be that the REIT marketers are savvier than the marketers of energy stocks. That's possibly the case. But I believe there is more to it than that.

Connection to tangible property

Some people argue that REITs are different from other stocks because they represent tangible property. Well, yeah, REITs do represent shopping malls filled with useless junk and condos filled with single people desperately looking for dates, and hospitals charging $10 for a Kleenex, and I suppose that makes them different from, say, stock in Anheuser-Busch or Procter & Gamble. But the reality is that REITs are stocks. And to a great degree, they behave like stocks. If REITs are different from other stocks, unusually high dividends and lack of market correlation are the likely distinctions — not their tangibility. After all, aren't beer and toothpaste "tangible"?

Calculating a proper REIT allocation

You don't really need REITs for the income they provide. Some people have this notion that withdrawing dividends from savings is somehow okay but withdrawing principal is not. Don't make that mistake. The reality is that if you withdraw $100 from your $1,000 account, it doesn't matter whether it came from cash dividends or the sale of stock. You're left with $900 either way.

REMEMBER

If you need cash, you can always create your own "artificial dividend" by selling any security you like (preferably one that has appreciated). Not that I have anything against dividends — they're fine — but they shouldn't be your primary reason for purchasing REITs.

Your primary motivations for buying REITs should be diversification and potential growth. In the past, the diversification afforded by REITs has been significant, as has the growth. In this section, I help you consider how much of your portfolio you may want to allot to REITs.

Judging from the past

If you could go back 20 years in a time machine, I'd have you put, heck, *everything* in Apple. But REITs would not have been a bad option, either. Looking forward, of course, the picture's a bit less clear. However, I think you can presume, regardless of future performance, that REITs will continue to move in somewhat different cycles than other stocks.

I think you can also presume fairly safely that REITs will continue to produce healthy gains, over the long run. As with all stocks, anything can happen in the short run. Anything.

Putting all the factors together, I suggest that most investors devote perhaps 15 percent to 22 percent of the equity side of their portfolios to REITs. If your portfolio is 60/40 (60 percent stocks and 40 percent bonds), that would translate to a REIT position of 9 percent to 13 percent of your *entire* portfolio.

What if, like many people, you're a homeowner whose home represents most of your net worth? You may want to play it a little light on the REITs, but don't let the value of your home affect your portfolio decisions to any great degree.

Splitting it up: Domestic and international REIT funds

International REITs are worth breaking out of your international stock holdings for all the same reasons that U.S. REITs are worth having tucked into a larger portfolio of U.S. stocks. The REIT allotment you give to your portfolio might be evenly split between U.S. and international REITs, in keeping with the 50/50 split between U.S. and non-U.S. stocks that I suggest for your overall portfolio.

As I discuss in Chapter 5, about 45 percent of the world's stocks are non-U.S.; in my mind, it stands to reason that an optimally diversified portfolio will have good exposure to foreign stocks. If you follow my advice, you might (assuming you have a 60/40 portfolio) have two REIT funds, and each might be given a 3 percent to 5 percent allocation in your portfolio. Alternatively, you might have just one global REIT fund making up 6 percent to 10 percent of your portfolio, which will give you both your U.S. and foreign-REIT exposure in one shot.

Oh, for you mathletes who think I've just made a mistake: Yes, yes, I know that I just said 6 percent to 10 percent of your (60/40) ETF portfolio might be made up of REIT funds, while several paragraphs earlier, I suggested that as much as 9 percent to 13 percent of your portfolio might be devoted to REITs. The reason for the discrepancy: You're also going to get some REIT exposure, above and beyond what you get from your REIT funds, in your broad stock-market ETFs. If, for example, you were to buy an S&P 500 index fund, about 3 percent of that fund would be made up of stock from REITs.

Picking REIT ETFs for your portfolio

If you want REITs in your portfolio, you won't get a whole lot of them unless you purchase a REIT fund. Despite the fact that there are roughly 160 of them, publicly traded REITs simply don't make up that large a segment of the economy.

So, if you want the diversification power of this special asset class, you need to go out of your way to get it. But thanks to ETFs, doing so shouldn't be much of a hassle, and you get many of ETFs' other benefits in the bargain, including rock-bottom expenses.

TIP

The tax-efficiency of ETFs can help limit the amount you're taxed on any capital gains you enjoy on your REIT fund, but it can't do anything to diminish the taxes you'll owe on the (nonqualified) dividends. For that reason, all REIT funds — ETFs or otherwise — are best kept in tax-advantaged retirement accounts, such as your traditional IRA, Roth IRA, or 401(k) plan.

Although about 50 REIT ETFs are currently available to U.S. investors, a handful really stand out for their low costs and reasonable indexes. In fact, making the selection shouldn't be all that hard.

TIP

The three U.S. domestic REIT ETFs I recommend are strikingly similar, and any one would fill the bill nicely when it comes to investing in the U.S. REIT market:

>> Schwab U.S. REIT ETF (ticker symbol: SCHH)

>> Fidelity MSCI Real Estate Index ETF (ticker symbol: FREL)

>> Vanguard REIT Index ETF (ticker symbol: VNQ)

TIP

If you follow my advice and split your REIT allocation between U.S. and international funds, the next three international and global REIT ETFs will definitely come in handy. The first two funds invest only in markets outside the United States and pair quite nicely with any of the domestic REITs I discuss earlier. The iShares fund is divided between U.S. and non-U.S. REITs, so it provides one-stop shopping for REIT investments (although at a higher cost than you'd pay for the Vanguard and Xtrackers options).

>> Vanguard Global ex-U.S. Real Estate ETF (ticker symbol: VNQI)

>> Xtrackers International Real Estate ETF (ticker symbol: HAUZ)

>> iShares Global REIT ETF (ticker symbol: REET)

All That Glitters: Gold, Silver, and Other Commodities

Historically, gold has been seen as the ultimate hedge against both inflation and market turmoil. Most people through the ages have bought gold just as I did: as coins or sometimes in bricks. Alternatively, in more recent decades, they may have invested in shares of gold-mining companies.

All these methods became optional for gold investors with the introduction of the first gold ETF in November 2004. Suddenly it became possible to buy gold at its spot price — in an instant — with very little commission and no need to fret about storage or insurance. Thanks to ETFs, you can now also buy silver or platinum in the same way.

In fact, you can invest in just about any commodity you please. You can invest in just about any precious or industrial metal: tin, nickel, you name it. Even natural gas, or crude oil, if that's your cup of Texas tea, can be purchased (sort of) with an ETF, as can coffee futures and contracts on wheat, sugar, or corn. Indeed, it seems the only commodity that's *not* available for purchase by the retail investor is weapons-grade plutonium.

In the following sections, I discuss the whys and wherefores of investing in commodity ETFs, as well as certain commodity pools and exchange-traded notes (which differ from ETFs). I also explain why investing in ETFs that feature stocks of commodity-producing companies and countries may be a somewhat better long-term play than investing in the commodities themselves.

Gold, gold, gold!

Stocks and bonds rise and fall. Currencies ebb and flow. Economies go boom and then bust. Inflation tears nest eggs apart. And through it all, gold retains its value. Or so we're told.

I believe that the best you can expect from gold over the very long term is that it will maintain its purchasing power. But hey, that's not a bad thing when every other investment is tanking. Gold, as it happens, does show little long-term correlation to other assets. And when the going gets really tough — or even seems that way — when people run from most investments, they often turn to gold. Then, as a self-fulfilling prophecy, the price rises.

REMEMBER

In the final analysis, it probably wouldn't hurt you to hold gold in your portfolio. But please don't buy the nonsense that gold "must go up." It will go up. It will go down. It will go up again. Have a ball — just don't bank your retirement on it, okay? (Personally, I don't own shares in a gold ETF, but I haven't ruled it out.)

TIP

If you allot a small percentage of your portfolio to gold — no more than, say, 5 percent please (actually make that 5 percent *total* precious metals) — and keep that percentage constant, you'll likely eke out a few dollars over time. Every year, if the price of gold falls, you might buy a bit; if the price rises, perhaps you sell. That strategy is called *rebalancing,* and I recommend it for all your portfolio allocations. (See my discussion of yearly portfolio rebalancing in Chapter 11.)

And if everything goes to hell in a handbasket, your gold may offer you some protection.

A vastly improved way to buy the precious metal

When, in November 2004, State Street Global Advisors introduced the first gold ETF, it was a truly revolutionary moment. You buy a share just as you would buy a share of any other security, and each share gives you an ownership interest in one-tenth of an ounce of gold held by the fund. Yes, the gold is actually held in various bank vaults. You can even see pictures of one such vault filled to near capacity (very cool!) on www.spdrgoldshares.com.

If you're going to buy gold, this is far and away the easiest and most sensible way to do it.

You currently have several ETF options for buying gold. Two that would work just fine include the original from State Street — the SPDR Gold Shares (ticker symbol: GLD) — and a second from iShares introduced months later — the iShares Gold Trust (ticker symbol: IAU). Both funds are essentially the same. Flip a coin (gold or other), but then go with the iShares fund, simply because it costs less: 0.25 percent versus 0.4 percent.

The taxman cometh

Strange as it seems, the IRS considers gold to be a collectible for tax purposes. A share of a gold ETF is considered the same as, say, a gold Turkish coin from 1923 (don't ask). So what, you ask? As it happens, the long-term capital gains tax rate on collectibles is 28 percent and not the more favorable 15 percent afforded to capital gains on stocks.

TIP

Holding the ETF should be no problem from a tax standpoint (gold certainly won't pay dividends), but when you sell, you could get hit hard on any gains. Gold ETFs, therefore, are best kept in tax-advantaged accounts, such as your IRA. (Note that this advice won't serve you well if gold prices tumble and you sell. In that event, you'd rather have held the ETF in a taxable account so you could write off the capital loss. Life is complicated, isn't it?)

Silver: The second metal

Talk about a silver bullet. In early 2006, after years of lackluster performance, the price of silver suddenly, within three short months, shot up 67 percent. Why? Largely, the move served as testimony to the growing power of ETFs!

The price jump anticipated the introduction of the iShares Silver Trust (ticker symbol: SLV) ETF in April 2006. SLV operates much the same as the iShares COMEX Gold Trust (ticker symbol: IAU). When you buy a share of SLV, you obtain virtual ownership of 10 ounces of silver.

To be able to convey that ownership interest, iShares had to buy many ounces of silver (initially 1.5 million), and that pending demand caused the silver market to bubble and fizz. Within several weeks after the introduction of the ETF, the price of silver continued to rise, reaching a 23-year high in May 2006 ($14.69 an ounce) before tumbling in the following weeks. The volatility has continued to this day as the price has darted above and below $40 an ounce.

Quick silver on the move

To say that silver is volatile is a gross understatement. In 1979, the price of an ounce of silver was about $5. It then rose tenfold in less than a year — to as high as $54 an ounce in 1980 — after the infamous Hunt brothers had cornered the silver market (until they were caught, because, y'know, it's illegal to corner the market in just about anything). The price then fell again. Hard.

Fast-forward to April 2011. The price of silver, having risen steadily and sharply since the introduction of the first silver ETF, had topped $48 an ounce and seemed headed back to the highs of 1980. And then — pop! — within a mere several days, the price fell about 30 percent to slightly under $34. Then it rose back up in the following months to $42, and then, in September 2011 — pop! — in a mere two days, it fell back down to $30.

If there is any reason to stomach such volatility, it stems from the fact that silver has a very low correlation to other investments. For the three years prior to my writing these words, the price of silver has had very, very little correlation to stocks (except for some modest correlation to the stocks of silver-producing countries, such as Chile); almost no correlation to bonds; and even a decidedly limited correlation (0.75) to the price of gold.

If you must . . .

If you're going to take a position in silver, the iShares ETF is the way to go. The expense ratio of 0.5 percent will eat into your profits or magnify your losses, but it will still likely be cheaper than paying a commission to buy silver bars or coins and then paying for a good-sized lockbox.

TIP

In the very long run, I don't think you're likely to do as well with silver as you would with either stocks or bonds. Note, however, that unlike gold, silver has many industrial uses. Demand for silver can come from diverse sources — not just jewelers and collectors — which can cause the metal's price to fluctuate with changing expectations for industrial production. Because the uses for silver effectively "consume" the metal, the laws of supply and demand may influence the future prospects of silver prices in a way that doesn't apply to gold. In the end, silver may prove useful as a hedge, maybe even better than gold. But I would urge you to invest very modestly; no more than 5 percent of your portfolio should be allocated to precious metals. Keep in mind that the same strange tax law pertains to silver as to gold. Any capital gains will be taxed at the "collectibles" rate of 28 percent. You may want to keep your silver shares in a tax-advantaged account.

Oil and gas: Truly volatile commodities

The United States Oil Fund (ticker symbol: USO) opened on the American Stock Exchange on April 10, 2006. Even though the fund is technically not an ETF but a very close cousin called a *commodity pool*, in my mind that date marks a sort of end to the Age of Innocence for ETFs. The United States Oil Fund, as official as that sounds, is run by a group called Victoria Bay Asset Management, which I'll turn to in just a moment.

WARNING

Don't mistake this fund for something like the Vanguard Energy ETF (ticker symbol: VDE) or the Energy Select Sector SPDR (ticker symbol: XLE) funds (see Chapter 6), both of which invest in oil companies like ExxonMobil and Chevron. Don't mistake this fund for something like the precious metal commodity funds discussed in the preceding sections. Victoria Bay, wherever that is, is not filled with oil. Whereas Barclays and State Street maintain vaults filled with gold and silver, Victoria Bay deals in paper: futures contracts, to be exact.

In other words, this company uses your money to speculate on tomorrow's price of oil. If the price of oil rises in the next several weeks, you should, theoretically, earn a profit commensurate with that rise, minus the fund's costs of trading and its expense ratio of 0.75 percent. When the price of oil and gas go on a tear, this fund promises to give you a piece of that action, perhaps offering warm comfort every time you pull up to the pump and have to yank out your credit card.

WARNING

The issuer of the USO fund is not a major investment bank. Victoria Bay Asset Management, LLC, is "a wholly-owned subsidiary of Wainwright Holdings, Inc., a Delaware Corporation . . . that also owns an insurance company organized under Bermuda law." The fund's prospectus, especially the part about the management of Victoria Bay, makes for *very* interesting reading. I would not invest in this fund, and neither should you.

The sad saga of contango

As fate would have it, the promise of the United States Oil Fund has turned out to be nothing like the reality. Consider this: The price of an actual barrel of oil rose from about $40 in January 2009 to nearly $100 in June 2011. In the same time period, USO's share price went from about $35 to $38 — not much of an increase.

That meager return, however, might be considered pure gravy compared to the return suffered by investors in Victoria Bay's United States Natural Gas Fund (ticker symbol: UNG) introduced on April 18, 2007. Through mid-2011, this fund's share price, which started at about $90 a share, had fallen to — are you ready? — roughly $11 a share. Investors in UNG have had anything but a gas.

The explanation for USO's stagnant share price and UNG's sink-like-a-rock share price can be found not only in the lackluster résumés of their managers and the dynamics of supply and demand for natural gas but also in something called *contango*. That's a word that nearly all investors in commodity ETFs, at least those that rely on futures contracts, wish to heck they never heard.

Contango refers to a situation where distant futures prices for a particular commodity start to run well ahead of near futures prices. In other words, if you want to maintain a futures position that looks one month out, you buy futures contracts for the next month that expire in 30 days. Then one month later you replace them with contracts that contango has made more expensive. The effect is sort of like holding a fistful of sand and watching the sand sift through your fingers until you're left with nothing but an empty hand.

As a result of contango, many commodity investors have lost money, and some have lost lots of money, in recent years — even in cases where, as with oil, the price of the commodity itself rose. The illustrious managers at Victoria Bay led their investors to slaughter. But more experienced managers were also caught with their trousers down.

WARNING

For you, the ETF investor, I would advise much caution before investing in commodities, especially in funds that use futures and other derivatives.

Taxing your tax advisor

ETFs that use futures typically generate special tax forms called *K-1 forms*. If you ask anyone who has ever filed a tax return and needed to account for earnings from K-1 investments, they'll tell you that these forms are a pain in the butt. Not only have investors in UNG been stung by falling share prices, but also they've often found that they were paying their tax advisors considerably more than in previous years, simply to file the dastardly K-1s.

As if that weren't bad enough, any gains on the sale of funds that use futures are taxed largely at short-term capital gains rates, even if the funds were held for more than a year — just another one of those IRS quirks. (Granted, not many people have had this problem recently because gains are hard to come by with these funds.)

(Somewhat) safer: General commodity index funds

Just as diversification works to dampen the risks of stock investing, it can similarly smooth out — to a degree — the ups and downs of investing in commodities. If you're willing to accept contango, the K-1 forms, and the natural volatility of most commodities (other than perhaps clay or granite), I urge you at least to diversify. In this section, I tell you about several funds that allow you to tap into a broad spectrum of commodities.

PowerShares DB Commodity Index Tracking Fund (ticker symbol: DBC)

Make no mistake, the DBC fund, issued in February 2006, is one volatile investment. (It lost about 32 percent in 2008; is that volatile enough for you?) Not a true ETF, this fund (like USO) is a *commodity pool* that deals in commodities futures.

Unlike USO, or the gold and silver ETFs, the PowerShares offering has a bit of diversity to protect you if one commodity suddenly heads south. That diversity, alas, is limited. The fund entails 14 commodity classes, but the top five are all energy-related (at the time of writing): light oil (12.4 percent), heating oil (12.4 percent), Brent crude (12.4 percent), gasoline (12.4 percent), and natural gas (5.5 percent). That adds up to about 55 percent. The remaining 45 percent is allocated to various metals and agricultural products.

TIP

DBC's expense ratio — 0.85 percent — is close to outrageous by ETF standards (and mine), but cheap is hard to find in this category. I like the idea of a general commodity fund, but I'm not wild about DBC.

iPath commodity ETNs

In June 2006, Barclays issued two funds that may offer better options for investing directly in commodities — or, more specifically, investing in a diversified mix of commodities using futures. They're the iPath S&P GSCI Total Return Index ETN (ticker symbol: GSP) and the iPath Dow Jones–UBS Commodity Index Total Return ETN (ticker symbol: DJP).

These offerings are *exchange traded notes* (ETNs) and are very different from iShares ETFs. (Note that the iShares ETFs were originally a product of Barclays and were then purchased by BlackRock, Inc. Barclays held onto its lineup of ETNs.) ETNs are actually debt instruments, more like bonds than anything else. By buying them, you're lending Barclays your money, and you're counting on Barclays to give it back. (If Barclays were to go under, you'd lose.) That's not the case with iShares or any other ETF, where the ETF provider is acting more as a custodian of your funds than anything else.

Barclays is rated a stable company (AA– by S&P; AA3 by Moody's), so I wouldn't worry too much about its going under (although anything is possible, of course). Your bigger worry is the future direction of commodity prices. Barclays promises to use "any tool necessary" to use your money to track commodity prices. Presumably, it works something like the PowerShares fund in that it uses primarily futures contracts. But Barclays won't say. ETNs are not transparent like ETFs, so you don't know exactly what you're holding.

Why do I like these funds more than the PowerShares fund? It's not because of the expense ratio. At 0.75 percent, the Barclays funds are only a tad less expensive. Here are the three reasons I prefer the Barclays funds:

>> I have faith in the company, which is huge, well managed, and profitable.

>> The Barclays funds, by promising to curtail capital gains and dividends, are likely much more tax-efficient than the PowerShares fund.

>> The Barclays ETNs offer somewhat better diversification. Both ETNs invest in a number of commodities, from oil and natural gas to gold and silver to cocoa and coffee.

Of the two Barclays funds, I prefer the DJP for its well-established index and the balanced weightings of its holdings: energy (34 percent), livestock (6 percent), precious metals (15 percent), industrial metals (17 percent), and agriculture (28 percent). Still, even when diversified, commodities are volatile, and their long-term returns are not as well established as the long-term returns on stocks and bonds.

TIP

If you buy into a Barclays ETN, you should do so for the right reason: lack of correlation to your other investments. Both of the iPath funds have shown almost no correlation to either stocks or bonds. For more information on these funds, Barclays has a special website: https://ipathetn.barclays.

TIP

As with precious-metals funds, devoting 5 percent of your portfolio to either of the iPath funds would be plenty. No more than that, please. Oh, one little caveat: Not long ago, the IRS changed its ruling on certain ETNs, making them much less tax-efficient. At the moment, the ruling doesn't pertain to commodity ETNs, but someday it may. If you're not going to stash them in a tax-advantaged retirement account, you could be in for an unpleasant surprise — you just never know.

(Quasi) actively managed commodity funds

Given all the challenges with investing in commodities by using exchange-traded vehicles, I'm inclined to believe that active management may be just the place to go if you want to invest in commodities. (And, by the way, you don't need to do so; you can invest indirectly in commodities in ways that may make more sense. More on that topic in just a moment.)

If you want direct commodity exposure, consider that a number of the newest ETFs and ETNs are promising to deal with some of the problems of the first-generation commodity funds. The leader in this brigade is iPath, which in April 2011 introduced a new lineup of ETNs called Pure Beta indexes. I wouldn't quite call these funds actively managed, but they aren't quite passively run either. The Pure Beta ETNs promise to "mitigate the effects of certain distortions in the commodity markets" (this language refers to contango) by rolling over futures contracts in an allegedly more intelligent manner (less mechanically) than the older commodity funds that used futures.

It's too soon to say whether Barclays's strategy will prove successful, but I'm keeping my eye on the iPath Pure Beta Broad Commodity ETN (ticker symbol: BCM), which uses this new-fangled strategy to track a basket of commodities consisting of energy (37 percent), agricultural products (24 percent), precious metals (20 percent), industrial metals (16 percent), and livestock (2.5 percent). The management fee is 0.75 percent. I'm ignoring the rest of the Barclays Beta lineup that allows you to speculate on individual commodities, such as lead, nickel, and aluminum.

Another ETN worth considering for commodity exposure is the ELEMENTS S&P CTI ETN (ticker symbol: LSC). This fund tracks the S&P Commodity Trends Indicator–Total Return index. The fund tracks 16 different commodities, using futures contracts. Unlike Barclays's funds, LSC uses a momentum strategy, buying "long" those commodities rising in price and selling "short" those commodities falling in price.

Backtesting of the index showed that this strategy, known as a *managed futures strategy*, has been successful for investing in commodities. (Of course, backtested strategies are notorious for performing less well in real time than their hypothetical numbers suggest.) The fund was born in October 2008, and although I feel that the strategy shows promise, it's far from proven. And just like any other kind of futures investing, but even more so, a managed futures strategy will not necessarily reflect ups and downs in the spot prices of commodities.

Because LSC is an ETN and not an ETF, keep in mind that you get your money back only if the issuer remains solvent. This fund is issued and backed by HSBC Bank USA, which has the very same high credit ratings as Barclays.

Playing the commodity market indirectly

In a recent interview with the *Journal of Indexes*, famed investment guru Burton G. Malkiel, professor of economics at Princeton and author of *A Random Walk Down Wall Street*, had this to say about commodity investing: "I think [commodities] should be in every portfolio, but for individuals, my sense is that the way they should get them is through ensuring that they have in their portfolios companies that mine or manufacture the commodities."

He is not alone. Frustrated with the problems of commodity investing I've outlined in this chapter, and doubtful that commodity investing in the very long run will provide returns commensurate with the risk, many investment advisors of late have turned to Malkiel's solution. The drawback is that stocks in commodity-producing companies are not going to show the same lack of correlation, or offer the same diversification power, as pure commodities do. Investing in commodities this way is a trade-off.

TIP

Lately, I've been splitting the difference: putting perhaps 3 percent to 4 percent of a portfolio in pure commodities (using one of the funds I identify earlier in this chapter) and perhaps another 3 percent to 4 percent in one of the funds I outline next.

Oil and gas ETFs

More than a dozen ETFs allow you to invest in the stocks of oil and gas companies. Among them are these options:

>> Vanguard Energy ETF (ticker symbol: VDE)

>> Energy Select Sector SPDR (ticker symbol: XLE)

>> iShares Dow Jones U.S. Energy Index (ticker symbol: IYE)

>> PowerShares Dynamic Energy Exploration & Production (ticker symbol: PXE)

>> iShares Dow Jones U.S. Oil Equipment & Services Index Fund (ticker symbol: IEZ)

>> iShares S&P Global Energy Index Fund (ticker symbol: IXC)

>> Global X Oil Equities ETF (ticker symbol: XOIL)

The funds all sound different from each other, but when you look at each of their rosters, they're actually quite similar, and I feel equally lukewarm about all of them.

REMEMBER

Keep in mind that the energy sector represents a large segment of the U.S. economy. Energy companies make up about 10 percent of the capitalization of the U.S. stock market. So, just being invested in the market gives you decent exposure to energy.

Mining ETFs

Several ETFs allow you to invest in mining companies. These include

» Global X Pure Gold Miners ETF (ticker symbol: GGGG)

» Market Vectors Gold Miners ETF (ticker symbol: GDX)

» SPDR S&P Metals and Mining ETF (ticker symbol: XME)

» Global X Silver Miners ETF (ticker symbol: SIL)

To me, these funds may make more sense in a portfolio than the energy ETFs, but they aren't my preferred way of tapping into commodity-producing companies. For my preference, keep reading.

Materials or natural resources ETFs

To give me extra exposure to companies that mine for gold and silver, produce oil and gas, and either produce or distribute other commodities, I prefer broader natural resource funds. (I say "extra exposure" because I already get exposure in my other stock funds.) If commodity prices pop, the broader natural resource funds generally do well, and I'm not taking on too much risk by banking on any one commodity or commodity group. A natural resources fund may also be called a *materials fund.*

Options in this category include these ETFs:

» Materials Select Sector SPDR (ticker symbol: XLB)

» iShares Dow Jones U.S. Basic Materials (ticker symbol: IYM)

» Vanguard Materials ETF (ticker symbol: VAW)

» iShares S&P North American Natural Resources (ticker symbol: IGE)

TIP

One of my favorites in this category is the SPDR S&P Global Natural Resources ETF (ticker symbol: GNR). This fund has an expense ratio of 0.5 percent. About 45 percent of its holdings are in the United States or Canada, and the remaining 55 percent are spread out through both the developed world and emerging markets. It offers exposure to a good variety of commodity firms: oil and gas (32 percent), fertilizers and agricultural chemicals (19 percent), diversified metals and mining (16 percent), and so on.

Going Active with ETFs

The first ETF in the United States was launched in 1993. It was the S&P 500 index fund SPY. And for the next 15 years, all ETFs were index funds. But then, in 2008, years of wheedling the Securities and Exchange Commission (SEC) paid off, and Wall Street was finally allowed to issue its first actively managed ETF.

It was foreshadowing, and ironic, that the very first actively managed ETF was issued by Bear Stearns. Within several months, the financial collapse of the investment banking industry, led by Bear Stearns, was well on its way to creating the worst bear market (more irony) of our lifetimes. That first ETF died, folding (with money returned to investors) in October 2008, as Bear Stearns, after 85 years in business, collapsed and itself folded.

Since that time, I've seen the opening (and closing) of dozens upon dozens of actively managed ETFs. At present, there are about 650 actively managed ETFs. That's nearly one-quarter of the ETF universe. But those active funds have failed to accumulate a whole lot in assets. According to Morningstar Direct, those 650 or so funds hold less than 4 percent of all investors' money stored in ETFs.

WARNING

If you're going to go with active management, active ETFs can be less expensive and more tax-efficient than their corresponding mutual funds. That offers reason for hope. On the flip side, active ETFs have a big disadvantage in that they can't, like a mutual fund, close the fund to new investors. As a result, actively managed ETFs can get bloated. The manager may be forced to take on new holdings or increase positions they don't really want to increase.

On balance, you must keep in mind that historically, actively managed funds as a group have not done nearly as well as index funds. That being said, active management may sometimes have an edge, especially in some areas of the investment world, such as micro caps, a universe too small to have been well studied, or commodities. And much of the advantage of index investing has been in its ultra-low costs — something that actively managed ETFs could possibly emulate. Investors will see over time if active management improves its track record.

If you want to go with an actively managed fund, I ask you to at least keep in mind the lessons learned from indexing and what has made indexing so effective over time. Basically, you want certain index-like qualities in any actively managed fund you pick:

>> **Choose a fund with low costs.** With so many ETFs allowing you to tap into stocks or bonds for a fraction of a percentage point a year, you do not need or want any fund that charges much more. Any stock fund that charges more than, oh, 0.6 percent, or any bond fund that charges more than about 0.3 percent, is asking too much, and the odds that such a fund will outperform in the long run are very slim. You should probably go elsewhere.

>> **Watch your style.** Make sure that any fund you choose fits into your overall portfolio. Studies show that index funds tend to do better than active funds in both large caps and small caps, but in small caps, you have a better chance that your active fund will beat the indexes. That's because large caps are more thoroughly scrutinized by investors, so finding a company with hidden strengths would be like finding a $50 bill on the sidewalk at 42nd and Broadway.

>> **Check the manager's track record — carefully.** Make sure that the track record you're buying is long term. (Any fool can beat the S&P 500 in a year. Doing so for ten years is immensely more difficult.) I'd look at performance in both bull and bear markets, but your emphasis should be on average annual returns over time compared with the performance of the fund's most representative market index over the same period. And note that a fund's returns will be determined largely by its asset class. In other words, a small-value fund should outperform the S&P 500 over time because it's riskier, and risk equals return, generally. The more important question is whether that small-value fund has beaten the small-value indexes over time.

>> **Don't go overboard with active management.** Studies show *so* conclusively that index investing kicks butt that I would be very hesitant to build anything but a largely indexed portfolio, using the low-cost index ETFs that I suggest throughout this book.

3

Making the Most of Your ETF Portfolio

Sift through samples of investment situations and strategies to help visualize the portfolio that will best serve your needs.

Give retirement account options a good look-see.

Get a firm handle on risk and return so you can best balance your portfolio.

Determine when to sit back and wait — and when the time is right to rebalance your portfolio.

Survey exchange-traded fund (ETF) options for a different take on investing.

IN THIS CHAPTER

» Revisiting risk and return

» Employing Modern Portfolio Theory

» Visualizing different portfolio options

» Comparing various retirement account options

» Taking action if your employer's 401(k) plan stinks

Chapter 9

Checking Out Sample ETF Portfolio Menus

I enjoy crafting portfolios not only because it involves multicolored pie charts (I've always had a soft spot for multicolored pie charts) but also because the process involves so much more than running a piece of wood through a jigsaw and hoping not to lose any fingers. Portfolio construction is — or should be — a highly individualized, creative exercise that takes into consideration many factors: economics, history, statistics, and psychology among them.

The ideal portfolio (if such a thing exists) for a 30-year-old who makes $75,000 a year is very different from the portfolio for a 75-year-old whose income is $30,000 a year. The optimal portfolio for a 40-year-old worrywart differs from the optimal portfolio for a 40-year-old devil-may-care type. The portfolio of dreams following a long bull market when interest rates are low may look a wee bit different from a prime portfolio following a bear market with high interest rates.

Every financial professional I know goes about portfolio construction in a somewhat different way. In this chapter, I walk you through the steps that I take and that have worked well for me.

So, How Much Risk Can You Handle and Still Sleep at Night?

The first questions I ask myself — and the first questions anyone building a portfolio should ask — are these:

» How much return does the portfolio-holder need to see?

» How much volatility can the portfolio-holder stomach?

Very few things in the world of investments are sure bets, but this one is: The amount of risk you take or don't take will have a great bearing on your long-term return. You simply aren't going to get rich investing in bank certificates of deposit (CDs). On the other hand, you aren't going to lose your nest egg in a single week either. The same cannot be said of a tech stock — or even a bevy of tech stocks wrapped up in an exchange-traded fund (ETF).

A well-built ETF portfolio can help to mitigate risks but not eliminate them. Before you build your portfolio, ask yourself how much risk you need to take to get your desired return — and then take no more risk than that.

REMEMBER

Please forget the dumb old rules about portfolio building and risk. How much risk you can or should take on depends on your wealth, your age, your income, your health, your financial responsibilities, your potential inheritances, and whether you're the kind of person who tosses and turns over life's upsets. If anyone gives you a pat formula — "Take your age, subtract it from 110, and that, dear friend, is how much you should have in stocks" — please take it with a grain of salt. Things aren't nearly that simple. (Although if you're going to go with *any* formula, the one I just provided is far better than most!)

A few things that just don't matter

Before I lay out what matters most in determining appropriate risk and appropriate allocations to stocks, bonds, and cash (or stock ETFs and bond ETFs), I want to throw out just a few things that really *shouldn't* enter into your thinking, even though they play into many people's portfolio decisions:

>> The portfolio of your best friend, which has done great guns

>> Your personal feelings on the current administration, where the Fed stands on the prime interest rate, and which way hemlines on women's dresses are moving this fall

>> The article you clipped out of *Lotsa Dough* magazine that tells you that you can earn 50 percent a year by investing in . . . whatever

Listen, your best friend may be in a completely different economic place than you are. Their well-polished ETF portfolio, laid out by a first-rate financial planner, may be just perfect for them and all wrong for you.

As far as the state of the nation and where the Dow is headed, you simply don't know. Neither do I. The talking heads on TV pretend to know, but they don't know squat. Nor does the author of that article in the glossy magazine (filled with ads from fund companies) that tells you how you can get rich quickly in the markets. The secrets to financial success cannot be had by forking over $4.95 for a magazine.

REMEMBER

Over the course of the past century, the stock market has returned an average of about 10 percent annually (7 percent or so after inflation). Bonds have returned about half as much. A well-diversified portfolio, by historical standards, has returned something in between stocks and bonds — maybe 7 percent to 8 percent (4 percent to 5 percent after inflation). With some of the advice in this book, even though market performance in the future may fall a bit shy of the past, you could see personal returns roughly approximating these numbers. But don't take inordinate risk with any sizable chunk of your portfolio in the hopes that you're going to earn 50 percent a year after inflation — or even before inflation. It won't happen.

On the other hand, don't pooh-pooh a 7 percent to 8 percent return. Compound interest is a truly miraculous thing. Invest $20,000 today, add $2,000 each year, and within 20 years, with "only" a 7.5 percent return, you'll have $171,566. (If inflation is running in the 3 percent ballpark, that $171,566 will be worth about $110,000 in today's dollars.)

The irony of risk and return

In a few pages, I provide you with some sample portfolios appropriate for someone who should be taking minimal risk as opposed to someone who should be taking more risk. At this point, I want to digress for a moment to say that in a perfect world, those who need to take the most risk would be the most able to take it on. In the real world, sadly ironic though it is, those who need to take the most risk really can't afford to.

Specifically, a poor person needs whatever financial cushion they have. They can't afford to risk the farm (not that they have a farm) on a portfolio of mostly stocks. A rich person, in contrast, can easily invest a chunk of discretionary money in the stock market, but they really don't need to because they're living comfortably without the potential high return. It just isn't fair. Yet no one is to blame, and nothing can be done about it. It is what it is.

The 25x rule

REMEMBER

Whatever your age, whatever your station in life, you probably wouldn't mind if your investments could support you. But how much do you need in order for your investments to support you? That's actually not very complicated and has been very well studied: You need about 25 times whatever amount you expect to withdraw each year from your portfolio, assuming you want that portfolio to have a good chance of surviving at least 20 to 25 years.

That is, if you need $40,000 a year — in addition to Social Security and any other income — to live on, you should have $1 million in your portfolio when you retire, assuming you retire in your mid-60s. You can have less, but you may wind up eating too far into the principal if the market tumbles — in which case you should be prepared to live on less, or get a part-time job.

(Factor in the value or partial value of your home only if it is paid up and if you foresee a day when you can downsize.)

The rationale behind the 25x rule is this: It allows you to withdraw 4 percent from your portfolio the first year, and then adjust that amount upward each year to keep up with inflation. The studies show that a well-diversified portfolio from which you take such withdrawals has a good chance of lasting at least 20 years, which is how long you may need the cash flow if you retire in your 60s and live to your mid-80s.

If you think you might live beyond your mid-80s — and especially if you're part of a couple, there's a good chance that one of you will live beyond your mid-80s — then you might want more than 25 times. If you want to retire prior to your mid-60s, then having more than 25 times your anticipated annual withdrawals would be an excellent idea. It would also be an excellent idea to limit your initial withdrawal, if you can, to 3.5 percent a year, just in case you live a long life. If you want to play it really safe, limit your withdrawal to 3 percent.

In truth, I'd much rather see you have 30 times your anticipated yearly withdrawals in your portfolio before you retire. But for many Americans who haven't seen a real pay increase in years, this is a lofty goal. For that reason, I say go with 25 times, but be prepared to tighten your belt if you need to.

TIP

If you're still far away from that 25 times mark, and you aren't in debt, and your income is secure, and you aren't burning out at work, and you have enough cash to live on for six months if you had to, then with the rest of your loot, you might tilt toward a riskier ETF portfolio (mostly stock ETFs). You need the return.

TIP

If you have your 25 times (or better yet, 30 times) annual cash needs already locked up or close to it, and you're thinking of giving up your day job soon, you should probably tilt toward a less risky ETF portfolio (more bond ETFs). After all, you have more to lose than you have to gain. You do need to be careful, however, that your investments keep up with inflation. Savings accounts are unlikely to do that.

If you have way more than 30 times annual expenses, congratulations! You have many options, and how much risk you take will be a decision that's unrelated to your material needs. You may, for example, want to leave behind a grand legacy, in which case you might shoot for higher returns. Or you may not care what you leave behind, in which case leaving your money in a tired savings account or "investing" in a high-performance but low-yielding Ferrari wouldn't make much difference.

Other risk/return considerations

I doubt I can list everything you should consider when determining the proper amount of risk to take with your investments, but here are a few additional things to keep in mind:

>> **What is your safety net?** If worse came to worst, do you have family or friends who would help you if you got in a real financial bind? If the answer is yes, you can add a tablespoon of risk.

>> **What is your family health history? Do you lead a healthy lifestyle?** These are the two greatest predictors of your longevity. If your parents lived to 100 and you don't smoke and you do eat your vegetables, you may be looking at a long retirement. Add a dollop of risk — you'll need the return.

>> **How secure is your job?** The less secure your employment, the more you should keep in nonvolatile investments (like short-term bonds or bond funds); you may need to draw from them if you get the pink slip next Friday afternoon.

>> **Can you downsize?** Say you're close to retirement, and you live in a McMansion. If you think that sooner or later you'll sell it and buy a smaller place, you have some financial cushion. You can afford to take a bit more risk.

The limitations of risk questionnaires

Yes, I give my clients a risk questionnaire. And then I go through it with them to help them interpret their answers. Lots of websites offer investment risk questionnaires, but instead of having anyone interpret the answers, a computer just spits out a few numbers: You should invest *x* in stocks and *y* in bonds. Yikes!

Please, please, don't allow a computer-generated questionnaire to determine your financial future! I've tried many of them, and the answers can be wacky.

What I'm saying is that after reading this book, if you aren't sure where you belong on the risk–return continuum, perhaps you should hire an experienced and impartial financial advisor — if only for a couple of hours — to review your portfolio with you. (I write more about seeking professional financial help in Chapter 12.)

A Few Keys to Optimal Investing

When you have a rough idea of where you should be riskwise, your attention should turn next to fun matters such as Modern Portfolio Theory, reversion to the mean, cost minimization, and tax-efficiency. Allow me to explain.

Incorporating Modern Portfolio Theory

The subject I'm about to discuss is a theory much in the same way that evolution is a theory: The people who don't believe it — and, yes, there are some — are those who decide to disregard all the science. Modern Portfolio Theory (MPT) says that if you diversify your portfolio — putting all kinds of eggs into all kinds of baskets — you reduce risk and optimize return.

REMEMBER

You get the most bang for your buck, according to MPT, when you mix and match investments that have little correlation. In other words, if you build your portfolio with different ETFs that tend to do well (and not so well) in different kinds of markets, you'll have a lean and mean portfolio.

MPT has been challenged. At times, there are stretches of days, even weeks and months, when different asset classes — U.S. stocks, foreign stocks, bonds, commodities, and real estate — may all move up and down nearly in lockstep. This was the case, unfortunately, in the last serious bear market — 2008. Like a flock of geese, just about every investment you could imagine headed south at the same time.

Correlations can change over time — and lately, the major asset classes have shown alarmingly high rates of correlation — but you shouldn't simply scrap the idea that diversification and the quest for noncorrelation are crucial. However, you may want to be cautious about relying too much on diversification. Yes, you can diversify away a lot of risk. But you should also have certain low-risk investments in your portfolio, investments that hold their own in any kind of market. Low-risk investments include Federal Deposit Insurance Corporation (FDIC)–insured savings accounts; money-market funds; short-term, high-credit-quality bonds; and bank CDs.

Minimizing your costs

Most ETFs are cheap, which is one of the things I love about them. The difference between a mutual fund that charges 1 percent and an ETF that charges 0.1 percent adds up to a *lot* of money over time. One of my favorite financial websites, www.moneychimp. com, offers a fund-cost calculator. Invest $100,000 for 20 years at 8 percent and deduct 0.1 percent for expenses; you're left with $457,540. Deduct 1 percent, and you're left with $386,968. That's a difference of $70,571. The after-tax difference, given that most ETFs (or at least the ones I tend to recommend) are highly tax-efficient index funds, would likely be much greater.

Because the vast majority of ETFs I'm recommending fall into the super-cheap to cheap range (generally 0.03 percent to 0.2 percent), the differences among ETFs won't be quite so huge. Still, in picking and choosing ETFs, cost should always be a factor. And that's especially true with bond funds during these days of pathetically low interest rates. Pay more than 0.2 percent for a short-term Treasury fund and you're likely to see *no* return for the coming months!

Striving for tax-efficiency

Keeping your investment dollars in your pocket and not lining Uncle Sam's is one big reason to choose ETFs over mutual funds. ETFs are, by and large, much more tax-efficient than active mutual funds. But some ETFs are going to be more tax-efficient than others. I provide coverage of this issue later in this chapter.

REMEMBER

For now, let me say that you must choose wisely which ETFs get put into which baskets. In general, high-dividend and interest-paying ETFs (real estate investment trust [REIT] ETFs, taxable-bond ETFs) are best kept in tax-advantaged accounts.

Timing your investments (just a touch)

If you've read much of this book already, by now, you realize that I'm largely an *efficient market* kind of guy. I believe that the ups and downs of the stock and bond market — and of any individual security — are, in the absence of true inside information, unpredictable. (And trading on true inside information is illegal.) For that reason, among others, I prefer index ETFs and mutual funds over actively managed funds.

However, that being said, I also believe in something called *reversion to the mean*. This is a statistical phenomenon that colloquially translates to the following: What goes up must come down; what goes *way* up, you need to be careful about investing too much money in.

At the time of this writing, for example, large-cap growth stocks, especially tech stocks like Microsoft, Alphabet (Google), and Tesla, have been flying high for several years. Real estate has also been doing very, very well. These are good reasons why you may want to be just a wee bit cautious about overstocking your portfolio in these particular asset classes.

TIP

I'm *not* suggesting that you go out and buy any ETF that has underperformed the market for years, or sell any ETF that has outperformed. But to a small degree, you should factor in reversion to the mean when constructing a portfolio.

For example, say you decide that your $100,000 portfolio should include a 15 percent allocation in the Vanguard Mega Cap 300 ETF (ticker symbol: MGC) and an equal allocation in the Vanguard Small Cap ETF (ticker symbol: VB), and you happen to be entering the market after an incredible several-year bull market in large-cap stocks, with small caps falling far behind. If anything, I'd be inclined to slightly overweight small-cap stocks, putting perhaps 16 percent or 17 percent in VB and maybe 13 percent to 14 percent in MGC.

Please don't go overboard. I'm suggesting that you use reversion to the mean to tweak your portfolio percentages very gently — not ignore them! This "going against the crowd" investment style is popularly known as *contrarian investing*.

Finding the Perfect Portfolio Fit

Time now to peek into my private world, as I reveal some of the ETF-based portfolios I've worked out for clients over the years (and updated, of course, as some newer ETFs proved to be superior to the old). You should look for the client that you most resemble, and that example will give you some *rough* idea of the kind of advice I would give you if you were my client. All names, of course, have been changed to protect privacy. For the sake of brevity, I provide you with only a thumbnail sketch of each client's financial situation.

Considering the simplest of the simple

Before I get into anything complicated or present any actual client portfolios, I want to introduce an easier-than-easy ETF portfolio (see Table 9-1). What I've constructed is a perfectly fine, workable investment model with decent (although not great) diversification. It may be enough for anyone without a great amount in savings (say, less than $50,000), or someone who has more but wants to keep things as simple as simple can be.

I include (in order of appearance) large-cap stocks, small-cap stocks, international stocks (large and small), and bonds (both conventional and inflation-adjusted).

REMEMBER

This portfolio can be tailored to suit the aggressive investor who can deal with some serious ups and downs in the hopes of achieving high long-term returns; the conservative investor who can't stand to lose too much money; or the middle-of-the-road investor. Keep in mind that you should always have three to six months in living expenses sitting in cash or near-cash (money markets, short-term CDs, an internet checking account, or a very short-term high-quality bond fund). You should also have all your credit card and other high-interest debt paid off. The rest of your money is what you may invest.

TABLE 9-1 A Simple ETF Portfolio

	Aggressive	Middle-of-the-Road	Conservative
Dimensional U.S. Core Equity Market (ticker symbol: DFAU)	24%	16%	12%
Vanguard Small Cap ETF (ticker symbol: VB)	16%	14%	8%
Vanguard Total International Stock Index Fund ETF (ticker symbol: VXUS)	24%	16%	12%
Vanguard FTSE All-World ex-U.S. Small Cap Index ETF (ticker symbol: VSS)	16%	14%	8%
BNY Mellon Core Bond ETF (ticker symbol: BKAG)	14%	28%	40%
iShares ESG Aware 1–5 Year USD Corporate Bond (ticker symbol: SUSB)	6%	12%	20%

Racing toward riches

High-risk/high-return ETF portfolios are made up mostly of stock ETFs. After all, stocks have a very long history of clobbering most other investments — *if* you give them enough time. Any portfolio that is mostly stocks should have both U.S. and international stocks, large cap and small cap, and value and growth, for starters. If the portfolio is diversified into industry sectors (an acceptable strategy, as I discuss in Chapter 6), a high-risk/high-return strategy would emphasize fast-growing sectors such as technology.

Let's consider the case of Jason, a single, 38-year-old pharmaceuticals salesman. Jason came to me after getting burned badly by several high-cost mutual funds that performed miserably over the years. Still, given his steady income of $120,000 and his minimal living expenses (he rents a one-bedroom apartment in Allentown, Pennsylvania), Jason has managed to sock away $220,000. His job is secure. He has good disability insurance. He anticipates saving $20,000 to $30,000 a year over the next several years. He enjoys his work and intends to work until normal retirement age. He plans to buy a new car (for around $40,000) in the next few months, but otherwise has no major expenditures earmarked.

Jason can clearly take some risk. Following is the ETF-based portfolio that I designed for him, which is represented in Figure 9-1. Note that I had Jason put four to six months of emergency money, plus the $40,000 for the car, into a money-market account, and that amount is not factored into this portfolio.

Also note that although this portfolio is made up almost entirely of ETFs, I do include one Pennsylvania municipal bond mutual fund to gain access to this asset class that's not yet represented by ETFs. Municipal bonds issued in Jason's home state are exempt from both federal and state taxes, which makes particular sense for Jason because he earns a high income and has no appreciable write-offs.

Finally, although this portfolio is technically 76 percent stocks and 24 percent bonds, I include a 4 percent position in emerging-market bonds, which can be considerably more volatile than your everyday bond. As such, I don't really think of this as a 76/24 portfolio, but more like an 80/20 portfolio, which is just about as volatile a portfolio as I like to see.

>> **Broad-based U.S. stock market:** 34 percent
- **Dimensional U.S. Core Equity Market (ticker symbol: DFAU):** 18 percent
- **Vanguard Small Cap Value ETF (ticker symbol: VBR):** 8 percent
- **Vanguard Small Cap ETF (ticker symbol: VB):** 8 percent

>> **Broad-based foreign stocks:** 34 percent
- **Vanguard Total International Stock Index Fund ETF (ticker symbol: VXUS):** 14 percent
- **iShares MSCI EAFE Value ETF (ticker symbol: EFV):** 5 percent
- **Vanguard FTSE All-World ex-U.S. Small Cap Index ETF (ticker symbol: VSS):** 15 percent

>> **Special sector funds:** 8 percent
- **Vanguard REIT ETF (ticker symbol: VNQ):** 4 percent
- **Vanguard International Real Estate ETF (ticker symbol: VNQI):** 4 percent

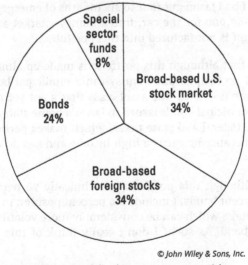

© John Wiley & Sons, Inc.

FIGURE 9-1: A portfolio that assumes some risk.

>> **Bonds:** 24 percent

- **BNY Mellon Core Bond ETF (ticker symbol: BKAG):** 10 percent

- **iShares ESG Aware 1–5 Year USD Corporate Bond (ticker symbol: SUSB):** 5 percent

- **Vanguard PA Long-Term Tax-Exempt Admiral Fund (ticker symbol: VPALX):** 5 percent

- **Vanguard Emerging Markets Government Bond ETF (ticker symbol: VWOB):** 4 percent

Sticking to the middle of the road

Next, I present Jay and Racquel, who are ages 64 and 63, are married, and have successful careers. Even though they're old enough to be Jason's parents, their economic situation actually warrants a quite similar high-risk/high-return portfolio. Both husband and wife, however, are risk-averse.

Jay is an independent businessman with several retail properties (valued at roughly $1.6 million); Racquel is a vice president at a major publishing house. Their portfolio: $1.1 million and growing. Within several years, the couple will qualify for combined Social Security benefits of roughly $93,500 — the highest a couple can collect if they start collecting at age 70. Racquel also will receive a fixed pension annuity of about $35,000. The couple's goal is to retire within two to three years, and they have no dreams of living too lavishly; they will have more than enough money. The fruits of their investments, by and large, should pass to their three grown children and any charities named in their wills.

Being risk-averse, Jay and Racquel keep 30 percent of their portfolio in high-quality municipal bonds. They handed me the other 70 percent ($560,000) and told me to invest it as I saw fit. My feeling was that 30 percent high-quality bonds was quite enough ballast, so I didn't need to add to their bond position by very much. So, I constructed a portfolio of largely domestic and foreign stock ETFs. The size of their portfolio (versus Jason's) warranted the addition of a few more asset classes, including a foreign-bond fund and a market-neutral fund.

I didn't include any U.S. REITs, given that so much of the couple's wealth is already tied up in commercial real estate. Figure 9-2 presents the portfolio breakdown.

>> **Municipal bonds:** 30 percent

>> **Broad-based U.S. stock market:** 28 percent

- **Dimensional U.S. Core Equity Market (ticker symbol: DFAU):** 16 percent

- **Vanguard Small Cap Value ETF (ticker symbol: VBR):** 6 percent

- **Vanguard Small Cap ETF (ticker symbol: VB):** 6 percent

>> **Broad-based foreign stocks:** 34 percent

- **Vanguard Total International Stock Index Fund ETF (ticker symbol: VXUS):** 10 percent

- **iShares MSCI EAFE Value ETF (ticker symbol: EFV):** 5 percent

- **Vanguard FTSE All-World ex-U.S. Small Cap Index ETF (ticker symbol: VSS):** 9 percent

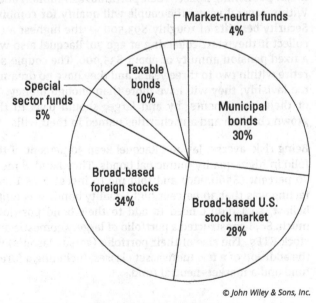

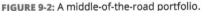
© John Wiley & Sons, Inc.

FIGURE 9-2: A middle-of-the-road portfolio.

- **>>** **Special sector fund:** 5 percent
  - **●** **Vanguard International Real Estate ETF (ticker symbol: VNQI):** 5 percent
- **>>** **Taxable bonds:** 10 percent
  - **●** **BNY Mellon Core Bond ETF (ticker symbol: BKAG):** 5 percent
  - **●** **Vanguard Total International Bond Index ETF (ticker symbol: BNDX):** 5 percent
- **>>** **Market-neutral fund:** 4 percent
  - **●** **Merger Fund (ticker symbol: MERFX):** 4 percent

Taking the safer road: Less oomph, less swing

We financial professional types hate to admit it, but no matter how much we tinker with our investment strategies, no matter how fancy our portfolio software, we can't entirely remove the luck factor. When you invest in anything, there's always a bit of a gamble involved. (Even when you decide *not* to invest, by, say, keeping all your money in cash, stuffed under the proverbial mattress, you're gambling that inflation won't eat it away or a house fire won't consume it.) Thus, the best investment advice ever given probably comes from Kenny Rogers: "You got to know when to hold 'em, know when to fold 'em."

The time to hold 'em is when you have just enough — when you've pretty much met, or come close to meeting, your financial goals.

I now present Richard and Maria, who are just about the same age as Jay and Racquel. They're 64 and 59, married, and nearing retirement. Richard, who sank in his chair when I asked about his employment, told me that he was in a job he detests in the ever-changing (and not necessarily changing for the better) newspaper business. Maria was doing part-time public relations work. I added up Richard's Social Security, a small pension from the newspaper, Maria's part-time income, and income from their investments, and I told Richard that he didn't have to stay at a job he hates. There was enough money for him to retire, provided the couple agreed to live somewhat frugally, and provided the investments — $700,000 — could keep up with inflation and not sag too badly in the next bear market.

I should add that the couple owned a home, completely paid for, worth approximately $400,000. They both agreed that they could downsize, if necessary.

For a couple like Richard and Maria, portfolio construction is a tricky matter. Go too conservative, and the couple may run out of money before they die. Go too aggressive, and the couple may run out of money tomorrow. It's a delicate balancing act. In this case, I took Richard and Maria's $700,000 and allocated 25 percent — $175,500 — to a Vanguard immediate fixed annuity. (The annuity was put in Richard's name, with 50 percent survivorship benefit for Maria. They agreed that if Richard dies before Maria, she'll sell the home and buy or rent something more economical.) The rest of the money — $525,000 — I allocated to a broadly diversified portfolio largely constructed using ETFs. Figure 9-3 shows the portfolio breakdown.

» **Broad-based U.S. stock market:** 14 percent
   - **Engine No. 1 Transform 500 ETF (ticker symbol: VOTE):** 10 percent
   - **Vanguard Small Cap Value ETF (ticker symbol: VBR):** 4 percent

» **Broad-based foreign stocks:** 14 percent
   - **Vanguard Developed Markets Index ETF (ticker symbol: VEA):** 10 percent
   - **Vanguard Emerging Markets Index ETF (ticker symbol: VWO):** 4 percent

» **Special sector fund:** 5 percent
   - **iShares Global Consumer Staples ETF (ticker symbol: KXI):** 5 percent

» **Bonds:** 42 percent
   - **BNY Mellon Core Bond ETF (ticker symbol: BKAG):** 12 percent
   - **iShares Global Green Bonds ETF (ticker symbol: BGRN):** 10 percent
   - **Schwab U.S. TIPS ETF (ticker symbol: SCHP):** 10 percent
   - **Vanguard Mortgage-Backed Securities ETF (ticker symbol: VMBS):** 5 percent

- **iShares ESG Aware 1–5 Year USD Corporate Bond (ticker symbol: SUSB):** 5 percent
>> **Market-neutral fund:** 5 percent
  - **Merger Fund (ticker symbol: MERFX):** 5 percent
>> **Vanguard immediate fixed annuity:** 20 percent (with 50 percent survivorship benefit)

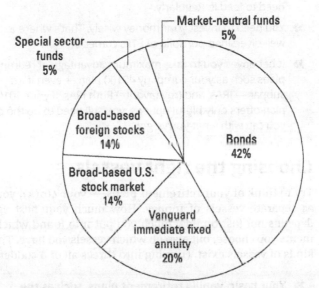

FIGURE 9-3: A portfolio aimed at safety.

Aiming for Economic Self-Sufficiency in Retirement

How much you need in your portfolio to call yourself economically self-sufficient ("retired," if you prefer) starts off with a very simple formula: $A \times B = \$\$\$\$$. A is the amount of money you need to live on for one year. B is the number of years you plan to live without a paycheck. $\$\$\$\$$ is the amount you should have before bidding the boss adieu. There you have it.

Of course, that formula is *way* oversimplified. You also need to factor in such things as return on your future portfolio, inflation, Social Security, taxes, and potential inheritances.

Taking the basic steps

Whatever amount you set as your goal, you need to do three basic things to achieve it:

>> Perhaps obvious, although most people prefer to ignore it: You have to *save*. A retirement portfolio doesn't just pop up from out of nowhere and grow like Jack's beanstalk. You need to feed it. Regularly.

>> You need to invest your money wisely. That's where a well-diversified portfolio of ETFs comes in.

>> It behooves you to take maximum advantage of retirement plans such as your company 401(k) plan — even if it's subpar — IRAs, and (my favorite) Roth IRAs. If your 401(k) plan offers only pitiful options, you still need to do the best you can with what you've got.

Choosing the right vessels

Try to think of your retirement plans — your 401(k), your IRA — as separate vessels of money. How much your nest egg grows depends not just on how much you put into it and which investments you choose, but also on which vessels you have. Three basic kinds of vessels exist. (I'm big into threes all of a sudden.)

>> **Your basic, vanilla retirement plans, such as the company 401(k), the traditional IRA, or, for the self-employed, the Simplified Employee Pension (SEP)-IRA or individual 401(k):** These are all *tax-deferred* vessels — you don't pay taxes on the money in the year you earn it; instead, you pay taxes at whatever point you withdraw money from your account, typically only after you retire.

>> **Roth IRA, 529 college plan, and health savings accounts (HSAs):** Those are *tax-free* vessels — as long as you play by certain rules (discuss them with your accountant), anything you plunk into these vessels (money on which you've generally already paid taxes) can double, triple, or (oh, please!) quadruple, and you'll never owe the IRS a cent.

>> **Non-retirement brokerage or savings bank account:** Except for certain select investments, such as municipal bonds (munis), all dividends or interest earned in these vessels will be taxable. And if your investments grow over time — yes, this includes munis — you may owe capital gains tax when you sell.

How much can your choice of vessels affect the ultimate condition of your nest egg? *Lots.* Even in a portfolio of all ETFs. True, ETFs are marvelously tax-efficient instruments. Often, in the case of stock ETFs, they eliminate the need to pay any capital gains tax (as you would with most mutual funds) for as long as you hold the ETF. Still, there may be taxes to pay at the end of the game when you finally cash out. And in the case of certain ETFs (such as any of the taxable-bond ETFs) that pay either interest or high dividends, you'll certainly pay taxes along the way.

Suppose you're an average, middle-class person with a marginal income tax rate of 30 percent (federal + state + local). Next, suppose that you have $50,000 on which you've already paid taxes, and you're ready to squirrel it away for the future. You invest this money in the Vanguard Intermediate-Term Corporate Bond ETF (ticker symbol: VCIT), which yields (hypothetically) 6 percent over the life of the investment, and you keep it for the next 15 years. Now, if that ETF were held in your regular brokerage account and you had to pay taxes on the interest every year, at the end of 15 years you'd have a pot worth $92,680. Not too shabby. But if you held that very same $50,000 bond ETF in your Roth IRA and let it compound tax-free, after 15 years you'd have $119,828 — an extra $27,148. And you would pay no income tax on this cash hoard when you eventually drew from it.

Unfortunately, the amount of money that you can put into retirement accounts is limited, although the law has allowed the sum to grow in recent years. For example, as I write this book, the maximum annual contribution to the most commonly used retirement accounts, the IRA and the Roth IRA, is $6,000 if you're younger than 50 and $7,000 if you're 50 or older. (The amount is subject to change each year.) Other retirement plans, such as the 401(k), 403(b), or SEP-IRA, have higher limits, but there is always a cap. (Ask your accountant about these plan limits; the formulas can get complicated.)

Knowing what should go where

Given these limitations, which ETFs (and other investments) should get dibs on filling up your retirement accounts, and which are best deployed elsewhere? Follow these four primary principles (I've given up on threes), and you can't go too wrong:

>> **Any investment that generates a lot of (otherwise taxable) income belongs in your retirement account.** Any

of the taxable-bond ETFs, REIT ETFs, and high-dividend-stock ETFs are probably best held in your retirement account. *Note:* Value stocks generally yield more in dividends than growth stocks. Also include any actively managed funds with a high turnover.

>> **Keep your emergency funds out of your IRA.** Any money that you think you may need to withdraw in a hurry should be kept out of your retirement accounts. Withdrawing money from a retirement account can often be tricky, possibly involving penalties if done before age 59½, and usually triggering taxation. You don't want to have to worry about such things when you need money by noon tomorrow because your teenage son just totaled the family car.

>> **House investments with the greatest potential for growth in your tax-free Roth IRA.** This may include your small-cap value ETF, your technology stock fund, or your emerging-markets ETF. Roth IRA money won't ever be taxed (assuming no change in the law), so why not try to get the most bang for your ETF buck?

>> **Foreign-stock ETFs are perhaps best kept in your taxable account.** That's because the U.S. government will reimburse you for any taxes your fund paid out to foreign governments, but only if you have that fund in a taxable account. Over the long run, this "rebate" can add about half a percentage point a year to the returns you get on these funds; it doesn't sound like a lot, but it can add up over time.

REMEMBER

Before you decide where to plunk your investments, refer to the following caveat: Tax laws change all the time. Because of the constant changes in tax laws, I advise you to review your portfolio every year or two to make sure that you have your assets in the right "vessels." Of course, there are other good reasons to review your portfolio, as well.

Retirement accounts

Here are ETFs and other investments that are generally best kept in a retirement account:

>> **Taxable-bond ETFs:** Examples include
  • Vanguard Intermediate-Term Corporate Bond ETF (ticker symbol: VCIT)
  • BNY Mellon Core Bond ETF (ticker symbol: BKAG)

- » **ETFs that invest in REITs:** Examples include
  - Vanguard REIT Index ETF (ticker symbol: VNQ)
  - Schwab U.S. REIT ETF (ticker symbol: SCHH)
  - iShares Global REIT (ticker symbol: REET)
- » **High-dividend ETFs:** Examples include
  - Vanguard High Dividend Appreciation ETF (ticker symbol: VIG)
  - SPDR S&P Dividend ETF (ticker symbol: SDY)
  - iShares Dow Jones Select Dividend Index Fund (ticker symbol: DVY)
- » **Actively managed funds, especially actively managed mutual funds.**

Taxable accounts

Here are ETFs and other investments that are generally best kept in a taxable account:

- » **Cash reserve for emergencies.**
- » **Municipal-bond ETFs:** Examples include
  - iShares S&P National Municipal Bond Fund (ticker symbol: MUB)
  - SPDR Nuveen Barclays Capital Municipal Bond (ticker symbol: TFI)
  - PowerShares Insured National Municipal Bond Portfolio (ticker symbol: PZA)
- » **Foreign-stock ETFs:** Examples include
  - Vanguard FTSE Developed Markets ETF (ticker symbol: VEA)
  - iShares Core MSCI Emerging Markets ETF (ticker symbol: IEMG)
  - Cambria Global Value ETF (ticker symbol: GVAL)

Could go into either kind of account

Here are ETFs that can go into your retirement accounts if you have the room, but the priority should be given to other, less tax-efficient funds:

>> **Stock ETFs, except for the highest-dividend-paying funds:** Examples include

- Vanguard Mega Cap 300 Growth ETF (ticker symbol: MGK)
- Nuveen ESG Large-Cap Growth ETF (ticker symbol: NULG)
- Vanguard Small Cap Growth ETF (ticker symbol: VBK)

>> **U.S. Treasury-bond funds:** Remember that you pay federal tax on the interest, but not state or local tax. Examples include

- Vanguard Intermediate-Term Treasury Index ETF (ticker symbol: VGIT)
- Schwab Intermediate-Term U.S. Treasury ETF (ticker symbol: SCHR)
- Schwab Long-Term U.S. Treasury ETF (ticker symbol: SCHO)

>> **Very short-term taxable-bond funds ("near cash"):** Examples include

- Schwab Short-Term U.S. Treasury ETF (ticker symbol: SCHO)
- Vanguard Short-Term Corporate Bond Index Fund (ticker symbol: VCSH)
- iShares ESG Aware 1–5 Year USD Corporate Bond ETF (ticker symbol: SUSB)

Curing the 401(k) Blues

Got one of those 401(k) plans at work, certain to eat you up alive in fees, about as well diversified as a lunar landscape? Don't despair. All is not lost. Here's what I suggest:

>> **Take the boss's money with a smile.** Make a big effort to shovel in at least the minimum required to get your full company match (which will differ from company to company). If you don't contribute enough to receive your employer's full matching contribution, you are, in essence, leaving free money on the table. Even if the investment options are horrible, you'll still end up well ahead of the game if your employer is kicking in an extra 25 percent or 50 percent.

>> **Invest to the best of your ability, however poor the menu.** Among the horrible choices, pick the least horrible. Choose those that will give you exposure to different asset classes. Choose index funds if available. Strongly favor whichever funds are least expensive.

TIP

If you need help understanding the different offerings in your 401(k) plan, ask someone in the human resources department, or the plan administrator, to help you. If you can't get a clear answer (you very well may not), perhaps hire a financial planner for at least a short consult.

>> **Argue for better options.** Tell the human resources people (diplomatically, of course) if their plan is a dog. They should look for another plan that includes either ETFs or (sometimes just as good) low-cost index mutual funds.

REMEMBER

>> **Check your statements.** It doesn't happen often, thank goodness, but yes, sometimes employers steal from their employees' retirement funds. Or give your employer the benefit of the doubt: Maybe they're just incompetent (and it's just a coincidence that mistakes seem always to reduce your account balance and never go in your favor). Check your statements regularly, and make sure that the money you're contributing is actually being credited to your account.

>> **Plan your rollover.** If you leave your job, you may have the option of keeping your 401(k) plan right where it is. But 90 percent of the time, you'll do much better by rolling your 401(k) into a self-directed IRA and then building yourself a well-diversified ETF portfolio.

WARNING

One important caveat: You can't withdraw IRA money without penalty until you're 59½, whereas some (but not all) 401(k) plans allow you to withdraw your money penalty-free at age 55 if you decide to retire at that point. Don't be too quick to initiate a rollover if you think you may need to tap your funds in the years between 55 and 59½.

TIP

If you do initiate a rollover, and you have your own company's stock in your 401(k), you may want to leave just that part behind. You'll get a nice tax break at retirement.

Chapter **10**

Getting a Handle on Risk, Return, and Diversification

October. This is one of the peculiarly dangerous months to speculate in stocks. The others are July, January, September, April, November, May, March, June, December, August, and February.

—MARK TWAIN

A peculiarly good writer, but also a peculiarly bad money manager, Twain sent his entire fortune down the river on a few bad investments. A century and a half later, investing, especially in stocks, can still be a peculiarly dangerous game. But today you have low-cost indexed ETFs and a lot more knowledge about the power of diversification. Together, these two things can help lessen the dangers and heighten the rewards of the stock market. In this chapter, I hope to make you a better stock investor — at least better than Mark Twain.

Risk Is Not Just a Board Game

Well, okay, actually Risk *is* a board game, but I'm not talking here about *that* Risk. Instead, I'm talking about investment risk. And in the world of investments, risk means one thing: volatility. Volatility is what takes people's nest eggs, scrambles them, and serves them up with humble pie. Volatility is what causes investors insomnia and heartburn. Volatility is the potential for financially crippling losses.

Ask people who had most of their money invested in stocks in 2008. For five years prior, the stock market had done pretty darned well. Investors were just starting to feel good again. The last market downfall of 2000–2002 was thankfully fading into memory. And then — *pow!* — the U.S. stock market tanked by nearly 40 percent over the course of the year. Foreign markets fell just as much. Billions and billions were lost. Some portfolios (which may have dipped more than 40 percent, depending on what kind of stocks they held) were crushed. Many people who had planned for retirement had to adjust their plans.

There was nothing pretty about 2008.

In early 2020, when the COVID-19 pandemic hit, investors got another taste of how quickly the markets can turn. It wasn't quite as bad as 2008 or 2000–2002 (between February and March, the Dow lost "only" 37 percent), and it lasted for just a short time, but it was still a shocker.

REMEMBER

Is risk to be avoided at all costs? Well, no. Not at all. Risk is to be mitigated, for sure, but risk within reason can actually be a *good* thing. That's because risk and return, much like Romeo and Juliet or Coronas and lime, go hand in hand. Volatility means that an investment can go way down or way up. You hope it goes way up. Without some volatility, you resign yourself to a portfolio that isn't poised for any great growth. And in the process, you open yourself up to another kind of risk: the risk that your money will slowly be eaten away by inflation.

WARNING

If you're ever offered the opportunity to partake in any investment scheme that promises you oodles and oodles of money with "absolutely no risk," run! You're in the presence of a con artist or a fool. Such investments do not exist.

The trade-off of all trade-offs: Safety versus return

To get to the holy grail — a big, fat payoff from your investments — you need to take on the fire-breathing dragon of risk. There simply is no way that you're going to make any sizable amount of money off your investments without a willingness to get hurt. The holy grail is not handed out to people who stuff money in their mattresses or carry their pennies to the local savings bank.

If you look at different investments over the course of time, you find an uncanny correlation between risk (volatility risk, not inflation risk) and return. Safe investments — those that really do carry genuine guarantees, such as U.S. Treasury bills, Federal Deposit Insurance Corporation (FDIC)–insured savings accounts, and certificates of deposit (CDs) — tend to offer very modest returns (often — especially these days — negative returns after accounting for inflation). Volatile investments — like stocks and "junk" bonds, the kinds of investments that cause people to lose sleep — tend to offer handsome returns if you give them enough time.

REMEMBER

Time, then, is an essential ingredient in determining appropriate levels of risk. You would be wise to keep any cash you're going to need within the next six months to a year in a savings bank, or possibly in an ETF such as the iShares Barclays 1–3 Year Treasury Bond Fund (ticker symbol: SHY), a short-term bond fund that yields a modest return but is very unlikely to lose value. You should *not* invest that portion of your money in any ETF that is made up of company stocks, such as the popular SPY or QQQ. True, SPY or QQQ can (and should), over time, yield much more than SHY, but they're also much more susceptible to sharp price swings. Unless you aren't going to need your cash for at least a couple of years (and preferably not for six or seven or more years), you're best off avoiding any investment in the stock market, whether it be through ETFs or otherwise.

So, just how risky are ETFs?

Asking how risky, or how lucrative, ETFs are is like trying to judge a soup knowing nothing about the soup's ingredients, only that it's served in a blue china bowl. The bowl — or the ETF — doesn't create the risk; what's inside it does. Thus, stock and real estate ETFs tend to be more volatile than bond ETFs. Short-term bond

ETFs are less volatile than long-term bond ETFs. Small-stock ETFs are more volatile than large-stock ETFs. International ETFs often see more volatility than U.S. ETFs. And international emerging-market ETFs see more volatility than international developed-nation ETFs.

Figure 10-1 shows some examples of various ETFs and where they fit on the risk–return continuum. Note that it starts with bond ETFs at the bottom (maximum safety, minimum volatility), and nearer the top, it features the EAFE (Europe, Australia, Far East) Index and the South Korea Index Fund. (An investment in South Korean stocks not only involves all the normal risks of business but also includes currency risk, as well as the risk that some deranged North Korean dictator may decide he wants to pick a fight. Buyer beware.)

High Risk (and highest return potential)

iShares MSCI South Korea Index Fund (EWY)

iShares MSCI EAFE Index Fund (EFA)

Vanguard Mid Cap ETF (VO)

SPDR S&P 500 (SPY)

iShares Barclays 7-10 Year Treasury Bond Fund (IEF)

iShares Barclays 1-3 Year Treasury Bond Fund (SHY)

Low Risk (with more modest return potential)

© John Wiley & Sons, Inc.

FIGURE 10-1: The risk levels of a sampling of ETFs.

Keep in mind when looking at Figure 10-1 that I'm segregating these ETFs — treating them as stand-alone assets — for illustration purposes. As I discuss later in this chapter (when I discuss something called Modern Portfolio Theory), stand-alone risk measurements are of limited value. The true risk of adding any particular ETF to your portfolio depends on what is already in the portfolio. (That statement will make sense by the end of this chapter. I promise!)

Smart Risk, Foolish Risk

There is safety in numbers, which is why teenage boys and girls huddle together in corners at school dances. In the case of teenagers, the safety is afforded by anonymity and distance. In the case of indexed ETFs and mutual funds, safety is provided (to a limited degree only!) by diversification in that they represent ownership in many different securities. Owning many stocks, rather than a few, provides some safety by eliminating something that investment professionals, when they're trying to impress, call *nonsystemic risk*.

Nonsystemic risk is involved when you invest in any individual security. It's the risk that the CEO of the company will be strangled by their pet python, that the national headquarters will be destroyed by a falling asteroid, or that the company's stock will take a sudden nosedive simply because of some internet rumor started by an 11th-grader in the suburbs of Des Moines. Those kinds of risks (and more serious ones) can be effectively eliminated by investing not in individual securities but in ETFs or mutual funds.

REMEMBER

Nonsystemic risk contrasts with *systemic risk*, which, unfortunately, ETFs and mutual funds cannot eliminate. Systemic risks, as a group, simply can't be avoided, not even by keeping your portfolio in cash. Examples of systemic risk include the following:

>> **Market risk:** The market goes up, the market goes down, and whatever stocks or stock ETFs you own will generally (though not always) move in the same direction.

>> **Interest-rate risk:** If interest rates go up, the value of your bonds or bond ETFs (especially long-term bond ETFs such as TLT, the iShares 20-year Treasury ETF) will fall.

>> **Inflation risk:** When inflation picks up, any fixed-income investments that you own (such as any of the conventional bond ETFs) will suffer. And any cash you hold will start to dwindle in value, buying less and less than it used to.

>> **Political risk:** If you invest your money in Canada, France, or Japan, there's little chance that revolutionaries will overthrow the government anytime soon. When you invest in the stock or bond ETFs of certain other countries (or when you hold

currencies from those countries), you'd better keep a sharp eye on the nightly news.

>> **Grand-scale risk:** The government of Japan wasn't overthrown, but that didn't stop an earthquake and ensuing tsunami and nuclear disaster from sending the Tokyo stock market reeling in early 2011. Similarly, in 2020, COVID-19 hit most of the world's stock markets hard — some harder than others.

Although ETFs can't eliminate systemic risks, don't despair. For even though nonsystemic risks are a bad thing, systemic risks are a decidedly mixed bag. Nonsystemic risks, you see, offer no compensation. A company is not bound to pay higher dividends, nor is its stock price bound to rise simply because the CEO has taken up mountain climbing or hang gliding.

REMEMBER

Systemic risks, on the other hand, do offer compensation. Invest in small stocks (which are more volatile and, therefore, incorporate more market risk), and you can expect (over the very long term) higher returns. Invest in a country with a history of political instability, and (especially if that instability doesn't occur) you'll probably be rewarded with high returns in compensation for taking added risk. Invest in long-term bonds (or long-term bond ETFs) rather than short-term bonds (or ETFs), and you're taking on more interest-rate risk. That's why the yield on long-term bonds is almost always greater.

In other words:

Higher systemic risk = Higher historical returns

Higher nonsystemic risk = Zilch

That's the way markets tend to work. Segments of the market with higher risks *must* offer higher returns or else they wouldn't be able to attract capital. If the potential returns on emerging-market stocks (or ETFs) were no higher than the potential returns on short-term bond ETFs or FDIC-insured savings accounts, would anyone but a complete nutcase invest in emerging-market stocks?

Understanding How Risk Is Measured

In the world of investments, risk means volatility, and volatility (unlike angels or love) can be seen, measured, and plotted. People in the investment world use different tools to measure volatility, such as standard deviation, beta, and certain ratios such as the Sharpe ratio. Most of these tools are not very hard to get a handle on, and they can help you better follow discussions on portfolio building that appear elsewhere in this book. Ready to dig in?

Standard deviation: The king of all risk measurement tools

So, you want to know how much an investment is likely to bounce? The first thing you do is look to see how much it has bounced in the past. Standard deviation measures the degree of past bounce and, from that measurement, gives you some notion of future bounce. To put it another way, standard deviation shows the degree to which a stock/bond/mutual fund/ETF's actual returns vary from its average returns over a certain period of time.

Table 10-1 presents two hypothetical ETFs and their returns over the last six years. Note that both portfolios start with $1,000 and end with $1,101. But note, too, the great difference in how much they bounce. ETF A's yearly returns range from –3 percent to 5 percent while ETF B's range from –15 percent to 15 percent. The standard deviation of the six years for ETF A is 3.09; the standard deviation for ETF B is 10.38.

Predicting a range of returns

What does the standard deviation number tell you? Take ETF A as an example. The standard deviation of 3.09 tells you that in about two-thirds of the months to come, you should expect the return of ETF A to fall within 3.09 percentage points of the mean return, which was 1.66. In other words, about 68 percent of the time, returns should fall somewhere between 4.75 percent (1.66 + 3.09) and –1.43 percent (1.66 – 3.09). As for the other one-third of the time, anything can happen.

TABLE 10-1 Standard Deviation of Two Hypothetical ETFs

Balance, Beginning of Year	Return	Balance, End of Year
ETF A		
$1,000	5%	$1,050
$1,050	–2%	$1,029
$1,029	4%	$1,070
$1,070	–3%	$1,038
$1,038	2%	$1,059
$1,059	4%	$1,101
ETF B		
$1,000	10%	$1,100
$1,100	6%	$1,166
$1,166	–15%	$991
$991	–8%	$912
$912	15%	$1,048
$1,048	5%	$1,101

It also tells you that in about 95 percent of the months to come, the returns should fall within two standard deviations of the mean. In other words, 95 percent of the time, you should see a return of between 7.84 percent [1.66 + (3.09 × 2)] and –4.52 percent [1.66 – (3.09 × 2)]. The other 5 percent of the time is anybody's guess.

Making side-by-side comparisons

The ultimate purpose of standard deviation, and the reason I'm describing it, is that it gives you a way to judge the relative risks of two ETFs. If one ETF has a three-year standard deviation of 12, you know that it's roughly twice as volatile as another ETF with a standard deviation of 6 and half as risky as an ETF with a standard deviation of 24. A real-world example: The standard deviation for most short-term bond funds falls somewhere around 0.7. The standard deviation for most precious-metals funds is somewhere around 26.

Important caveat: Don't assume that combining one ETF with a standard deviation of 10 with another that has a standard deviation of 20 will give you a portfolio with an average standard deviation of 15. It doesn't work that way at all, as you see when I introduce Modern Portfolio Theory later in this chapter. The combined standard deviation will not be any greater than 15, but it could (if you do your homework and put together two of the right ETFs) be much less.

Beta: Assessing price swings in relation to the market

Unlike standard deviation, which gives you a stand-alone picture of volatility, beta is a relative measure. It's used to measure the volatility of something in relation to something else. Most commonly that "something else" is the S&P 500. Very simply, beta tells you that if the S&P rises or falls by x percent, then your investment, whatever that investment is, will likely rise or fall by y percent.

The S&P is considered your baseline, and it's assigned a beta of 1. So, if you know that Humongous Software Corporation has a beta of 2, and the S&P shoots up 10 percent, Jimmy the Greek (if he were still with us) would bet that shares of Humongous are going to rise 20 percent. If you know that the Sedate Utility Company has a beta of 0.5, and the S&P shoots up 10 percent, Jimmy would bet that shares of Sedate are going to rise by 5 percent. Conversely, shares of Humongous would likely fall four times harder than shares of Sedate in response to a fall in the S&P.

In a way, beta is easier to understand than standard deviation; it's also easier to misinterpret. Beta's usefulness is greater for individual stocks than it is for ETFs, but nonetheless it can be helpful, especially when gauging the volatility of U.S. industry-sector ETFs. It is much less useful for any ETF that has international holdings. For example, an ETF that holds stocks of emerging-market nations is going to be volatile, trust me, yet it may have a low beta. How so? Because its movements, no matter how swooping, may happen independently of movement in the U.S. market. (Emerging-market stocks tend to be more tied to currency flux, commodity prices, interest rates, and political climate.)

The Sharpe, Treynor, and Sortino ratios

The Sharpe, Treynor, and Sortino ratios measure what you get for your risk. The following sections give you the scoop.

The Sharpe ratio

Back in 1966, a goateed Stanford professor named Bill Sharpe developed a formula that has since become as common in investment-speak as runs batted in (RBIs) are in baseball-speak. The formula looks like this:

> (Total portfolio return – Risk-free rate of return) ÷ Portfolio standard deviation = Sharpe ratio

The risk-free rate of return generally refers to the return you could get on a short-term U.S. Treasury bill. If you subtract that from the total portfolio return, it tells you how much your portfolio earned above the rate you could have achieved without risking your principal. You take that number and divide it by the standard deviation (discussed earlier in this chapter). And what *that* result gives you is the Sharpe ratio, which essentially indicates how much money has been made in relation to how much risk was taken to make that money.

Suppose Portfolio A, under manager Bubba Bucks, returned 7 percent last year, and during that year Treasury bills were paying 5 percent. Portfolio A also had a standard deviation of 8 percent. Okay, applying the formula, you get this:

> (7% – 5%) ÷ 8% = 2% ÷ 8% = 0.25

That result wasn't good enough for Bubba Buck's manager, so the manager fired Bubba and hired Donny Dollar. Donny, who just read this book, takes the portfolio and dumps all its high-cost active mutual funds. In their place, Donny buys ETFs. In his first year managing the portfolio, he achieves a total return of 10 percent with a standard deviation of 7.5. But the interest rate on Treasury bills has gone up to 7 percent. Applying the formula:

> (10% – 7%) ÷ 7.5% = 3% ÷ 7.5% = 0.4

The higher the Sharpe ratio, the better. Donny Dollar did his job much better than Bubba Bucks did his.

The Treynor ratio

The Treynor approach was first used by — you guessed it — a guy named Jack Treynor in 1965. Instead of using standard deviation in the denominator, it uses beta. The Treynor ratio shows the amount of money that a portfolio is making in relation to the risk it carries relative to the market. To put that another way, the Treynor ratio uses only systemic risk, or beta, while the Sharpe ratio uses total risk.

Suppose that Donny Dollar's portfolio, with its 10 percent return, had a beta of 0.9. In that case, the Treynor ratio would be this:

$$(10\% - 7\%) \div 0.9 = 3\% \div 0.9 = 0.03 \div 0.9 = 0.033$$

Is 0.033 good? That depends. It's a relative number. Suppose that the market, as measured by the S&P 500, also returned 10 percent that same year. It may seem like Donny isn't a very good manager. But when you apply the Treynor ratio (recalling that the beta for the market is always 1), you get a lower number:

$$(10\% - 7\%) \div 1 = 3\% \div 1 = 0.03 \div 1 = 0.03$$

That result indicates that although Donny earned a return that was similar to the market's, he took on less risk. Put another way, he achieved greater returns per unit of risk. Donny's boss will likely keep him.

The Sortino ratio

Another variation on the Sharpe ratio is the Sortino ratio, which basically uses the same formula:

(Total portfolio return – Risk-free rate of return) ÷ Portfolio standard deviation (downside only) = Sortino ratio

Note that instead of looking at historical ups and downs, it focuses only on the downs. After all, say members of the Sortino-ratio fan club, you don't lose sleep fretting about your portfolio rising in value. You want to know what your downside risk is. The Sortino-ratio fan club has been growing in size, but as yet, it's difficult to find Sortino-ratio calculations for any given security, including ETFs. I'm sure it will get easier over time, because comparing downside risk among various ETFs can be a helpful tool.

Meeting Modern Portfolio Theory

For simplicity's sake, I've discussed the choice of one ETF over another (SHY or SPY?) based on risk and potential return. In the real world, however, few people, if any, come to me or to any financial planner asking for a recommendation on a single ETF. More commonly, I'm asked to help build a portfolio of ETFs. And when looking at an entire portfolio, the riskiness of each individual ETF, although important, takes a back seat to the riskiness of the entire portfolio.

In other words, I would rarely recommend or rule out any specific ETF because it's too volatile. How well any specific ETF fits into a portfolio — and to what degree it affects the risk of a portfolio — depends on what else is in the portfolio. What I'm alluding to here is something called *Modern Portfolio Theory*: the tool I use to help determine a proper ETF mix for my clients' portfolios. You and I will use this tool throughout this book to help you determine a proper mix for your portfolio.

Tasting the extreme positivity of negative correlation

Modern Portfolio Theory is to investing what the discovery of gravity was to physics. Almost. What the theory says is that the volatility/risk of a portfolio may differ dramatically from the volatility/risk of the portfolio's components. In other words, you can have two assets with both high standard deviations and high potential returns, but when combined, they give you a portfolio with modest standard deviation but the same high potential return. Modern Portfolio Theory says that you can have a slew of risky ingredients, but if you throw them together into a big bowl, the entire soup may actually splash around very little.

REMEMBER

The key to whipping up such pleasant combinations is to find two or more holdings that do not move in sync: One tends to go up while the other goes down (although both holdings, in the long run, will see an upward trajectory). In the figures that follow, I show how you'd create a fantasy ETF portfolio consisting of two high-risk/high-return ETFs with perfect negative correlation. It's a fantasy portfolio because perfect negative correlations among asset classes don't exist; they simply serve as a target.

Figure 10-2 represents hypothetical ETF A and hypothetical ETF B, each of which has high return and high volatility. Notice that even though both are volatile assets, they move up and down at different times. This fact is crucial because combining them can give you a nonvolatile portfolio.

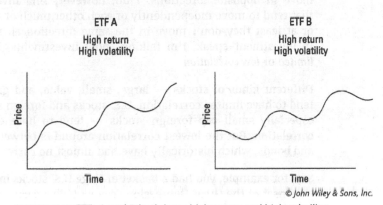

© John Wiley & Sons, Inc.

FIGURE 10-2: ETFs A and B both have high return and high volatility.

Figure 10-3 shows what happens when you invest in both ETF A and ETF B. You end up with the perfect ETF portfolio — one made up of two ETFs with perfect negative correlation. If only such a portfolio existed in the real world! (*Note:* I'm ignoring for the moment the so-called inverse ETFs, which promise negative correlation, but don't always deliver.)

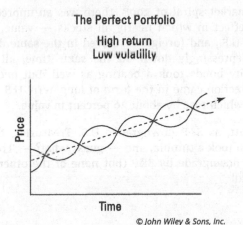

© John Wiley & Sons, Inc.

FIGURE 10-3: The perfect ETF portfolio, with high return and no volatility.

Settling for limited correlation

When the U.S. stock market takes a punch, which happens on average every three years or so, most U.S. stocks fall. When the market flies, most stocks fly. Not many investments regularly move in opposite directions. I do, however, find investments that tend to move independently of each other much of the time, or at least they don't move in the same direction all the time. In investment-speak, I'm talking about investments that have *limited* or *low correlation*.

Different kinds of stocks — large, small, value, and growth — tend to have limited correlation. U.S. stocks and foreign stocks — especially small-cap foreign stocks — tend to have even less correlation. But the lowest correlation around is between stocks and bonds, which historically have had almost no correlation.

Say, for example, you had a basket of large U.S. stocks in 1929, at the onset of the Great Depression. You would've seen your portfolio lose nearly a quarter of its value every year for the next four years. Ouch! If, however, you were holding high-quality, long-term bonds during that same period, at least that side of your portfolio would have grown by a respectable 5 percent a year. A portfolio of long-term bonds held throughout the growling bear market in stocks of 2000 through 2003 would've returned a hale and hearty 13 percent a year. (That's an unusually high return for bonds, but at the time the stars were in perfect alignment.)

During the market spiral of 2008, there was an unprecedented chorus-line effect in which nearly all stocks — value, growth, large, small, U.S., and foreign — moved in the same direction: down . . . depressingly down. At the same time, all but the highest-quality bonds took a beating as well. But once again, portfolio protection came in the form of long-term U.S. government bonds, which rose by about 26 percent in value.

In August 2011, as S&P downgraded U.S. Treasuries, the stock markets again took a tumble, and — guess what? — Treasuries, despite their downgrade by S&P (but none of the other raters), spiked upward!

Reaching for the elusive Efficient Frontier

Correlation is a measurable thing, represented in the world of investments by something called the *correlation coefficient*. This number indicates the degree to which two investments move in the same or different directions. A correlation coefficient can range from −1 to 1.

REMEMBER

A correlation of 1 indicates that the two securities are like the Radio City Rockettes: When one kicks a leg, so does the other. Having both in your portfolio offers no diversification benefit. On the other hand, if investment A and investment B have a correlation coefficient of −1, that means they have a perfect negative relationship: They always move in the opposite directions. Having both in your portfolio is a wonderful diversifier. Such polar-opposite investments are, alas, very hard to find.

A correlation coefficient of zero means that the two investments have no relationship to each other. When one moves, the other may move in the same direction, the opposite direction, or not at all.

As a whole, stocks and bonds (not junk bonds, but high-quality bonds) tend to have little to negative correlation. Finding the perfect mix of stocks and bonds, as well as other investments with low correlation, is known among financial pros as looking for the *Efficient Frontier*. The Frontier represents the mix of investments that offers the greatest promise of return for the least amount of risk.

Fortunately, ETFs allow you to tinker easily with your investments so you can find just that sweet spot.

Accusations that Modern Portfolio Theory is dead are greatly exaggerated

Since the market swoon of 2008, some pundits have claimed that Modern Portfolio Theory is dead. This claim is nonsense. As I mention earlier, U.S. government bonds more than held their own during this difficult period. And even though all styles of stock moved down in 2008, they moved at different paces. And the degree to which they recovered has differed significantly. The same thing happened again in 2020 with the COVID-19 dip. You'll see these differences in the charts in the upcoming sections "Filling in your style box" and "Buying by industry sector."

The investors who were hurt terribly in 2008 were those who sold their depressed stocks and moved everything into cash or "safe" bonds. Those bonds, at least long-term government bonds, then lost about 16 percent of their value in 2009. Those who flipped from stocks to bonds would've been doubly wounded. But those who kept the faith in Modern Portfolio Theory and rebalanced their portfolios, as I discuss in Chapter 11, would not have been so badly wounded. These investors would've been buying stock in 2008 instead of selling it. And any investor with a fairly well-balanced portfolio of stocks and bonds would've recouped their losses within two years after the market bottomed in March 2009. In 2020, buyers and holders saw their losses reverse even more quickly — a sign, I believe, of things to come.

Mixing and Matching Your Stock ETFs

Reaching for the elusive Efficient Frontier means holding both stocks and bonds — domestic and international — in your portfolio. That part is fairly straightforward and not likely to stir much controversy (although, for sure, experts differ on what they consider optimal percentages). But experts definitely don't agree on how best to diversify the domestic-stock portion of a portfolio. Two competing methods predominate:

>> One method calls for the division of a stock portfolio into domestic and foreign, and then into different styles: large cap, small cap, mid cap, value, and growth.

>> The other method calls for allocating percentages of a portfolio to various industry sectors: health care, utilities, energy, financials, and so on.

My personal preference for the small to midsize investor, especially the ETF investor, is to go primarily with the styles. But there's nothing wrong with dividing a portfolio by industry sector. And for people with good-sized portfolios, a mixture of both, without going crazy, may be optimal.

Filling in your style box

Most savvy investors make sure to have some equity in each of the nine boxes of the grid in Figure 10-4, which is known as the *style box* or *grid* (sometimes called the *Morningstar Style Box*).

Large-cap value	Large-cap blend	Large-cap growth
Mid-cap value	Mid-cap blend	Mid-cap growth
Small-cap value	Small-cap blend	Small-cap growth

© John Wiley & Sons, Inc.

FIGURE 10-4: The style box or grid.

REMEMBER

The reason for the style box is simple enough: History shows that companies of differing capitalization (cap) size (in other words, large companies and small companies), and value and growth companies, tend to rise and fall under different economic conditions. I define *cap size, value,* and *growth* in Chapter 3, and I devote Chapters 3 and 4 to showing the differences among styles, how to choose ETFs to match each one, and how to weight those ETFs for the highest potential return with the lowest possible risk.

Table 10-2 shows how well various investment styles, as measured by four Vanguard index ETFs that track each style, have fared in the recent past. Note that a number of ETFs are available to match each style.

TABLE 10-2 Recent Performance of Various Investment Styles

	2016	2017	2018	2019	2020
Large-cap growth	6.17%	27.75%	–3.32%	37.26%	40.27%
Large-cap value	16.95%	17.14%	–5.45%	25.83%	2.29%
Small-cap growth	10.79%	21.93%	–5.78%	32.86%	35.4%
Small-cap value	24.8%	11.84%	–12.28%	22.77%	5.91%

Buying by industry sector

The advent of ETFs has largely brought forth the use of sector investing as an alternative to the grid. Examining the two models toe-to-toe yields some interesting comparisons — and much food for thought.

One study on industry-sector investing, by Chicago-based Ibbotson Associates, came to the very favorable conclusion that sector investing is a potentially superior diversifier to grid investing because times have changed since the 1960s when style investing first became popular. As Ibbotson concluded:

> Globalization has led to a rise in correlation between domestic and international stocks; large-, mid-, and small-cap stocks have high correlation to each other. A company's performance is tied more to its industry than to the country where it's based, or the size of its market cap.

The jury is still out, but I give an overview of the controversy in Chapter 6. Here, I invite you to do a little comparison of your own by looking at Tables 10-2 and 10-3. Note that by using either method of diversification, some of your investments should smell like roses in years when others stink. Also, recall what I state earlier about how all stocks crashed in 2008 but recovered at significantly different paces; this is true of various styles and sectors. And it's certainly true for various geographic regions. Modern Portfolio Theory is not dead!

Table 10-3 shows how well various industry sectors (as measured by the returns of Vanguard index ETFs that match the index of each of the respective sectors) fared in recent years. Yes, there are ETFs that track each of these industry sectors — and many more.

TABLE 10-3 Recent Performance of Various Market Sectors

	2016	2017	2018	2019	2020
Health care	−3.32%	23.35%	5.49%	22%	18.34%
Real estate	8.53%	4.90%	−5.97%	28.89%	−4.64%
Information technology	13.75%	37.04%	2.43%	48.75%	46.09%
Energy	28.93%	−2.35%	−20.01%	9.37%	−33.03%

Don't slice and dice your portfolio to death

REMEMBER

One reason I tend to prefer the traditional style grid to industry-sector investing, at least for the nonwealthy investor, is that there are simply fewer styles to contend with. You can build yourself, at least on the domestic side of your stock holdings, a pretty well-diversified portfolio with just four ETFs: one small value, one small growth, one large value, and one large growth. With industry-sector investing, you would need a dozen or so ETFs to have a well-balanced portfolio, and that may be too many.

I hold a similar philosophy when it comes to global investing. Yes, you can, thanks largely to the iShares lineup of ETFs, invest in about 50 individual countries. (And in many of these countries, you can furthermore choose between large-cap and small-cap stocks, and in some cases, value and growth.) Too much! I prefer to see most investors go with larger geographic regions: U.S., developed markets, emerging markets, and so on.

You don't want to chop up your portfolio into too many holdings, or the transaction costs (even if trading ETFs commission-free, there are still small, frictional costs when you trade) can start to bite into your returns. Rebalancing gets to be a headache. Tax filing can become a nightmare. And, as many investors learned in 2008 — okay, I'll admit it, as *I* learned in 2008 — having a very small position in your portfolio, say, less than 2 percent of your assets, in any one kind of investment isn't going to have much effect on your overall returns anyway.

TIP

As a rough rule, if you have $50,000 to invest, consider something in the ballpark of a 5- to 10-ETF portfolio, and if you have $250,000 or more, perhaps look at a 15- to 25-ETF portfolio. Many more ETFs than this won't enhance the benefits of diversification but will entail additional trading costs every time you rebalance your holdings. (See my sample ETF portfolios for all sizes of nest eggs in Chapter 9.)

Chapter **11**

Exercising Patience and Discovering Exceptions

Many, if not most, day-traders (who just *love* exchange-traded funds [ETFs], especially the really kooky ones) believe in something called *technical analysis:* the use of charts and graphs to predict movements in securities. The basic idea behind the charts comes from a best-selling book on technical analysis.

I once had the honor of interviewing one of the biggest names in technical analysis. This guy writes books, gives seminars, and tells everyone that he makes oodles and oodles of money by following charting patterns and buying and selling securities accordingly. At the time I interviewed him, I had been a journalist for 20 years, writing for many of the top U.S. magazines, covering many topics. If you develop one thing being a journalist for two decades, it is a very well-honed b.s. radar. I can tell you after spending an hour on the phone with this "expert" that he is perhaps making oodles and oodles of money with his books and seminars, but he is *not* making oodles and oodles of money with his charts.

And neither will you.

The key to success in investing isn't to do a lot of trading based on secret formulas that are every bit as fruitless as alchemy. The key is to keep your investment costs low (ETFs will do that for you), diversify your portfolio (ETFs can do that, too), lose as little as possible to taxes (ETFs can help there, too), and exercise patience (that part's up to you).

In this chapter, I present the evidence to back up my contention that buying and holding, more or less, with regular rebalancing, is the thing to do. Yes, that's true even in today's uber-turbulent markets. You'll see that the true champions of the investing world are those with the most patience.

The Tale of the Average Investor (A Tragicomedy in One Act)

I talk a bit in this book about *correlation*, the tendency for two things (such as two ETFs or other investments) to move in the same direction. A correlation of 1 indicates a *perfect* correlation: Think of a kitten swiping at itself in the mirror. Another perfect correlation is the correlation between stock prices and the public's willingness to purchase those stocks.

For some strange reason, the market for stocks (and stock funds, such as ETFs) does not work the same way as, say, the market for cars, shoes, or pineapples. With most products, if the seller drops the price, the public is likely to increase consumption. With stocks and stock funds, when the price *rises*, the public increases consumption.

For example, after tech stocks had their fabulous run in the 1990s, only then — in the latter part of the decade — did money start pouring into tech stocks. After the bubble had burst and tech stocks were selling cheaper than tarnished dirt, people were selling right and left, and no one was buying. As I write these words, I'm seeing the price and valuations of a handful of companies — Microsoft, Alphabet (Google), Facebook, Amazon, and Tesla — reach levels not seen since 1999. (Valuations refer to stock prices as they compare to companies' earnings.) As soon as the bubble bursts on these, well, it'll be red-tag-sale day once again.

Returns that fall way short of the indexes

Every year, the investment research group Dalbar compares the returns of indexes to the returns that mutual-fund investors see in the real world. In their 2020 study, the Dalbar research crew found that the average stock mutual-fund investor for the 30 years prior to December 31, 2019, earned 5.04 percent a year. This compares to the more than 9.96 percent that someone would've earned just plunking their money in an S&P 500 index fund for those two decades and leaving it put. Bond-fund investors did worse in relation to the bond indexes: 0.38 percent versus 5.91 percent.

There's recently been some controversy from Morningstar and some other research groups over Dalbar's methodology, but those researchers still come to the conclusion that the average fund investor falls far behind the indexes.

How to explain such lackluster investor returns? In part, the culprit is the average investor's inclination to invest in pricey and poor-performing mutual funds. An even larger problem is that the average investor jumps ship too often, constantly buying when the market is hot, selling when it chills, and hopping back on board when the market heats up again. They're forever buying high and selling low — not a winning strategy, by any means.

ETFs can solve the first part of the problem. They are, as long as you pick the right ones, not pricey. In fact, they cost very little. Most ETFs are also guaranteed not to underperform the major indexes because they mirror those indexes. As for the jumping-ship problem, however, I fear that ETFs can actually *exacerbate* the problem.

ETFs can make failure even easier!

ETFs were brought into being by marketing people from the Toronto Stock Exchange who saw a way to beef up trading volume. Unlike mutual funds, which can be bought and sold only at day's end, ETFs trade throughout the day. In a flash, you can plunk a million in the stock market. A few seconds later, you can sell it all. Yippee!

In other words, Dalbar's future studies looking at 30-year returns — now that ETFs have really caught on with the average investor — may be even more dismal. Keep in mind that just because ETFs can be traded throughout the day doesn't mean you *have* to or that you *should* trade them!

REMEMBER

The vast majority of ETF trades are made by institutional investors: managers of mutual funds or hedge funds, multibillion-dollar endowments, pension funds, and investment banks. These are highly trained, incredibly well-paid professionals who do nothing all day but study the markets.

When you go to buy, say, the Financial Select Sector SPDR ETF (ticker symbol: XLF), which represents stocks in the financial sector, you're betting that the price is going to go up. If you're day-trading, you're betting that the price will go up that very same day. If you're selling, you're betting that the price will fall that day. Someone, most likely a highly educated financial professional with an army of researchers and computers more powerful than the FBI's — someone who does nothing but study financial stocks 80 hours a week (for which reason their spouse is about to walk out the door) — is on the other end of your transaction. As you sell, he — I'll call him Chad — is buying. Or, as you buy, he's selling.

Obviously, Chad's vision of the next few hours and days is different from yours. Chad may not know that his spouse is about to leave him for a professional hockey player, but if either of you has any idea which way financial stocks are headed, well, do you really think that you know something Chad doesn't? Do you really think that you're going to get the better end of this deal?

Obviously, lots of ETF traders think they're pretty smart because ETFs are among the most frequently traded of all securities. But that's not necessarily a good thing. Read on.

The lure of quick riches

WARNING

If you jump onto the internet, as I just did, and type in the words *day-trading secrets,* you'll see all kinds of websites and newsletters offering you all kinds of advice (much of it having to do with reading charts) that's sure to make you rich. Add *ETF* to your search, and you'll quickly see that an entire cottage industry has formed to sell advice to wannabe ETF day-traders.

According to these websites and newsletters, following their advice has yielded phenomenal returns in the past (and they'll give you specific *big* numbers proving it). And following their advice in the future (after you've paid your hefty subscription fee) will likewise yield phenomenal returns.

TECHNICAL STUFF

If you're wondering, by the way, who regulates investment websites and newsletters and the performance figures they publish, wonder no more. No one does. The U.S. Supreme Court decided in 1985 that, just as long as a newsletter is providing general and not personal advice, the publisher is protected by the free-speech provisions of the First Amendment.

REMEMBER

John Rekenthaler, a VP at Morningstar, once told me (and I love how he put it): "Investment newsletter publishers have the same rights as tabloid publishers. There's nothing illegal about a headline that reads 'Martian Baby Born with Three Heads!' and there's nothing illegal about a headline that reads 'We Beat the Market Year In and Year Out!'" Both should be read with equal skepticism.

Patience Pays, Literally

The flip side of flipping ETFs is buying and holding them, which is almost certain, in the long run, to bring results far superior to market timing. It's the corollary to choosing ETFs over stocks. Study after study shows that the markets are, by and large, *efficient*. What does that mean? So many smart players are constantly buying and selling securities, always on the lookout for any good deals, that your chances of beating the indexes, whether by market timing or stock picking, are very slim.

One of many studies on the subject, "The Difficulty of Selecting Superior Mutual Fund Performance," by Thomas P. McGuigan, appeared in the *Journal of Financial Planning*. McGuigan found that only 10 percent to 11 percent of actively managed mutual funds outperform index funds over a 20-year period. (*Active managers* are professionals who try to pick stocks and time the market.)

REMEMBER

You can probably safely assume that the professionals do better than the amateurs, and even the professionals fail to beat the market 90 percent of the time.

Timing doesn't work because markets are largely random. The unpredictability of the stock market (and the bond market, for that matter) never ceases to amaze me. Just when things seem certain to take off, they sink. Just when they seem certain to sink, they fly.

In 2021, the world was locked in a struggle against COVID-19 that first hit the United States in February 2020. The first month or two were brutal to the stock market. Portfolios fell dramatically as sector by sector succumbed, first to panic and then to a sharp reduction in consumption and production. Airlines, hotels, retail, and financials were hit the hardest, but every industry suffered. From mid-February to mid-March 2020, over the course of a mere 33 days, the broad U.S. stock market fell 34 percent. And then . . . the market came raging back.

The market reached break-even just a few months later, in mid-August 2020, and then continued to rise. By the end of December 2020, the S&P 500 had risen more than 18 percent from the start of the year. And then it continued to rise more. From January 2021 to the end of July 2021, the market rose yet *another* 18 percent.

This is not atypical. Stocks react, and often overreact to bad news. And then, after a time, stocks come back.

Remember September 11, 2001? The Dow immediately dropped more than 7 percent. Six months later, the Dow was up by 10.5 percent. On September 24, 1955, President Eisenhower's heart attack led to a one-day drop of 6.5 percent. Six months later, the Dow was up 12.5 percent. I could give example after example.

In 2008, the market had its worst dip since the Great Depression; the S&P 500 tumbled nearly 37 percent for the year. But it came back, gaining 26 percent in 2009 and about 15 percent in 2010. Had you rebalanced in 2008, shaving off bonds and buying up stocks at rock-bottom prices, your portfolio (provided it was well diversified) would likely have fully recovered within two years.

REMEMBER

That's not to say that the market will *always* come back. One of these days, well, even Rome eventually fell. But history shows that the stock market is a mighty resilient beast. I suggest that you build a portfolio of ETFs — including stock and bond ETFs — and hang tight. Sooner or later (barring some truly major economic upheaval), you'll very likely be rewarded.

Exceptions to the Rule (Ain't There Always)

Earlier in this chapter, I discuss the virtues of a buy-and-hold approach to ETF investing. But that doesn't mean that you should purchase a bunch of ETFs and *never* touch them. Switching from one ETF to another won't get you a clock radio or a leather wallet, but there can be other benefits to making some occasional moves, for sure.

In the following sections, I discuss certain circumstances where it makes sense to trade ETFs rather than buy and hold. For example, you need to rebalance your portfolio, typically on an annual basis, to keep risk in check, and on occasion you may want to swap ETFs to harvest taxes at year-end. I also discuss the ways in which life changes may warrant tweaking a portfolio. And finally, I introduce you to the world of ETF options, where frequent trading is a way of life.

Rebalancing to keep your portfolio fit

Few investors walked away from 2008 smelling like a rose. But those who were slammed, truly slammed, were those who had more on the stock side of their portfolios than they should have. It happens, and it happens especially after bull markets, as investors saw in the several years prior to 2008 — and as they're seeing today.

Let's take the case of Joan. In 2011, when she was 54 years old, she sat down and looked at her financial situation and goals. She determined that she warranted a 60/40 (60 percent stock/ 40 percent bond) portfolio and duly crafted a darned good one. But then she got lazy. She held that portfolio without touching it through the stock-market boom years that followed, and as a result, her portfolio morphed from a 60/40 mix to an 80/20 mix by the start of 2021.

Now Joan is at the cusp of retirement, sitting on a portfolio that's way too risky. If the market were to tumble today as it did in, say, 2008, she might lose 40 percent of her worth. Starting retirement with a portfolio that's down 40 percent wouldn't be an enviable position to be in. If the market falls and doesn't come back anytime soon, she may have to sell her stock ETFs at very depressed prices, locking in her losses. And she'll have absolutely no "dry powder" (cash) with which to reload her stock portfolio for potential future gains.

REMEMBER

It's in large part to prevent such big falls, and lack of "dry powder," that you need to rebalance. That is, on a regular basis, you need to do exactly the opposite of what most investors do: You need to sell off some of your winners and buy up the losers. By doing so, not only do you cap your risk, but studies show that you may also juice your returns. By systematically buying low and selling high, you may, over the long run, increase your average annual returns by as much as 1.5 percent. That's not a bad return at all for an exercise that shouldn't take you more than a couple hours! (*Note:* I say "as much as 1.5 percent" because the profitability of rebalancing will depend on how many asset classes you own and the correlations they have to each other.)

How rebalancing works

What Joan should've done once a year or so was rebalance her portfolio so that the initial 60/40 (stock/bond) mix was reset. She should never have allowed any one slice of her portfolio to overtake the rest. She should've periodically pulled her portfolio back into balance.

To illustrate how this should be done, I'll use the simple middle-of-the-road ETF portfolio that I introduce in Chapter 9. At the start of the year, the portfolio is just where you want it to be: 60 percent diversified stocks, 40 percent bonds. But it turns out to be a banner year for stocks, and especially for small-cap U.S. stocks. At the end of the year, as you can see in Table 11-1, the portfolio looks quite different.

What to do? Bring things back into balance, starting with the bond position. That's because the split between stocks and bonds has the greatest impact on portfolio risk. In this example, you need to increase the bond allocation from 32 percent back up to 40 percent. If you have a year-end portfolio of $100,000, that means you'll buy $6,000 in municipal bonds to bring that allocation up to $30,000 or 30 percent of your portfolio. You'll also buy $1,000 of the BNY Mellon Core Bond ETF and $1,000 of the Vanguard Total International Bond Index ETF, so that your taxable bonds will be back to $10,000 total, or 10 percent of the portfolio.

TABLE 11-1 A Shifting Portfolio Balance

ETF	Percent of Portfolio
Beginning of Year One (in Balance)	
Municipal bonds	**30 percent**
Broad-based U.S. stock market	**28 percent**
Dimensional U.S. Core Equity Market (ticker symbol: DFAU)	16 percent
Vanguard Small Cap Value ETF (ticker symbol: VBR)	6 percent
Vanguard Small Cap ETF (ticker symbol: VB)	6 percent
Broad-based foreign stocks	**23 percent**
Vanguard Total International Stock Index Fund ETF (ticker symbol: VXUS)	10 percent
iShares MSCI EAFE Value ETF (ticker symbol: EFV)	4 percent
Vanguard FTSE All-World ex-U.S. Small Cap Index ETF (ticker symbol: VSS)	9 percent
Special-sector fund	**5 percent**
Vanguard International Real Estate ETF (ticker symbol: VNQI)	5 percent
Taxable bonds	**10 percent**
BNY Mellon Core Bond ETF (ticker symbol: BKAG)	5 percent
Vanguard Total International Bond Index ETF (ticker symbol: BNDX)	5 percent
Market-neutral fund	**4 percent**
Merger Fund (ticker symbol: MERFX)	4 percent
End of Year One (Out of Balance)	
Municipal bonds	**24 percent**
Broad-based U.S. stock market	**33 percent**
Dimensional U.S. Core Equity Market (ticker symbol: DFAU)	17 percent
Vanguard Small Cap Value ETF (ticker symbol: VBR)	8 percent

(continued)

TABLE 11-1 *(continued)*

ETF	Percent of Portfolio
Vanguard Small Cap ETF (ticker symbol: VB)	8 percent
Broad-based foreign stocks	**26 percent**
Vanguard Total International Stock Index Fund ETF (ticker symbol: VXUS)	11 percent
iShares MSCI EAFE Value ETF (ticker symbol: EFV)	5 percent
Vanguard FTSE All-World ex-U.S. Small Cap Index ETF (ticker symbol: VSS)	10 percent
Special sector fund	**6 percent**
Vanguard International Real Estate ETF (ticker symbol: VNQI)	6 percent
Taxable bonds	**8 percent**
BNY Mellon Core Bond ETF (ticker symbol: BKAG)	4 percent
Vanguard Total International Bond Index ETF (ticker symbol: BNDX)	4 percent
Market-neutral fund	**3 percent**
Merger Fund (ticker symbol: MERFX)	3 percent

TIP

Where will the $8,000 come from? That depends. You could sell off part of your stock position, which may be necessary given that things are pretty seriously out of balance. But do keep in mind that selling off winning positions in a taxable account will require you to pay capital gains — and possibly a small commission on the ETF trades. So, to the extent possible, try to rebalance by shoring up your losing positions with fresh deposits or with dividends and interest earned on your portfolio.

How often to rebalance

REMEMBER

The question of how often to rebalance has been studied and restudied, and most financial professionals agree that once a year is a good time frame, at least for those still in the accumulation phase of their investing careers. Anything less frequent than that increases your risk as positions get more and more out of whack.

Anything more frequent than annually, and you may lower your returns by interrupting rallies too often and increasing your "friction" costs (spreads, possible commissions, and taxes).

Keep these costs in mind as you rebalance. Tweaking a portfolio by a few dollars here and there to achieve "perfect" balance may not make sense.

Another way to approach rebalancing is to seek to address any allocations that are off by more than 10 percent, and don't sweat anything that's off by less. In other words, if your muni-bond position is given an allocation in the portfolio of 30 percent, I wouldn't worry too much about rebalancing unless that percentage falls to 27 percent or rises to 33 percent.

Rebalancing for retirees

TIP

If you're in the *decumulation* phase of your investing career (that's a fancy way of saying that you're living off of your savings), you may want to rebalance every 6 months instead of every 12. The reason: Rebalancing has a third purpose for you, in addition to risk reduction and performance juicing. For you, rebalancing is a good time to raise whatever cash you anticipate needing in the upcoming months. In times of super-low interest rates on money-market and savings accounts, such as we've seen in recent years, it can be profitable to rebalance more often so you don't need to keep as much cash sitting around earning squat.

Contemplating tactical asset allocation

Astute readers — such as you — may now be wondering this: If you can juice your returns by rebalancing (systematically buying low and selling high), can you perhaps juice your returns even more by *over*-rebalancing? In other words, suppose you design a 60/40 portfolio, and suddenly stocks tank. Now you have a 50/50 portfolio. Might you consider not only buying enough stock to get yourself back to a 60/40 portfolio, but also (because stocks are so apparently cheap) buying even *more* stocks than you need for simple rebalancing purposes?

Investment professionals call this kind of maneuver "tactical asset allocation." It's the art of tilting a portfolio given certain economic conditions. Tactical asset allocation is different from market timing only in the degree to which action is required. With tactical asset allocation, you make a gentle and unhurried shift in one direction or another, whereas market timing entails a more radical and swift shifting of assets. Tactical asset allocation, done right, may add to your bottom line, but market timing will almost always cost you. The division between the two can be a fine line, so proceed with caution.

Understanding the all-important P/E ratio

If a certain asset class has been seeing returns much, much lower than its historical average, you may want to very slightly over-weight that asset class. If, for example, you're considering over-weighting U.S. stocks, it makes more sense to do it when U.S. stocks are selling relatively cheaply. Typically, but not always, an asset class may be "selling cheap" after several years of under-performing its historical returns.

But is there any way to find a more objective measure of "selling cheap"? Investment legend Benjamin Graham liked to use something called the *price-to-earnings* (P/E) *ratio*. When the market price of a stock (or all stocks) is high, and the earnings (or profits for a company or companies) are low, you have a high P/E ratio; conversely, when the market price is down but earnings are up, you have a low P/E ratio. Graham, as well as his student Warren Buffett, preferred to buy when the P/E ratio was low.

Throughout this book, I urge you to consider tilting your entire stock portfolio, on a permanent basis, toward lower P/E stocks, otherwise known as *value stocks*. Here, I'm talking not about a permanent tilt but a mild, temporary one. It stands to reason that if value stocks outperform other stocks — and, historically, they've done just that — and if the entire stock market appears to be a value market, then that market may outperform in the foreseeable future.

Work by Yale University economist Robert J. Shiller has lent credence to the notion that buying when the P/E ratio is low raises your expected returns. In fact, Shiller has tinkered with the way the P/E ratio is defined so that the earnings part of the equation looks back over a decade (rather than the typical one year) and then factors in inflation. Shiller's research, based on tracking market returns with varying P/E ratios over the decades, indicates that when his adjusted P/E ratio is low, the stock market is more likely to produce gains over the following decade. When the P/E ratio is high (it reached an all-time high in 1999, for example), you may be looking forward to a decade of very low (or no) returns. Sure enough, the first decade of the millennium produced a rather flat market.

Applying the ratio to your portfolio

Although Shiller's theories have been debated, it stands to reason that, if they're applied carefully, you may just do yourself a favor to slightly overweight all stocks when the P/E ratio is low and to underweight all stocks when the P/E ratio is high. But against the probability that Shiller's formula holds, you need to weigh the very real transaction costs involved in shifting your portfolio. On balance, I wouldn't suggest engaging in tactical asset allocation very often — and then only if the numbers seem to be shouting at you to act.

TIP

One very quick way to check the P/E ratio for the entire stock market would be to look up an ETF that tracks the entire market, such as the Vanguard Total Stock Market ETF (ticker symbol: VTI), on Vanguard's website (www.vanguard.com) or on just about any financial website (such as www.morningstar.com). Or, to see both the traditional and the potentially more powerful "Shiller PE Ratio," go to www.multpl.com. (The P/E ratio is sometimes called the "multiple.")

The historical average for the S&P 500 P/E Ratio is about 16. It's roughly 34 at the time of writing. The historical average for Shiller's adjusted P/E is about 17. It is 38 at the time of writing. So, unless those numbers have changed by the time you're reading this chapter, you don't want to overweight stocks right now. However, if stock prices fall and earnings rise, and you start to see the P/E fall back to historical norms or below, you may want to gently — very gently — tweak your portfolio toward the more aggressive side.

TIP

If, all things being equal, you determine that you should have a portfolio of 60 percent stocks, and if the adjusted P/E falls to the low teens, then consider adding 2 to 3 percentage points to your stock allocation, and that's all. If the market P/E falls to 14 or less, then maybe, provided you can stomach the volatility, consider adding yet another percentage point or two, or even three, to your "neutral" allocation. If the adjusted P/E rises back up to where it was in 1999 — about 44 — then you may want to lighten up on stocks by a few points. Please keep to these parameters. Tilting more than a few percentage points — particularly on the up side (more stocks than before) — increases your risks beyond the value of any potential gains.

The IRS's "wash rule" and harvesting tax losses

So, you had a bad year on a particular investment? You had a bad year on *many* of your investments? Allow Uncle Sam to share your pain. You only need to sell these investments by December 31, and you can use the loss to offset any capital gains. Or, if you've had no capital gains, you can deduct the loss from your taxable ordinary income for the year, up to $3,000.

But there's a problem. Because of the IRS's "wash rule," you can't sell an investment on December 31 and claim a loss if you buy back that same investment or any "substantially identical" investment within 30 days of the sale. You may simply want to leave the sale proceeds in cash. That way, you save on any transaction costs and avoid the hassle of trading.

On the other hand, January is historically a very good time for stocks. You may not want to be out of the market that month. What to do? ETFs to the rescue!

The IRS rules are a bit hazy when it comes to identifying "substantially identical" investments. Clearly, you can't sell and then buy back the same stock. But if you sell $10,000 of ExxonMobil Corp. (ticker symbol: XOM) stock, you *can* buy $10,000 of an ETF that covers the energy industry, such as the Energy Select Sector SPDR (ticker symbol: XLE) or the Vanguard Energy ETF (ticker symbol: VDE). They're not the same thing, for sure, but either one can be expected to perform relatively in line with XOM (and its competitors as well) for the 30 days that you must live without your stock. And rest assured, no ETF could reasonably be deemed to be "substantially identical" to any individual stock.

I, of course, would prefer that you keep most of your portfolio in ETFs in the first place. Even then, if you follow my advice, and one year turns out to be especially bad for, say, large-cap value stocks, no problem. If you're holding the iShares S&P 500 Value Fund (IVE) and you sell it at a loss, you can buy the Vanguard Value ETF (VTV), hold it for a month, and then switch back if you want.

Two ETFs that track similar indexes (IVE tracks the S&P 500 Value Index; VTV tracks the CRSP U.S. Large Cap Value Index) are going to be very, very similar but not "substantially identical." At least the IRS *so far* has not deemed them substantially identical. But the

IRS changes its rules often, and what constitutes "substantially identical" could change tomorrow or the next day. It's usually a good idea to consult with a tax professional (which I am not) before proceeding with any tax-harvesting plans.

Revamping your portfolio with life changes

Rebalancing to bring your portfolio back to its original allocations, making tactical adjustments, and harvesting losses for tax purposes aren't the only times it may make sense to trade ETFs. Just as you may need a new suit if you lose or gain weight, sometimes you need to tailor your portfolio in response to changes in your life.

As I discuss in Chapter 9, the prime consideration in portfolio construction is whether you can and should take risks in the hope of garnering high returns or whether you must limit your risk with the understanding that your returns will likely be modest. (Diversification can certainly help to reduce investment risk, but it can't eliminate it.) Certain events may occur in your life that warrant a reassessment of where you belong on the risk–return continuum.

If a single person walks into my office and asks me to help build a portfolio, I will want to know if wedding bells will be ringing in the near future. If a married couple walks into my office, one of the first things I take note of is how close they sit together. And if the woman has a swollen belly, I really take notice.

No, I'm not being nosy. Marriage, divorce, and the arrival of babies are major life changes and need to be weighed heavily in any investment decisions. So, too, are the death of a spouse or parent (especially if that parent has left a hefty portfolio to the adult child); a child's decision to attend college; any major career changes; or the imminent purchase of a new house, new car, or Fabergé egg.

Betsy and Mark: A fairly typical couple

It's 2021, and Betsy and Mark are just married. They don't have a lot of money. But both are in their early thirties, in good health, gainfully employed, and without debt. They plan to merge their combined savings of roughly $41,500 and have asked me to help them invest it for the long haul.

The first thing we do is to decide how much money to take out to cover emergencies. Given their monthly expenses of roughly $3,500, we decide to earmark five months' of living expenses — $17,500 — and plunk that into an online savings account. That leaves us with $24,000 to invest.

This $24,000 is money they tell me they shouldn't need to touch until retirement. I urge them both to open a Roth individual retirement account (IRA). (Any money you put into a Roth IRA grows tax-free for as long as you want, and withdrawals are likewise tax-free.) I ask them to divide the $24,000 between the two accounts. Because each of them can contribute $6,000 per year, I have them both make double contributions — one immediate contribution of $6,000 each for the current year (they can make their 2021 contributions until April 15, 2022), and one contribution each for 2022. (They'll have to hold the second $6,000 each in cash until the morning of January 1, 2022.)

To keep things simple for now, because the couple has no investment experience, I limit the number of investments. The only difference: Mark tells me he wants to be as aggressive as can be, whereas Betsy is more ambivalent about taking a lot of risk. With this in mind, I give Mark greater exposure to stock, and less to bonds. I also give Betsy more stock than bonds, but less than I give Mark.

Betsy's Roth IRA	
Vanguard Total World Stock ETF (ticker symbol: VT)	$8,400
BNY Mellon Core Bond ETF (ticker symbol: BKAG)	$3,600
Mark's Roth IRA	
Vanguard Total World Stock ETF (ticker symbol: VT)	$9,600
BNY Mellon Core Bond ETF (ticker symbol: BKAG)	$2,400

As Betsy and Mark's portfolio grows, I would plan to add other asset classes (real estate investment trusts [REITs], Treasury Inflation-Protected Securities [TIPS], and so on) and other accounts.

One year later

Betsy is pregnant with twins! The couple is saving up for their first home, with a goal of making that purchase within 18 months.

Although IRAs are normally not to be touched before age 59½, an exception is made for first-time home purchases. Betsy and Mark could take out as much as $10,000 from each Roth IRA without having to pay either a penalty or tax on the gains.

I'd rather that they leave their Roth IRA money untouched, but the couple informs me that they think the money may need to be tapped. At this point, the money in each of the two Roth IRAs has grown from $12,000 to $14,000 each (for illustration purposes, I'm pretending that each investment grew by an equal amount), and Betsy and Mark can each contribute another $6,000 in fresh money, bringing the total of each account to $20,000. Because there is a possibility that $10,000 from each account may need to be yanked in one year, I decide to earmark most of the fresh money to a fairly nonvolatile short-term bond ETF.

Betsy's Roth IRA	
Vanguard Total World Stock ETF (ticker symbol: VT)	$7,000
BNY Mellon Core Bond ETF (ticker symbol: BKAG)	$3,000
Vanguard Short-Term Bond ETF (ticker symbol: BSV)	$10,000
Mark's Roth IRA	
Vanguard Total World Stock ETF (ticker symbol: VT)	$8,000
BNY Mellon Core Bond ETF (ticker symbol: BKAG)	$2,000
Vanguard Short-Term Bond ETF (ticker symbol: BSV)	$10,000

Another year later

The twins (Aiden and Ella) have arrived! Much to their surprise, Betsy's parents have gifted the couple $10,000 for the purchase of their home. The Roth IRA money needn't be touched. At this point, I would sell the short-term bond fund and add to their other positions. Also, provided the couple had another $6,000 each to contribute, I'd begin adding asset classes to the mix, perhaps introducing a TIPS ETF and a REIT ETF. If there's money left over to invest in a taxable brokerage account, I might add a tax-free muni ETF.

Hopefully, Betsy and Mark (and Aiden and Ella) will have many happy years together. And with each major life event, I would urge them to adjust their portfolio appropriately.

Are Options an Option for You?

Aside from the universe of ETFs, there's a parallel universe filled with things called *exchange-traded derivatives*. A *derivative* is a financial instrument that has no real value in and of itself; instead, its value is directly tied to some underlying item of value, be it a commodity, a stock, a currency, or an ETF.

The most popular derivative is called an *option*. Think of an option as sort of a movie ticket. You give the cashier $8.50 to see the movie, not to hold some dumb little piece of cardboard. Certainly the ticket itself has no intrinsic value. But the ticket gives access (the option) to see the movie.

REMEMBER

Most options in the investment world give you the right either to buy or sell a security at a certain price (the *strike price*) up to a certain specified date (the *expiration date*). Options are a prime example of a *leveraged* investment. In other words, if you buy an option, you're leveraging the little bit of money that you pay for the option — the *premium* — in the hopes of winning big money. If you're an option seller, you stand to make the amount of the small premium, but you risk losing big money. For the system to work, the sellers have to win much more often than the buyers — and they do.

Options on certain ETFs, most notably the SPY (which represents the S&P 500) and the QQQ (which represents the 100 largest company stocks traded on the Nasdaq), typically trade just as many shares on an average day as the ETFs themselves. On most days, options on ETFs like the QQQ and SPY trade more shares than any other kind of options, including options on individual stocks, commodities, and currencies.

You see, ETFs provide traders with the opportunity to trade the entire stock market, or large pieces of it, rather than merely individual securities. In the past, this was doable but difficult. You cannot trade a mutual fund on the options market as you can an ETF.

Much of this often frenetic trading in ETF options, at least on the buying side, is being done by speculators, not investors. If you have an itch to gamble in the hopes of hitting it big, then options may be for you. I warn you, however, that successful options trading takes an iron gut, a lot of capital, and a lot of expertise. And even if you have all that, you may still end up getting hurt.

Understanding puts and calls

All kinds of options exist, including options on options (sort of). The derivatives market almost seems infinite — as does the number of ways you can play it. But the two most basic kinds of options, and the two most popular by far, are *put options* and *call options*, otherwise known simply as *puts* and *calls*. I'm going to take just a moment to describe how these babies work.

Calls: Options to buy

With a call option in hand, you may, for example, have bought yourself the right to buy 100 shares of the PowerShares QQQ Trust (currently trading at $367) at $380 (the strike price) a share at any point between now and, say, December 16 (the expiration date). If QQQ rises above $380, you will, of course, take the option and buy the 100 shares at $380 each. After all, you can then turn around and sell them immediately on the open market for a nifty profit. If, however, the price of QQQ does not rise to $380 or above, then you aren't going to exercise your option. Why in the world would you? You can buy the stock cheaper on the market. In that case, your option expires worthless.

Puts: Options to sell

With a put option in hand, you may, for example, have bought yourself the right to *sell* 100 shares of QQQ (currently trading at $367) at $340 (the strike price) a share at any point between now and December 16 (the expiration date). By December 16, if QQQ has fallen to any price under $340, then you will likely choose to sell. If QQQ is trading above $340, then you'd be a fool to sell. In the latter case, your option will simply expire, unused.

Using options to make gains without risk

Those people who use calls as an investment (as opposed to gambling) strategy are assuming (as do most investors) that the market is going to continue its historical upward trajectory. But instead of banking perhaps 60 percent or 70 percent of their portfolio on stocks, as many of us do, they take a much smaller percentage of their money and buy calls.

If the stock market goes up, then they may collect many times what they invested. If the stock market doesn't go up, then they lose it all — but only a modest amount. Meanwhile, the bulk of their money can be invested in something much less volatile than the stock market, such as bonds.

Insuring yourself against big, bad bears

The put option is an option to sell. This investment strategy allows you to have money in the stock market (all of it, if you so desire), but you carry insurance in the form of puts. If the market tumbles, you're covered.

Suppose you want to invest everything in the Nasdaq index through the QQQ. Normally, an investor would have to be insane to bet everything on such a volatile asset. But with the right put options in place, you can actually enjoy explosive growth but limit your losses to whatever you want: 5 percent, 10 percent, 15 percent.

With a pocketful of puts, you can laugh a bear market in the face. If the QQQ drops by, say, 50 percent in the next week, you will have checked out long before, smiling as you hold your cash.

Seeming almost too good to be true

So, options allow you to capture the gains of the stock market with very limited risk. They allow you to invest in the market and not have to worry about downturns. What's not to love about options?

WARNING

Whoa, not so fast! You need to know a couple little things about options:

>> **They're expensive.** Every time you buy either a put or a call, you pay. The price can vary enormously depending on the strike price, the expiration date you choose, and the volatility of the ETF the option is based on. But in no case are options cheap. And the *vast majority* of options reach their expiration date and simply expire.

So, yes, options can save you in a bear market, and they can help you to capture a bull market, but either way, you're going to pay. Free lunches are very hard to come by!

>> **If you happen to make a gain on an option, the income will usually be considered a short-term gain by the IRS.** As such, you may pay twice the tax on it that you would on the long-term appreciation of a stock.

Weighing options against a diversified ETF portfolio

Don't misunderstand me. I'm not saying that the price you pay for options isn't worth it — even after taxes are considered. Options do provide investors with a variety of viable strategies. The real question, though, is whether using puts and calls makes any more sense than investing in a well-diversified portfolio of low-cost ETFs. Most financial professionals I know are skeptical. And that includes several who have traded heavily in options only to learn the hard way that it's a very tricky business.

To be sure, if I knew a bear market were coming, I would definitely buy myself a slew of put options. If I knew a bull market were in the offing, I would certainly buy a fistful of call options. But here's the problem: I don't know which way the market is going, and neither do you. And if I buy both puts and calls on a regular basis, I'm going to be forever bleeding cash.

Not only that, but if the market stagnates, then both my puts and calls will expire worthless. In that case, I'm going to be one really unhappy camper.

So, here's the way I look at it: The chances of success with a steady call strategy are one in three: I win if there's a bull market; I lose if there's a bear market; I lose if the market stagnates. Ditto for a put option strategy: I win if there's a bear market; I lose if there's a bull market; I lose if the market stagnates. It's hard to like those odds.

With a well-diversified portfolio of low-cost ETFs — stock, bond, REIT ETFs — I reckon my chances of success are more like two in three: I lose if there's a bear market; I win if there's a bull market; in the case of a stagnant stock market, *something* in my portfolio will likely continue to make money for me anyway.

The Part of Tens

Dig into common questions about exchange-traded funds (ETFs), like whether they're risky and how to choose among the hundreds of ETFs available.

Find out how to avoid common mistakes, like buying too much of the same thing.

Chapter **12**

Ten Common Questions about ETFs

W hen someone asks me what I'm working on, and I say, "A book about exchange-traded funds," sometimes their eyes glaze over, and then, if the topic isn't immediately steered in a new direction, I'm inevitably asked what the heck an exchange-traded fund is. And so I explain. The *next* question I'm asked is invariably one of the following.

Are ETFs Appropriate for Individual Investors?

REMEMBER

Although the name *exchange-traded funds* (ETFs) sounds highly technical and maybe a little bit scary, ETFs — at least the ones I tend to recommend in this book — are essentially friendly index mutual funds with a few spicy perks. They're *more* than appropriate for individual investors. In fact, given the low expense ratios and high tax-efficiency of most ETFs, as well as the ease with which you can use them to construct a diversified portfolio, these babies can be the perfect building blocks for just about any individual investor's portfolio.

Are ETFs Risky?

That all depends. Some ETFs are way riskier than others. It's a question of what kind of ETF we're talking about. Many ETFs track stock indexes, and some of those stock indexes can be extremely volatile, such as individual sectors of the U.S. economy (technology, energy, defense and aerospace, and so on) or the stock markets of emerging-market nations. Other ETFs track broader segments of the U.S. stock market, such as the S&P 500. Those can be volatile, too, but less so.

But other ETFs track bond indexes. Those tend to be considerably less volatile (and less potentially rewarding) than stock ETFs. One ETF (ticker symbol: SHY) tracks short-term Treasury bonds, and as such is only a little bit more volatile than a money-market fund.

Many newer-generation ETFs are *leveraged*, using borrowed money or financial derivatives to increase volatility (and potential performance). Those leveraged ETFs can be so wildly volatile that you're taking on risk of Las Vegas proportions.

REMEMBER

When putting together a portfolio, a diversity of investments can temper risk. Although it seems freakily paradoxical, you can sometimes add a risky ETF to a portfolio (such as an ETF that tracks the stocks of foreign small companies) and lower your overall risk! How so? If the value of your newly added ETF tends to rise as your other investments fall, that addition will lower the volatility of your entire portfolio. (Financial professionals refer to this strange but sweet phenomenon as *Modern Portfolio Theory*.)

Do I Need a Professional to Set Up and Monitor an ETF Portfolio?

Setting up a decent ETF portfolio, with the aid of this book, is very doable. You can certainly monitor such a portfolio as well. A professional, however, has special education, tools, and (I hope) objectivity to help you understand investment risk and construct a portfolio that fits you like a glove, or at least a sock. A financial planner can also help you properly estimate your retirement needs and plan your savings accordingly.

Be aware that many investment "advisors" out there are nothing more than salespeople in disguise. Don't be at all surprised if you bump into a few who express their disgust of ETFs! ETFs make no money for those salespeople, who make their living hawking expensive (often inferior) investment products. Your best bet for good advice is to find a *fee-only* (takes no commissions) financial planner. If you are more or less a do-it-yourselfer but simply want a little guidance, try to find a fee-only planner who will work with you on an hourly basis.

If you hire a fee-only advisor who takes your assets under management, know that the standard fee of 1 percent of assets under management has gone largely by the wayside. You shouldn't have to pay that much if you're only getting portfolio management. If your advisor also helps you with other financial matters, that's a different story. But do consider an hourly advisor first.

How Much Money Do I Need to Invest in ETFs?

You can buy as little as one share of any ETF, and many ETF shares sell for under $30. Some brokerage houses now allow for the purchase of fractional shares on the more common ETFs, so you could theoretically start an ETF portfolio with pennies.

You'll need a brokerage house to purchase ETFs, and some brokerage houses have minimums. But plenty of brokerage houses don't have minimums, including Schwab and Fidelity. Vanguard has no minimum, but you'll pay an annual service fee of $20 for any account that holds less than $10,000 (although you can waive the service fee if you agree to get all your documents electronically).

With Hundreds of ETFs to Choose From, Where Do I Start?

The answer depends on your objective. If you're looking to round out an existing portfolio of stocks or mutual funds, your ETF should complement that. Your goal is always to have a well-diversified collection of investments. If you're starting to build a portfolio, you want to make sure to include stocks and bonds and to diversify within those two broad asset classes.

There is not much in the world of stocks and bonds that can't be satisfied with ETFs. Try to have both U.S. and international stock ETFs. And within the U.S. stock arena, aim to have large-cap and small-cap, value and growth stocks (I explain these terms in Chapters 3 and 4). You can also diversify your stock ETFs by industry sector: consumer staples, energy, financials, and so on (see Chapter 6 for details).

On the bond side of your portfolio, you want both government-issued bonds and corporate bonds, and if you're in a higher tax bracket, you may want municipal bonds as well. For more conservative portfolios in which bonds play a major role, foreign bonds may offer added diversification. Many ETFs will give you exposure to all these kinds of bonds (for a full discussion, see Chapter 7).

Although most ETFs are somewhat reasonably priced, some are more reasonably priced than others. If you're going to pay 0.4 percent a year in operating expenses for a certain ETF, you should have a good reason for doing so. Many ETFs are available for under 0.2 percent and some for even less than 0.05 percent. A handful are *free!*

Where Is the Best Place for Me to Buy ETFs?

TIP

I suggest setting up an account with a financial supermarket such as Fidelity, Vanguard, Charles Schwab, or TD Ameritrade. Each of these allows you to hold ETFs, along with other investments — such as mutual funds or individual stocks and bonds — in one account.

Different financial supermarkets offer different services and charge different prices depending on how much you have to invest, how often you trade, and whether you do everything online or by phone. You need to do some shopping around to find the brokerage house that works best for you. (I provide more suggestions for shopping financial supermarkets in Chapter 2.)

Is There an Especially Good or Bad Time to Buy ETFs?

Well, the stock market is open for business between 9:30 a.m. and 4 p.m., Monday through Friday. That's Eastern time. It's generally best to trade your ETFs between 9:45 a.m. and 3:45 p.m. Avoid the opening and closing bells; there is often added volatility at those times.

Other than that, nope, there really is no particular good or bad time. It isn't like airline tickets (which many people say you should shop for on Tuesdays, and never on Fridays).

And how about a day after the market is up as opposed to down? Studies show rather conclusively that the stock and bond markets (or any segment of the stock or bond markets) are just about as likely to go up after a good day as they are after a bad day (or week, month, year, or any other piece of the calendar). Trying to time the market tends to be a fool's game — or, just as often, a game that some like to play with other people's money.

Do ETFs Have Any Disadvantages?

Because most ETFs follow an index, you probably won't see your ETF (or any of your index mutual funds) winding up number one on *Wise Money* magazine's list of Top Funds for the Year. (But you probably won't find any of your ETFs at the bottom of such a list, either.)

But perhaps the biggest disadvantage of ETFs is something that many consider an advantage. ETFs, unlike mutual funds, trade in a flash. If at, say, 2:34 on a Wednesday afternoon, you want to sell your entire portfolio, then you can have it done by 2:35. This is not a technical disadvantage — unless you have a trigger finger and are apt to make rash financial decisions. Yes, there are some people who sell out their stock ETFs after every downward blip in the market. If this is you, you'd be better off with mutual funds — or perhaps cash under your mattress!

Does It Matter Which Exchange My ETF Is Traded On?

No. Most ETFs are traded on the NYSE Arca (Archipelago) exchange, but plenty of others are traded on the Nasdaq. It doesn't matter in the slightest to you, the individual investor. The cost of your trade is determined by the brokerage house you use, and most brokerage houses are now charging zero for ETFs. The *spread* (the difference between the price a buyer pays and the price the seller receives) is determined in large part by the share volume of the ETF being traded. Regardless of the exchange, if the volume is small (such as would be the case for, say, the Global X Nigeria ETF), you may want to place a limit order rather than a market order.

Which ETFs Should I Keep in Which Accounts?

Generally, investments that generate income — whether interest, dividends, or capital gains — are best kept in a tax-advantaged retirement account, such as your individual retirement account (IRA) or 401(k) plan. That would include any bond, real estate investment trust (REIT), or high-dividend-paying ETF. You'll eventually need to pay income tax on any money you withdraw from those accounts, but it's generally better to pay later than sooner. In the case of a Roth IRA, which is often the best case of all, you'll never have to pay taxes on the earnings, the principal, what's in the account, or what you withdraw. Try to put your ETFs that have the greatest potential for growth — REIT ETFs are great candidates — into your Roth IRA.

REMEMBER

Because retirement accounts generally penalize you if you take money out before age 59½, anyone younger than that would want to keep all emergency money in a non-retirement account.

Chapter **13**

Ten Typical Mistakes Most Investors Make

R emember that personal investing course you took in high school? Of course, you don't! If you're a middle-ager like me, then your high school probably didn't offer such a course (although people who've graduated very recently may have had the opportunity). And that lack of education — combined with a surfeit of cheesy and oft-advertised investment industry products, plus an irresponsible and lazy financial press — leads many investors to make some very costly mistakes, such as the ones I share in this chapter.

Paying Too Much for an Investment

Most investors pay way, way too much to middlemen who suck the lifeblood out of portfolios, leaving too many folks with too little to show for their investments. By investing primarily in index exchange-traded funds (ETFs), you can spare yourself and your family this tragic fate. The most economical ETFs cost a fraction of what you would typically pay in yearly management fees to a mutual-fund company selling "active management." You never pay any *loads* (high commissions). And trading fees, which never were very much, have all but disappeared in the past year or two.

Failing to Properly Diversify

Thou shalt not put all thine eggs in one basket is perhaps the first commandment of investing, but it's astonishing how many sinners there are among us. ETFs allow for easy and effective diversification. By investing in ETFs rather than individual securities, you've already taken a step in the right direction. Don't blow it by pouring all your money into one narrow ETF representing a single hot sector! You want to invest in both stock and bond ETFs, and both U.S. and international securities. You want diversification on all sides.

REMEMBER

Invest, to the extent possible, mostly in *broad* markets: value, growth, small cap, large cap. On the international side of your portfolio, aim to invest more in regions than in individual countries (see Chapter 5). ETFs make such diversification easy.

Taking on Inappropriate Risks

Some people take on way too much risk, investing perhaps everything in highly volatile technology or biotech stocks. But many people don't take enough risk, leaving their money to sit in secure but low-yielding money-market funds or in the vault of their local savings and loan. If you want your money to grow, you may have to stomach some volatility.

REMEMBER

In general, the longer you can tie your money up, and the less likely you are to need to tap into your portfolio anytime soon, the more volatile your portfolio can be. A portfolio of ETFs can be amazingly fine-tuned to achieve the levels of risk and return that are appropriate for you.

Selling Out When the Going Gets Tough

It can be a scary thing, for sure, when your portfolio's value drops 10 percent or 20 percent . . . never mind the 40 percent that an all-stock portfolio would've lost in 2008 (demonstrating graphically why you shouldn't have an all-stock portfolio). Keep in mind that if you invest in stock ETFs, that scenario is going to happen. It has happened many times in the past; it will happen many times in the future. That's just the nature of the beast. If you sell when the going gets tough (as many investors do), you lose the game.

REMEMBER

The stock market is resilient. Hang tough! Bears are followed by bulls. Your portfolio — as long as you are well diversified — will almost surely bounce back, given enough time.

Paying Too Much Attention to Recent Performance

Many investors make a habit of bailing out of whatever market segment has recently taken a dive. Conversely, they often look for whatever market segment has recently shot through the roof, and that's the one they buy. Then, when *that* market segment tanks, they sell once again. By forever buying high and selling low, they see their portfolios dwindle over time to nothing.

When you build your portfolio, don't overload it with last year's ETF superstars. You don't know what will happen next year. Stay cool. You may notice that in this book, I do not include performance figures for any of the ETFs discussed (except in just a few circumstances to make a specific point). That omission is intentional. Many of the ETFs I discuss are only a few years old, and a few years' returns tell you *nothing*. On the other hand, the indexes tracked by certain ETFs go back decades. In those cases, I often do provide performance figures.

Not Saving Enough for Retirement

Compared to spending, saving doesn't offer a whole lot of joy. But you can't build a portfolio out of thin air. If your goal is one day to be financially independent, to retire with dignity, you probably need to build a nest egg equal to about 25 times your yearly budget. Doing so won't be easy. It may mean saving 15 percent of your paycheck for several decades. The earlier you start, the easier it will be.

Savings come from the difference between what you earn and what you spend. Keep in mind that both are adjustable figures. One great way to save is to contribute at least enough to your

401(k) plan at work to get your employer's full match, if any. Do it! Another is to note that material goodies, above and beyond what it takes to be comfortable, do not buy happiness and fulfillment. Honest. Psychologists have studied the matter, and their findings are rather conclusive.

Having Unrealistic Expectations of Market Returns

One reason many people don't save enough is that they have unrealistic expectations; they believe fervently that they're going to win the lottery or (next best thing) earn 25 percent a year on their investments. The truth: The stock market, over the past 100 years, has returned roughly 10 percent a year before inflation and 7 percent a year after inflation. Bonds have returned about 5 percent before inflation and 2 percent to 3 percent after inflation. A well-balanced portfolio, therefore, may have returned 7 percent or 8 percent before inflation and maybe 5 percent or so after inflation.

Five percent growth after inflation — with interest compounded every year — isn't too shabby. In 20 years' time, an investment of $10,000 growing at 5 percent will turn into $26,530 in constant dollars. Most of us in the investment field expect future returns to be more modest. But with a very well-diversified, ultra-low-cost portfolio, leaning toward higher-yielding asset classes, you may be able to do just as well as Mom and Dad did. If you want to earn 25 percent a year, however, you're going to have to take on inordinate risk. And even then, I wouldn't bank on it.

Discounting the Damaging Effect of Inflation

No, a dollar certainly doesn't buy what it used to. Think of what a candy bar cost when you were a kid. Think of what you earned on your first job. Are you old enough to remember when gas was 32 cents a gallon? Now look into the future, and realize that your nest egg, unless it's wisely invested, will shrivel and shrink.

Historically, certain investments do a better job of keeping up with inflation than others. Those investments, which include stocks, tend to be somewhat volatile. It's a price you need to pay, however, to keep the inflation monster at bay.

TIP

The world of ETFs includes many ways to invest in stocks, but if you find the volatility hard to take, you might temper it with a position in Treasury Inflation-Protected Securities (TIPS). You can buy a number of ETFs that allow for very easy investing in TIPS. (Read about them in Chapter 7.)

Not Following the IRS's Rules

When they leave their jobs, many employees cash out their 401(k) accounts, thereupon paying the Internal Revenue Service (IRS) a stiff penalty and immediately losing the great benefit of tax deferral. The government allows certain tax breaks for special kinds of accounts, and you really need to play by the rules or you can wind up worse off than if you had never invested in the first place.

People beyond 72 must be especially careful to take the required minimum distributions (RMDs) from their traditional IRAs or 401(k) plans. Calculators are available online; simply search the web for "RMD calculator." Unlike a retirement calculator, based on all kinds of assumptions, the RMD is a straightforward equation. Any online calculator can take you there, or ask your accountant or the institution where you have your retirement plan.

Not Incorporating Investments into a Broader Financial Plan

REMEMBER

Have you paid off all your high-interest credit card debt? Do you have proper disability insurance? Do you have enough life insurance so that, if necessary, your co-parent and children could survive without you? A finely manicured investment portfolio is only part of a larger picture that includes issues such as debt management, insurance, and estate planning. Don't spend too much time tinkering with your ETF portfolio and ignoring these other very important financial issues.

Index

About the Author

Russell Wild has been a fee-only (takes no commissions) financial advisor for the past 20 years. He heads Global Portfolios, LLC, an investment advisory firm based in Philadelphia. The firm name reflects Wild's strong belief in international diversification — using exchange-traded funds (ETFs) to build well-diversified, low-expense, tax-efficient, global portfolios.

In addition to the fun he has with his financial calculator, Wild is also an accomplished writer, having written hundreds of articles for national magazines, including *AARP: The Magazine, Consumer Reports, Men's Health, Men's Journal, Parade, Reader's Digest,* and *The Saturday Evening Post.* He has also contributed to numerous financial professional journals, such as *Financial Planning* and *Financial Advisor.*

The author or coauthor of two dozen nonfiction books, he also has written several other *For Dummies* titles in addition to this one, including *Bond Investing For Dummies* and *Index Investing For Dummies.* No stranger to mass media, Wild has shared his wit and wisdom on such shows as *Oprah, The View, CBS Morning News,* and *Good Day, New York,* as well as in hundreds of radio and blog interviews.

Wild holds an MBA with a concentration in finance from Arizona State's Thunderbird School of Global Management, in Glendale, Arizona; a bachelor of science (BS) degree in business/economics magna cum laude from American University in Washington, D.C.; and a graduate certificate in personal financial planning from Moravian College in Bethlehem, Pennsylvania. A member of the National Association of Personal Financial Advisors (NAPFA) since 2002, Wild is also a long-time member and past president of the American Society of Journalists and Authors.

Dedication

To the small investor, who has been bamboozled, bullied, and beaten up long enough. And to Lenore Wild of Boca Raton, who taught me early on that wordsmithery (such as using the word *wordsmithery,* rhymes with *rotisserie,* sort of . . .) can be lots of fun.

Author's Acknowledgments

I'd like a big round of applause for the editorial staff at John Wiley & Sons, Inc., for running such a well-oiled machine. We've worked on quite a few projects together now, and each one has been dust and drama free. As any author knows, that's not always the case in today's publishing world.

Thanks, too, to the Investment Company Institute, Cerulli Associates, and the helpful staff of many of the fund companies, indexers, and brokerage houses discussed throughout this book. Thanks, too, to Tensie Whelan, head of the Center for Sustainable Business at NYU Stern School of Business, for helping make this a better world, and for helping me to better understand the mechanics behind socially responsible investing.

And special thanks to Marilyn Allen of Allen O'Shea Literary Agency, my agent of many years and quite a few books.

Publisher's Acknowledgments

Senior Acquisitions Editor:
Tracy Boggier

Senior Managing Editor:
Kristie Pyles

Compilation Editor:
Georgette Beatty

Editor: Elizabeth Kuball

Production Editor:
Tamilmani Varadharaj

Cover Design: Wiley

Cover Images:
Frame: © aleksandarvelasevic/
Getty Images
Paper texture: © Dmitr1ch/
Getty Images
Inset: © 13ree_design/
Adobe Stock